Spiritual Direction

Spiritual Direction

A practical introduction

Sue Pickering

CANTERBURY
PRESS
Norwich

First published in 2008 by the Canterbury Press Norwich
(a publishing imprint of Hymns Ancient & Modern Limited,
a registered charity)
13–17 Long Lane, London EC1A 9PN

www.scm-canterburypress.co.uk

Second impression 2011

British Library Cataloguing in Publication data

A catalogue record for this book is available
from the British Library

ISBN 978-1-85311-885-2

Typeset by Regent Typesetting, London
Printed and bound by
CPI Antony Rowe, Chippenham, Wiltshire

Contents

Acknowledgements

To all my colleagues in Spiritual Growth Ministries, especially Sr Mary Concannon, thank you for your deep commitment to the formation of spiritual directors and for your trust in me.

To Cecilie Hadlow and my spiritual directors, Peter Mitchell, Judith-Anne O'Sullivan, Sheila Pritchard, Michael Bent and Marg Schrader – thank you for your 'holy listening'.

To my directees, thank you for letting me see the God of grace at work in your lives.

To Jemma Allen, Peter Benge, Simon Brown, Andrew Dunn, Brian Hamilton, Robyn Lewis, Bruce Maden, Clare O'Connor, Peter Osborne, Alan Upson, Ricky Waters, Jeff Whittaker, Di Woods and Mike Wright – thank you for sharing your experience and passion for bridge-building with God.

To Philip Richardson, Bishop of Taranaki, and to Andrew Pritchard, Convenor of Spiritual Growth Ministries, my brothers in Christ, thank you both for your wise advice, your patient attention to this book's birth, and your ongoing encouragement.

To David Moxon, Co-Presiding Archbishop of the New Zealand Dioceses and Bishop of Waikato – thank you for your gracious contribution to this book and to my life.

To those friends who prayed . . . and prayed . . . and prayed . . . you are part of every page.

To John and Matt – thank you for sharing me with this book for the past 18 months.

To God – Creator, Companion and Bringer of Inspiration – I bless you for your faithfulness and patience, for meeting me in my uncertainty and sustaining me in struggle. Any glory is yours – any errors are entirely mine.

Foreword

It is a privilege to provide an endorsement for Sue Pickering's reflections on spiritual direction today.

Sue is a most sensitive soul-friend to many, but has also thought at depth about the practice of soul-friendship in the complexities of the contemporary world. This book examines the history of spiritual direction, biblical examples and contemporary models as well as the practice of listening and responding to God, listening and responding to ourselves – all leading to the art of listening and responding to others in the Spirit.

It has been said of those in the First Testament, the Hebrew Scriptures, who listened deeply to others as a soul-friend, that they were like shade from the heat of the noon-day sun. The highest compliment you could pay such a deeply interested companion was the affirmation 'You are my shade'.

In the sometimes searing heat of today's climate, spiritual as well as ecological, a cool space away from the glare of life's pressures is an invaluable oasis. We can return to our journeys, and the heat and intensity of the trackless paths we need to make, having been refreshed and nurtured from this oasis time with a soul-friend.

Sue's book offers us a careful and finely tuned manual for the art of spiritual direction. There is such a thirst for this art now that this book deserves to be widely used and widely shared. If this happens, we will all be blessed and encouraged in our pilgrimage.

David J. Moxon
Bishop of Waikato
Archbishop of the
New Zealand Dioceses

Preface

Whatever your background or experience may be, the purpose of this book is to offer an introduction to spiritual direction, and to consider some of the key issues which arise as we listen to the faith journeys of those we companion. As we shall see, spiritual direction, though enjoying a resurgence, is not a passing fad but has always been part of the Christian tradition.

In this book we shall primarily be exploring spiritual direction in the context of a one-to-one conversation in which one person helps another reflect on and deepen his or her connection with God. We shall also look at how some of the principles and practices of contemplative spiritual direction can inform and enhance day-to-day ministry, including worship and preaching, pastoral care, chaplaincy and even community development. As such, this book is designed for clergy, chaplains, ordinands, lay people with pastoral responsibilities, those in training for pastoral ministry, and those who seek to reach out to their neighbourhood in mission and service.

Theological education and formation is being re-examined, reclaiming the original understanding of theology as a sacred blend of robust intellectual exploration of scripture, tradition and doctrine, together with personal spiritual development through prayer and reflection in the context of daily life. For this reason, this book is not only *about* spiritual direction but also provides material for *personal spiritual formation* by offering reflection ⚱ or discussion ☺ questions. Although it may be tempting to rush through these questions or exercises, I warmly encourage you to give them space in your schedule, honouring the invitation they represent to attend to your own spiritual growth. You will also find dialogues based on spiritual direction conversations, and I would invite you to pay attention to your own responses as you listen with your spiritual direction 'antennae' up.

We know that increasing attention is being paid to the future shape and health of the Church and to the need to be as Christ in our communities. The principles and practice of contemplative spiritual direction offer a rich resource for those involved in parish ministry, in 'fresh expressions' of Church and for those who are engaged in community development – helping them discern the leading of the Holy Spirit, and strengthening their relationship with God so they can, in turn, help others listen to God for themselves and take the risks inherent in new ventures.

There is one other point that needs to be made before going any further. Although it is not the intention of this book to propel you into deep emotional waters, nevertheless some people, because of their particular background, may be affected by apparently innocuous material. So, I encourage you to take care of yourself if something emerges which is challenging or painful and, if possible, to find another person with whom you can discuss any issues, for example a trustworthy friend, prayer partner, spiritual director or counsellor.

Inevitably a book emerges from a particular writer's set of experiences and attitudes. This material will no doubt reflect my preferences, my gender, age and personality, my theological position and the streams that weave through my life – marriage and motherhood, priesthood and prayer, teaching and offering spiritual direction, social times with friends, gardening, music, and walking our bouncy Labrador!

Also woven into the fabric of this book will be the insights and experience of others with whom I have shared my journey: writers whose books have touched my heart and my mind; men and women – lay, ordained or vowed religious – whom I have companioned in spiritual direction, or on the spiritual directors' formation programme which I co-ordinate; clergy and chaplains whose ministry includes spiritual direction principles and practices and whose experiences are referred to in various places; colleagues with whom I have shared workshops, discoveries and struggles; and those who have been my own spiritual directors and teachers over the years, providing inspiration, wisdom, timely encouragement and ongoing support.

To this mix you will bring your own expectations, your particular understandings, your resources of reason, faith and experience, and your hopes for ministry in and for Christ. May there be a holy conjunction as our worlds meet for this short space of time.

Introduction

There is no bridge to Skomer Island.

Settled in the swirling sea at the tip of Pembrokeshire and surrounded by power-ful Atlantic ocean currents, this small haven for puffins, guillemots and gannets can be reached only by boat. It was a place that had caught my imagination, and so, on a recent visit to South Wales, my husband and I planned to spend some time there. We had a five-day 'window of opportunity' to make the trip – more than enough time, or so we thought.

But we could not go on the Monday because the sanctuary was closed.
And not on Tuesday, Wednesday or Thursday – the birds were being counted.
And not on Friday because the weather was too rough.
And on Saturday we had to leave!

My dream of seeing the aerodynamic anomaly that is a puffin in flight remained unfulfilled. While my history-loving husband began to anticipate the delights of the next National Trust property on our itinerary, I was left to look at the sanctu-ary from a distance, to wonder about the reality of something only heard about but never experienced, to gaze out to sea searching for the unseen, and to wish there was a way across from where I was to where I longed to be.

For many years I have been offering spiritual direction and been closely in-volved in the formation of spiritual directors. As I prepared to write this book, I wondered how I might engage you, the reader, with a practice and approach that I believe can shape, inform and inspire your ministry – not just now, but for the rest of your life.

Of all the approaches I could have taken, I elected to begin with a *story*. Why? Because spiritual direction is about listening to people's stories, listening for glimpses of grace and hints of the holy, listening for the breakthrough presence of God in the midst of ordinary life. The Skomer Island story described one such 'breakthrough' moment in my life, an experience which served to intensify my longing for a fresh connection with the Holy One, and started me thinking about others who seem stranded, disconnected from the God of grace, and unaware of God's attempts to reach out to them.

So many of those we meet are stuck on the present-day 'mainland' of material-ism and busyness, cut off from a sanctuary of the spirit where they can be truly nurtured and grow strong. Such people may have a distant awareness of things related to the Church and to faith, mediated perhaps through the example of elderly relatives, or media images and commentary. Young or old, they may have heard stories of people touched by God and wondered how they might feel that sense of connection, or whether there could be any credibility in such accounts; they may – or may not – be aware of a longing in their deepest being for something more, something 'other' which we might name the fullness of life in relationship with God.

Others may have had some encounter with that 'something other' but, lacking an appropriate vocabulary or a listener who could help them hold and deepen the experience and engage with the questions it raises, have let that instant of deep connection sink into the background of their minds. The 'more real than real' becomes overlaid with the sediment of the clamouring voices and daily routines around them.

Others may occupy a different portion of the 'mainland' – a place that is famil-iar with the routines and rituals of institutional religion. Such folk may be faithful in attendance and giving; they may be active in the Church and in offering service to those in their neighbourhood. But they too may sense that there is more – more to being a Christian, more to prayer, and much more to God than they have encountered until now. They, too, long for some way of finding a bridge across the gap between their experience up to this point and the abundant life which God longs to give each one of us in and through Jesus Christ.

This book is all about addressing that God-given longing, helping people make connections, helping people find a way of exploring their spiritual experience, offering spiritual direction to those who are 'marooned on the mainland' and equipping those who are called to the subtle and satisfying work of companioning others on their journey home to God, the constant bridge-builder.

What is 'Spiritual Direction'?

1.1 A self-serving novelty or a God-inspired opportunity?

⸎ Before we begin to look at how other people define 'spiritual direction', take a few minutes to write down your own thoughts about the term. You may want to explore your experience, note the ideas you have about how spiritual direction is done or what it hopes to achieve, your emotional response to the term itself and any questions which come to mind.

Whatever your personal experience of spiritual direction, the fact that you are holding this book means you have more than a passing interest in this ministry. However, although spiritual direction has always been part of the Christian tradition, it is not well understood, to some extent because of the terms 'director' and 'directee' which are found in much spiritual direction literature and history and which will be used throughout this book.

The word 'director' in common usage does describe someone whose role is to be *directive*, to tell others what they should be doing. The film director, for example, has the responsibility of seeing that actors portray the characters in a way that honours the script and story. However, if we think of 'director' as describing someone who helps people find their own route to God, it may be easier to set aside negative connotations.

'Directee' is used as a shorthand way of referring to 'the person who comes to see a spiritual director'. Other terms could be used: 'client' is one option, but this tends to be more commonly used in a counselling or social work context; 'friend' is another possibility, but as we shall see in more detail later, some of the traditional elements of friendship, such as a mutual sharing of experience, are generally less appropriate in the spiritual direction relationship.

People, inside or outside the Church, may think spiritual direction has something to do with:

- being told what to do in my spiritual life by an expert;
- someone giving me ideas about how to pray;
- having a talk with the minister;

- being accountable to someone for my spiritual progress;
- only for super-spiritual people like nuns and ministers!

There are little grains of truth in some of the above ideas, but gross inaccuracies as well – so let's look at each one:

'Being told what to do in my spiritual life by an expert'

Christian spiritual directors would discount any claims of 'expert' or 'guru' status, being aware of their fallibility and frailty, and their dependence on God. One of the potential risks for spiritual directors is that directees may want to put them on a pedestal of piety. On the other hand, it is of little use to directees if their spiritual directors have little idea of the dynamics of the spiritual journey. A healthy balance of knowledge, humility, experience and attentiveness to God's leading helps spiritual directors support the directees' journey instead of attempting to create a personal following. Like John the Baptist, spiritual directors always point to the One who is greater.

'Someone giving me ideas about how to pray'

Spiritual direction certainly has to do with prayer but in the context of the *whole* of the directee's life: successes and failures, wounds and blessings, relationships, work, health, hopes and fears. This 'definition' of spiritual direction also implies a certain passivity in the directee, as if he or she is not going to be very involved in the decision-making but a docile recipient of someone's else's choices. This subtle expectation assumes that the spiritual director is going to make things happen for the directee, when in fact the Holy Spirit is the true director, drawing the directee to a richer encounter with God. Occasionally spiritual directors might offer some resources or ideas about methods of prayer, but this will only be in response to what directees have shared about their life, prayer experience, and God-given longings for deepening relationship.

'Having a talk with the minister'

People talk to a minister about all sorts of things, not solely their journeys of faith. In reality, people bring personal problems, complaints, bright suggestions for new programmes – the list is endless. Spiritual direction takes place when the minister and parishioner are both *intentional* about paying attention to what God is doing in the parishioner's life. Spiritual-direction conversations with members of their congregation can greatly encourage clergy as they hear stories of God's activity in parishioners' lives. Sadly, many ministers have not been equipped for this vital part of their ministry and may struggle to know how to maximize the opportunity which lies waiting in every pastoral encounter.

'Being accountable to someone for my spiritual progress'

Most of us value having someone with whom we can evaluate any endeavour, and the Christian life is no different. Looking at spiritual direction this way, however, paints a picture of the directee being accountable *to the spiritual director*, rather than *to God*. A simple change of preposition will make a world of difference – 'being accountable *with* someone . . .' places the director alongside the directee, as a witness to the directee's movement towards God, as an ally in the times of struggle.

'Only for super-spiritual people like nuns and ministers'

Two assumptions lie behind this particular misconception. One is that spiritual direction is appropriate only for those who are in full-time ministry. However, lay people, by virtue of their baptism, have entered 'the priesthood of all believers'; all people are equal in the sight of God and can participate in spiritual direction if they wish. The second assumption is that, just because people are ordained ministers or vowed religious, they automatically have a highly disciplined, effective and rewarding spiritual life which includes a lively relationship with God. This may not always be the case.

✠

More accurately, spiritual direction could be defined as taking place when one person (the director) prayerfully supports and encourages another person (the directee) to attend and respond to God. As a fellow pilgrim, the spiritual director accompanies the directee on this journey of faith. The real 'director' is God the Holy Spirit, who initiates and inspires the directee's deepening relationship with the Trinity, with his or her own self, with other people, and with the realities of life in the global village of the twenty-first-century. Christian spiritual direction seeks to help directees:

- dive deeper into prayer and draw closer to God in everyday life;
- discover God's care in the midst of difficulties;
- become aware of the sacred within the ordinary events of life;
- honestly share with God their feelings, doubts and questions;
- become more like Christ and experience the fruits of the Spirit;

- move from a preoccupation with their sinfulness to a grace-full life of love and service.

Some current writers about spiritual direction have rightly drawn attention to the risk that directees might, at least initially, be more interested in developing their own spirituality without thinking much about the communal implications of growing closer to God. After all, there is much in contemporary society that promotes individualism, and spiritual growth is not immune to these influences.

Spiritual direction, however, is *not* about leading people away from the realities of the everyday world, or offering individuals a 'feel-good' experience, or fostering spiritual arrogance. Neither is it a more socially acceptable or trendy alternative to therapy. Spiritual direction *is* designed to help directees listen and respond to God – who desires relationship, and who longs for people to express the truth of who they are as they share their gifts, experience and personhood with others.

So, while the goal of spiritual direction is to help people grow to become more like Christ, emphasis is also given to the consequences of this growth: the outworking of the directees' life at home and in their chosen vocation, in their decision-making, and their imprint on the earth.

✠

Reflection questions

- Compare what you noted about spiritual direction at the start of this chapter with what has been written so far. Note any questions which have arisen for you.
- If you have already been seeing a spiritual director, how has that experience affected your understanding of God, of prayer and of your ministry?
- 'The real "director" is God the Holy Spirit, who initiates and inspires the directee's deepening relationship with the Trinity, with his or her own self, with other people, and with the realities of life in the global village of the twenty-first century.' Take a few minutes to reflect on this quotation and then write your response to it.
- Recalling the bridge metaphor, what sort of bridge seems right to express something of your movement towards God and God's movement towards you?

Using crayons or felt-tip pens, spend some time sketching the bridge – you don't have to be 'good at art' to make some lines on the page! You may want to add some words to describe what is going on for you as you see this bridge take shape. Then ask yourself:

- Who is helping me to 'build a bridge' towards God, to recognize God's activity in my life?
- What brings me closer to the One who loves me?
- What makes it harder for me to draw closer to God?
- What part of the bridge is 'under construction' at the present time?

1.2 A glimpse behind the scenes – spiritual direction in the Christian tradition

History shows that throughout the centuries followers of the way of Christ have sought help from mature Christians who had a deep capacity to listen with their hearts, who were familiar with the signposts and struggles on the Christian journey towards holiness, and who could, when familiar landmarks disappeared in the darkness, provide a strong beacon to keep the light of God alive.

I do not intend to provide a comprehensive treatment of the history of spiritual direction. Other writers, notably Kenneth Leech, cover this ground and provide an excellent overview of the practice of spiritual direction in the Eastern and the Western Church. Peter Ball has also written a valuable account of spiritual direction in the Anglican tradition. Details of their books can be found in the Further Reading section. What follows instead is a selection of influences, communities and individuals, which I hope will demonstrate that spiritual direction is securely embedded in the Christian tradition, and whet your appetite to do some further exploration:

- Anthony (251–356) and other Desert Fathers and Mothers in the fourth and fifth centuries. Attention to God, having a place of security (the cell), meditation on the scriptures, and wrestling with one's inner darkness, were at the centre of the spirituality of the time, with rare words offered to seekers as a sacrament by the spiritual Abba (Father) or Amma (Mother), who *lived* prayer rather than taught it.
- The early saints of the Celtic Church such as Brigid of Ireland, Patrick, Columba of Iona, and Cuthbert of Lindisfarne. The role of the soul friend *anam cara* was central in Celtic spiritual life during this period, and pilgrimage was a reality for many.
- John Cassian brought the teachings of the Desert to the West, and his writing influenced Benedict.
- Benedict, at Monte Cassino in the sixth century, established a form of Western monasticism which continues to this day. His 'Rule' consisted of a daily rhythm of work, rest, prayer and study, including spiritual reading (*lectio divina*), and simple accountability to other members of the community.

- Bernard of Clairvaux and his Cistercian contemplative community were committed to simplicity in prayer and shared their spiritual struggles with a trusted member of their brotherhood.
- Francis of Assisi, Clare and Dominic in the twelfth century lived a common life of radical poverty and love inspired by the Holy Spirit, and encouraged people's growth towards God.
- Aeldred of Rievaulx stressed the loving compassion of a spiritual father for his children and the virtue of spiritual friendship.
- English mystic Richard Rolle (1295–1349) focused his life on the love of God. He was the author of *The Fire of Love* and was spiritual director for Cistercian nuns in his later years.
- The unidentified fourteenth-century author of a long letter of spiritual guidance, *The Cloud of Unknowing*, describes the call to contemplation.
- Julian (1342–1413), an Anchoress, lived simply in a small room attached to a church in Norwich, and was visited by many for spiritual counsel. Her deep conviction that God's love overcomes all trials fills her book, *Revelations of Divine Love*.
- Catherine of Siena (1347–80) offered spiritual direction in person and by letter.
- St Ignatius of Loyola (1495–1556) developed the *Spiritual Exercises*, essentially a handbook for spiritual directors accompanying retreatants as they pray imaginatively through a sequence of scripture passages and experience a deep interior journey with Christ.
- St Teresa of Avila (1515–82) and St John of the Cross (1543–91), Spanish mystics from the Carmelite tradition, describe the growth of the soul and the nature and value of 'dark night' experiences.
- Martin Luther (1483–1546), although suspicious of any person apart from Jesus Christ mediating between man and God, nevertheless wrote letters of spiritual guidance, for example *A Simple Way to Pray*, written to a barber friend, Peter, giving him recommendations for his spiritual life.
- Thomas Cranmer, wrote *The Book of Common Prayer*, the foundational prayer book for the Anglican Church – a devotional aid and vehicle of spiritual direction.
- George Herbert was a gifted scholar, musician and poet who lived from 1593 to 1633. He is remembered as a fine example of a loving, spiritually wise, pastoral priest, and his poetry in particular is still a valuable source for meditation.
- Richard Baxter (1615–91) was a dedicated parish priest and moderate Puritan whose work *The Reformed Pastor* promoted spiritually sensitive pastoral practice and implored priests to pay attention to their own spiritual life and relationship with God.
- Jeremy Taylor in the 1660s, tried to encourage priestly spiritual guidance, and

his book, *Rules and Exercises for Holy Living*, contains advice, prayers and meditations.[1]

- John Wesley, pioneer of eighteenth-century Methodism, included many letters of individual spiritual guidance in his personal correspondence
- Laywoman Evelyn Underhill (1875–1941) made a significant contribution to spiritual direction as she searched for the holy, whether in her own life and prayer, in her exploration of the lives and experiences of those who had followed a mystical path to God, or in the lives of those who sought her spiritual counsel. She gave retreats, taught and wrote books and articles on the spiritual life, saw people for one-to-one spiritual direction, or wrote them helpful letters, longing for people to find a sense of the *reality* of God.
- In 1915, Fr Reginald Ward, at the age of 34, and following an unmistakable call from God, began a full-time ministry of spiritual direction. For nearly 50 years he travelled around England, often seeing a dozen people a day for half an hour at a time. Over the course of his ministry, thousands of people received spiritual counsel.
- Twentieth-century contributors to the ministry and understanding of spiritual direction include C. S. Lewis, Joyce Huggett, Henri Nouwen, Thomas Merton, Joyce Rupp, Gerard Hughes, Peter Ball, Anne Long, Alan Jones, Margaret Guenther and more recently David Benner.

As I have been writing this inevitably selective list, I am mindful of the sacred practice of reciting the names of those who have gone before – we see this publicly for example at Ground Zero in New York each anniversary of 11 September 2001. Closer to home, countless small communities honour their dead on special days of commemoration such as Armistice Day or Anzac Day or All Souls'. In many tribal-based communities to this day, the reciting of the names of the dead has serious social implications, forming for the living a line of belonging, a *whakapapa*[2] or genealogy which gives meaning and a sense of connection with those who have protected the *taonga*, the things of value, for subsequent generations.

As you have been reading this list I hope you have felt a link with the great stream of faith and spiritual direction practice in which we stand. By offering spiritual direction we are not promoting a novel, esoteric or transitory method of connecting with the Divine; we are instead reclaiming an ancient ministry – the cure of souls.

✠

---

1 Leech, Kenneth, *Soul Friend: Spiritual Direction in the Modern World* (revised edition), Harrisburg, PA: Morehouse, 2001, p. 74.

2 As I have lived in New Zealand for 50 years it comes naturally to me to use Maori words to explain some familiar aspects of life. *Whakapapa* is what we would call our 'family tree' or genealogical story, *taonga* literally means 'treasure' or 'that which is precious'.

Reflection opportunities

- ⏳ Take a few minutes to write down the names of those people who have shaped or encouraged your spiritual life. When you have finished, offer a prayer of thanksgiving for their lives.
- ⏳ A harder task – this time, write down the names of those people whom you have helped on their spiritual journey. Once you have finished, talk to God about what you have discovered, and offer these people into God's care and faithful love.
- ⏳ Has anyone ever written you a letter of encouragement about your spiritual journey? What was it like to receive and read it?

  Have you ever sent anyone a letter of encouragement on their Christian walk? Spend some time sitting quietly with God and see if anyone's name comes to mind. Then think about how you might encourage that person.
- ⏳ Look up one of the people listed in section 1.2 and find out more about her/ his life and ministry.

1.3 The complex contemporary world

As we have begun to see, for much of its history the Church has tried to provide spiritual direction for its members. Guided by the Holy Spirit, clergy and, less frequently, laity, have endeavoured to use one-to-one conversations about the ordinary things of life as the raw material for spiritual growth.

But we are now living in an age of unprecedented change when so much of what has been accepted for hundreds of years is being challenged, even deconstructed. In the general population, social cohesion is affected by migration, changing employment patterns, poverty and family dysfunction. There have been changes in the roles of men and women, in the place of religion in society, and huge developments in science. We are in a period of human history when, paradoxically, there is a burgeoning interest in *spirituality* but at the same time a decline in institutional expressions of the Christian *religion*, at least in the West.

- ⏳ What do you understand by the terms 'spirituality' and 'religion'?

  Once you have written down your own ideas, have a look at what follows.

The word 'spirituality' comes from the Latin word '*spirare*' which means 'to breathe'. The word's origin reminds us that spirituality is not an optional extra, something added to our lives, but is at the very core of what it means to be human.

However, it is quite possible to define 'spirituality' without mentioning God. P. G. Reed, for example, writing in a nursing context, defines spirituality as:

> making meaning through a sense of relatedness/connectedness to dimensions that transcend the self in a way that empowers and does not devalue the individual. This relatedness may be experienced via three dimensions: intra-personally – by having purpose, satisfaction and values; interpersonally – through giving and receiving in relationships; and trans-personally – by a link with a higher being.[3]

From this definition we can begin to understand why the term 'spirituality' is attractive to those who suspect there is something greater than themselves, something which gives their lives focus and meaning, even if institutional religion has no appeal.

The late Godfrey Wilson, a former Anglican Assistant Bishop of Auckland, put spirituality into a specifically Christian context when he wrote:

> For me the concept of spirituality encompasses:
>
> i the way I understand God's nature and purpose, and my own existence within that purpose (my vision of what my life is 'for', if you like);
> ii the way I live out this understanding in relationship with God and my fellow human beings;
> iii the spiritual resources and discipline which energize and sustain me as I do so.
>
> It is important for me to grasp that my spirituality is forged in struggle, and is not something I can somehow first 'acquire' before committing myself.[4]

How does 'religion' differ from 'spirituality'? It is not uncommon, after all, to hear people say, 'Well, I'm not *religious* . . . !' When invited to talk further, many equate the practice of religion with formality and inflexibility rather than with growth, creativity and hope. Holding an organized set of beliefs, participating in corporate worship and regular personal prayer are often outside their experience.

Whether we like it or not, the term 'post-Christian' has entered the contemporary landscape. Church attendance in the West is declining along with religious adherence, and people are less likely to pass on to their children a coherent system of religious belief and practice. With this diminishing community-consciousness of Christian teachings and traditions, comes a host of questions regarding how ministry and mission might be offered in contexts which are no longer overtly

3 Reed, P. G., 'An Emerging Paradigm for the Investigation of Spirituality in Nursing', *Research in Nursing and Health* 15, 1992, pp. 340–57.

4 In *Spirituality*, Spiritual Growth Ministries Trust, New Zealand, Spiritual Directors Formation Programme course notes.

shaped by the values and practices which have sustained Western civilization for two millennia.

☺ In a small group brainstorm ideas about:
   i what you see going on in society that may be contributing to a rise of interest in 'spirituality' and/or the Western decline in institutional Christianity;
   ii what you are aware of in terms of changes in religious practice in the world at large.

✠

You may have noted some of the following:

- Western individualism's personal growth goals expanding to include spiritual growth.
- A dissatisfaction with the degree to which organized religion is able to meet the spiritual needs of individuals.
- A proliferation of media programmes with supernatural or occult themes.
- A growing awareness that material abundance cannot make up for spiritual poverty.
- A search for meaning in the midst of massive change in modern society.
- A search for connectedness when there is dislocation, migration and fragmentation of families.
- New reproductive technologies which challenge previously accepted understandings of what constitutes human life and raise complex ethical questions.
- A postmodern deconstruction of meta-narratives – the overarching ways of making sense of our world are being taken apart.
- A search for security, for 'answers' in the face of the uncertainty of things like terrorism.
- Changes to living patterns, with seven-day shopping and less time for church attendance and recreation.
- A recognition that even when society discounts people's spiritual experience, such experience remains, waiting to be taken seriously.
- Rise in Christianity in Asia and Africa as numbers of adherents fall in the West.
- New forms of the Christian Church emerging in various places around the world, often modelled on simplicity and hospitality.
- Increasing public awareness that 'one size does not fit all', that there are different ways of being Christian or Muslim, and that there are 'moderates', not just 'fundamentalists' in all religions.
- Media coverage of areas of dispute in the Christian Churches, for example the blessing of same-sex couples and the ordination of gay and lesbian people.

David Tacey, Associate Professor at La Trobe University and teacher of spirituality courses to many young people, writes of the 'spirituality' revolution:

> What wells up from secular society is not dressed up in the costume of formal
> religion, but sometimes seems to draw on pre-theological contents . . . In popu-
> lar spirituality, we find people who are interested in long-forgotten initiatory or
> mystery cults, in indigenous tribal religions, in paganism and wicca, in astrol-
> ogy, and in long-buried divinatory systems and gnostic traditions. In the New
> Age market, everything is filtered through our pathologies and complexes, and
> is designed to appeal to egotism and pride . . .
>
> The task of religion is not to stand on dignity and rail against the inferiority of
> spirituality. Instead, it *has* to get down to ordinary experience and *build bridges
> of communication* between the new flood and traditional mystery.[5]

In the midst of this complicated and unpredictable period in the world's history,
people are searching for meaning, for depth, for stability, for a way of being with
the mystery beyond themselves which we would name as God. Sadly, however,
few people are aware that, in its contemplative tradition, the Christian Church has
a rich resource to share with people who want to engage with this mystery and
further explore their spiritual experience.

Rather than being critical, or afraid to engage with those who are on a spiritual
search in areas that to many of us may be unfamiliar or downright scary, the
Church, trusting the truth of Christ to draw all people to himself, has to find ways
of connecting with people in their neighbourhood, helping them grapple with mystery and eventually grow in their interior life for the good of all. Spiritual direction
is one way of offering hospitality to those on the road, perhaps long before they
find 'the way', as this story illustrates:

> 'Jenny' was in third form when I met her. I was the college chaplain at the
> time. She was a bright kid adept at rubbing adults/teachers up the wrong way.
> Witchcraft was her passion but she was interested in all religions and asked for
> some Christian material to read. I gave her a New Testament and showed her
> the stories of Jesus. Over the ensuing months Jenny's interest in Jesus genuinely
> increased with every discussion. Ironically, her practice in witchcraft increased
> also. She joined the local youth group while still clinging to her 'craft' but even-
> tually strayed from the Christian scene altogether.
>
> I met her some years later and discovered she had become a house captain at
> her school, a sportswoman of national acclaim, was no longer practising witch-
> craft, had dedicated her life to Christ and was fellowshipping in a local church.

---

5 Tacey, David, *The Spirituality Revolution: The Emergence of Contemporary Spirituality*,
Sydney: HarperCollins, 2003, p. 25. Italics mine.

Jenny came to direction with no understanding of the process of spiritual direction, scant understanding of the Christian story but keen to talk about her spiritual journey.[6]

'Keen to talk about her spiritual journey.' That is often the catalyst for people who are searching, and how we respond to that longing is critical. In this case, the chaplain responded to Jenny's searching, not with judgement but by sharing with her 'the stories of Jesus' and letting the Spirit meet Jenny in her reality. This takes courage, confidence in God's grace and a deep conviction that the Spirit will continue to work in whoever we meet, long after our association with them is ended.

✠

Reflection questions

⚭ What aspects of the changes we have discussed have affected you or your family?

⚭ Reflect on your own spiritual journey. You may like to draw a timeline and mark on it moments of choice which took you towards or further away from God. To what extent have you explored alternative or 'New Age' spiritualities? If at some point your path took you away from the Church and its teachings, what did you learn from those alternatives, and what happened to start you on the return journey?

⚭ If you think of the Church community that you know best, how does the body of Christ, the people in that place, offer hospitality to the searching 'traveller on the road'?

⚭ Look again at Jenny's story. What experience do you have with people who are exploring other spiritualities? How do you relate to those who are on a spiritual path that differs radically from yours?

1.4 Spiritual direction and other helping relationships

People within the Church, those who are apparently already on 'the way', also need:

• a safe, non-judgemental context in which to explore new understandings of God;

---

6 Brown, Simon, *Mission and the Art of Spiritual Direction*, research project written as part of the requirements for the Spiritual Directors' Formation Programme, New Zealand: Spiritual Growth Ministries, 2002, p. 4. Full text available on <www.sgm.org.nz>. Used with permission.

- encouragement when prayer hits the ceiling and words of praise droop from overuse;
- support as they negotiate the theological implications of harrowing life events.

We know from studies among church leavers from Pentecostal, Charismatic and Evangelical[7] backgrounds, that unless churchgoers find a climate in which their stories and experience can be respected, their questions heard without judgement, their difficulties in prayer met with understanding not accusation, and their longing to grow affirmed and resourced, they simply leave. It is not a question of whether or not they still believe in God – most do; they leave because no one can help them navigate this new stage of their spiritual journey. Undirected, they move out and away.

Although there is an unprecedented need for competent, sensitive spiritual directors to help those who attend church regularly, those who come into the Church as seekers and those outside the Church with whom we might have even a casual connection, we still don't see spiritual direction being resourced or offered in parish, chaplaincy or community contexts. Instead we see a range of other valuable helping relationships such as supervision, discipling, mentoring and pastoral counselling.

Supervision

Ministry supervision helps people reflect regularly and in depth on their ministry, their skills and capacities for service, and the issues which are raised as they go about their daily work. The supervisee normally sets the agenda, and the supervisor is responsible for facilitating the process. It is often seen as a 'two heads are better than one' dynamic, and can include problem-solving and teaching. Issues discussed might include:

- Difficult relationships with colleagues/parishioners.
- Sad or frustrating pastoral situations.
- Boundary issues and dual relationships, for example where a parishioner is also the minister's doctor.
- Sexual attraction/other strong reactions.
- Provisions for good self-care.
- Identifying personal issues and discussing whether or not these need further work and with whom this might be done.

---

7 See for example research undertaken by Alan Jamieson, *A Churchless Faith: Faith Journeys Beyond the Churches*, London: SPCK, 2002.

Ministry supervision is necessary for safe practice and guards against any abuse of power by those working with people who may be vulnerable. Although a supervisee's spiritual life may come up in the conversation, unless the supervisor is also a spiritual director and the two agree to a change of focus, the supervisee would usually be encouraged to take any spiritual struggles or questions to his or her own spiritual director for a deeper exploration.

Discipling and mentoring

Discipling is likely to be most useful when people are new Christians and need to find out what is appropriate behaviour, learn the basics of the faith and how to apply those principles in daily life, cope with criticism from family or friends, and build up relationships with other Christians in a small group setting. The discipler is often seen as someone to look up to, someone whose faith is strong and who would be a good example to follow, so initially the relationship can have a 'teacher/student' or even 'parent/child' quality to it. Because of the relative frequency – often meeting weekly in a one-to-one or small group setting, the intensity of the relationship can lead to dependency, so access to good supervision is essential.

Mentoring is often initiated by someone who has a good grasp of the basics and wants to refine an aspect of their application; for example, a youth leader with a solid Christian upbringing may seek out a person with more experience of working with a particular age group, looking for encouragement and advice relevant to a particular context. There is often a 'master/apprentice' feel to this relationship, a learning from an experienced practitioner who acts as coach and adviser. The relationship may be ongoing or for a short period of time to address some particular issue.

Pastoral counselling

A significant development in the way pastoral counselling was offered in the UK took place in 1958 with the establishment of the Clinical Theology movement by Dr Frank Lake. Taking insights from Christian sources and the then current psychiatry, Lake hoped to improve the pastoral care being offered by clergy and, at the same time, assist clergy to recognize their own biases or neuroses. Courses were offered around Britain in the 1960s and early 1970s.[8]

---

8 For further details about this movement see Leech, *Soul Friend*, pp. 92–3 and Ball, Peter, *Journey Into Truth: Spiritual Direction in the Anglican Tradition*, London: Mowbray, 1996, p. 89.

From about the mid-1970s, as clergy grappled with their apparently diminishing role in society,[9] improving their counselling skills seemed an appropriate way to meet people's needs. Around the same time, the Clinical Pastoral Counselling movement was developing in the United States and, in the decades since then, many clergy and laity in various parts of the world have taken the opportunity to develop skills to improve their pastoral work. However, the hidden catch was that the model on which the Clinical Pastoral Counselling movement was based was primarily analytical, diagnostic and individualistic, borrowed from a Western medical setting and not grounded in the Christian spiritual traditions. It is not surprising, therefore, that much pastoral counselling became – and still remains – problem or crisis-focused, relying heavily on modern psychological and therapeutic theory and practices rather than on pastoral and ascetical theology for its rationale and delivery.

Of course many have benefited from pastoral counselling and from experiencing Clinical Pastoral Education (CPE) courses. However, the less helpful effects of this clinical background which I have noted above continue to seep into much modern pastoral counselling practice.

Professional Christian counsellors from different theoretical frameworks may well recognize the importance of the client's spiritual life, but in practice they are expected to help clients find ways to cope more effectively, and so their focus is not usually on the client's relationship with God. Like the shepherds in Genesis 29.1–3, who have to take the stone off the well before the sheep can access the water, such counsellors usually have to concentrate on helping clients get to the point where they can lift the 'stone' and deal with their problem or crisis. Helping them explore the nature of the deep resource available to them in God is not seen as the counsellors' role, nor may they have the time or specific expertise to accompany clients who, for example, want to begin to 'let the bucket down' into the well of prayer.

We also face the reality that, as most parishes don't have their own professional counselling services, parishioners will talk to the priest or pastoral assistant when they strike difficulties, looking for solutions to problems and a reduction in anxiety. Ministers naturally want to support people in emotional need, and help them develop strategies to overcome the presenting problems or crises. Such help is necessary of course, and I don't want in any way to devalue skilled counselling offered in a parish context, but the question has to be asked: 'Is there something else ministers might offer?'

---

9 Martin Thornton, writing in the 1980s, commented that the overall answer to a recent sociological survey asking if clergy fulfilled any useful function in society was 'No'. See *Spiritual Direction: A Practical Introduction*, London: SPCK, 1984, p. 5.

A regaining of focus: the 'cure of souls'

Eugene Peterson in his book *The Contemplative Pastor* writes hopefully of a re-examination of the core task of pastors, and identifies a shift away from a managerial model of church leadership back to the 'cure of souls':

> The primary sense of *cura* in Latin is 'care', with undertones of 'cure'. The cure of souls, then, is the Scripture-directed, prayer-shaped care that is devoted to persons singly or in groups, in settings sacred and profane. It is a determination to work at the center, to concentrate on the essential . . .[10]

> . . . the cure of souls is not a specialised form of ministry (analogous, for instance, to hospital chaplain or pastoral counsellor) but is the essential pastoral work. It is . . . a way of life that uses weekday tasks, encounters and situations as the raw material for teaching prayer, developing faith and preparing for a good death . . . It is also a term that identifies us with our ancestors and colleagues in ministry, lay and clerical, who are convinced that a life of prayer is the connective tissue between holy day proclamation and weekly discipleship.[11]

Martin Thornton, writing in the United Kingdom in the 1980s about the need for spiritual direction and passionately describing prayer as the 'peak of human achievement' has this to say:

> Spiritual direction is the way forward. It is the positive nurture of man's relation to God, the creative cultivation of *charismata*; the gifts and graces that all have received. It is the opposite of the sort of pastoral care which assumes that religion can only offer little bits of help in emergencies: the ambulance syndrome. And it is the obverse of what has come to be called pastoral counselling, or perhaps more fairly the necessary consummation of it; if counselling deals with problems, direction takes over as soon as they are solved.[12]

Pastoral counselling and spiritual direction do share a set of core skills such as creating rapport, encouraging openness, active listening, appropriate questioning, reflecting content and feelings, summarizing, etc. Both respect the uniqueness of the individual person's life story and desire for health and wholeness. Both are committed to confidentiality and ethical behaviour, using regular supervision or peer review of their practice. However, the central work, focus and structure are different, as the Table opposite illustrates.

---

10 Peterson, Eugene H., *The Contemplative Pastor: Returning to the Art of Spiritual Direction*, Grand Rapids, MI: Eerdmans, 1989, p. 57.

11 Peterson, *The Contemplative Pastor*, p. 59.

12 Thornton, *Spiritual Direction*, pp. 10–11.

	Counselling	Spiritual direction
Problems	The focus is on helping the client to find a way through the issues they have raised, to develop strategies and become better able to function.	Problems and difficulties may form part of what is discussed, but always the focus will turn to the questions of faith, of prayer, of wondering where God might be in the midst of the directee's experience. Valuable when there are no pressing problems, and the directee is learning to discern the movement of God in the midst of daily routines.
Prayer	Depending on the context and the background of the counsellor and client, prayer may or may not form part of the session.	Prayer is central to the process: a spiritual director prays for the directee between sessions, prepares prayerfully before each meeting, and the session is conducted in an atmosphere of prayer.
Presence of the Holy Spirit	Not usually referred to.	God as Third Party Presence is openly acknowledged; silence and space help both director and directee listen to the Spirit.
Pace and process	May occur weekly for some weeks or months, or longer in some therapeutic contexts such as Jungian analysis.	Usually once a month or at longer intervals depending on the needs of the directee; may, with regular reviews, extend for many years, so long as the directee is still growing in his or her relationship with God.

Reflection questions

◊ Reflect on your own experience of supervision, discipling, mentoring or pastoral counselling offered in a Christian context.

◊ For which of these four helping relationships do you currently feel best or least equipped?

What questions are raised for you as you recognize areas of inadequacy or competence?

◊ How easy is it to access good supervision and pastoral counselling in your context?

◊ Both Peterson and Thornton consider spiritual direction central to the work of pastoral ministry and the *distinctive function* of all priests, ministers, chaplains and pastoral workers.

What is your response to this assertion?

What are the implications for you in what Peterson and Thornton are saying?

1.5 Biblical examples of spiritual direction

There is no better place to deepen our understanding of spiritual direction than to look at the scriptures. We see one example of God at work in an unsuspecting individual's life in 1 Samuel 3.1–18, the story of the old priest Eli and the young Samuel who has been serving God in the temple ever since he was weaned. Eli is frail, nearly blind, and grieving because of what lies ahead for his faithless family. In the silence and darkness, Samuel hears a voice calling him by name. He runs to Eli thinking the old man has summoned him, only to be told, mysteriously, that Eli has done no such thing.

⚮ Read the story from 1 Samuel 3.6–18 and then ask yourself: 'If spiritual direction is all about helping someone find their way to God, what can I learn about spiritual direction in action from this passage?'

✠

You may have noticed things like:

- Eli knew enough about the ways of God *to recognize* that God was making a personal approach to the young Samuel; Eli also knew how to help the young boy *receive and respond* to that call.
- Eli was not afraid because he knew enough of God's character to trust God's goodness and purpose for Samuel.
- The gentleness in Eli's response suggests a genuine care for this young boy.
- In spite of Eli's diminishing strength and the difficulties he has with his disobedient sons, God still uses him as a bridge to reach Samuel; people offering spiritual direction to others don't have to be perfect.
- In spite of being familiar with temple life, Samuel as yet has no personal connection with the God whom he serves.
- This passage involves three people, not two: there is Eli, there is Samuel and there is God, a God who is not remote or absent, but, by the Spirit, present and active.
- This call has its origin in God, not in Samuel or in Eli. Always God initiates, makes a move towards us, is at work even in our darkness whether or not we recognize the touch of grace.

The second example comes from the New Testament, and the ministry and role of John the Baptist. With uncharacteristic consistency, all four Gospels portray John in the words of Isaiah 40.3 as a voice crying out in the wilderness, '. . . prepare the way of the LORD, make straight in the desert a highway for our God'. John has the prophetic task of helping people begin to recognize their own need of

18

God. People are drawn to him – perhaps initially because of his eccentric lifestyle, but increasingly because in him they sense a person who is in touch with God. Although some of the passages reveal him to be far from gentle and conciliatory, nevertheless in the baptism of repentance he provides a way for the crowds to take a step towards God.

🕯 Again take a few minutes to consider what can be learned about spiritual direction from this key New Testament character.

✠

You may have thought of some of the following:

- John knows his place in the order of things. 'The one who is more powerful than I is coming after me; I am not worthy to stoop down and untie the thong of his sandals. I have baptised you with water; but he will baptise you with the Holy Spirit' (Mark 1.7–8).
- Years of solitude and silence had helped him develop an attentiveness to the prompting of the Holy Spirit, particularly apparent when Jesus came to him for baptism. How easy it would have been for him to have let his own unworthiness sabotage the purposes of God.
- People were drawn to him in droves, yet the action of baptism could only take place one-on-one – there was the intimacy of human touch offering the promise of forgiveness and hope.
- John resisted any attempts to put him on a pedestal or ascribe to him 'Messiah' status. He knew the task God had given him – to point others towards Jesus so even in the face of others' adulation, he resolutely claimed the lesser role: 'You yourselves are my witnesses that I said, "I am not the Messiah, but I have been sent ahead of him . . . He must increase, but I must decrease"' (John 3.28, 30).
- John finds fulfilment and joy in being the 'friend of the bridegroom' (John 3.29).

Jesus as spiritual director

There are plenty of examples of Jesus acting as a spiritual director, but a few will get us started:

- His meeting with Nicodemus (John 3.1–21).
- His encounter with the rich young man (Mark 10.17–22).
- The walk with two disheartened disciples on the road to Emmaus (Luke 24.13–32).

☺ Use the table below as a guide for a discussion about the way Jesus acted as spiritual director for each of the people in the three passages of scripture. Consider how each person may have felt or what they might have thought, and list ideas about how Jesus engaged with each one; include any questions you might have about his approach.

	Directee	Jesus as spiritual director
John 3.1–21 Nicodemus		
Mark 10.17–22 Rich young man		
Luke 24.13–32 Disciples on the road to Emmaus		

🔥 After your discussion, compare your responses with the suggestions in the table below.

	Directee	Jesus as spiritual director
John 3.1–21 Nicodemus	Wary of the opinion of his peers; tentative, but searching for the truth; gradually realizing the unique character of Jesus; a teacher of the faith yet lacking understanding of spiritual growth; willing to take the risk of exposing his ignorance by asking a question.	Was not drawn in by Nicodemus's initial admiration; pointed to the kingdom of God; helped Nicodemus move from a literal to a symbolic understanding of 'to be born again'; taught Nicodemus about the Spirit; gently confronted him with his ignorance; re-stated the central fact of God's intention to save the world through Jesus . . .
Mark 10.17–22 Rich young man	Recognizes in Jesus someone who can help him; is very keen to do the right thing in his spiritual life; is pleased to be able to say he has kept the commandments; is confronted by his attachment to wealth; goes away sad . . . (but thoughtful?).	Was not drawn in by the young man's admiration; pointed to God, not himself; spoke the truth with compassion; did not chase after the young man but released him to wrestle with the reality of his attachment to material goods.

Luke 24.13–32 Disciples on the road to Emmaus	Preoccupied with their grief, disappointment and confusion; need to speak about the events in Jerusalem as they try to make sense of what had happened; reveal their understanding of who Jesus was; share their hopes about his resurrection and the story of the women visiting the tomb; want to talk more with Jesus and/or want to make sure their companion is offered hospitality; left remembering the *felt experience* of the encounter on the road – when their hearts were touched by the presence of Christ.	Approached them and walked alongside for a time, without revealing his identity; asked open-ended questions; in the context of companionship he confronted them with their lack of faith; helped them understand the scriptures; accepted their offer of hospitality; reconnected them with the events of the Last Supper and in doing so revealed his true identity; left them to reflect on their experience.

In the Reflection section that follows there is an opportunity to summarize your understanding of the way Jesus offered spiritual direction, but for now let us turn to look at another encounter in more detail.

⚭ From John 4, read the encounter between Jesus and the Samaritan woman. Although this passage will already be familiar to you, ask the Holy Spirit to help you to look at it with fresh eyes, perhaps putting yourself into the story – as the woman, one of the disciples or townspeople, or as Jesus.
When you are ready, list as many things as you can about how Jesus helped the woman to grow closer to an awareness of God and what effect the encounter had on her.

✠

You may have noted:

- Jesus breaks cultural and religious rules by talking to the woman.
- Their first exchange is about something she could relate to – physical thirst – and the surprise of his taking the initiative to approach her.
- As Jesus speaks about 'the gift of God', the woman begins to ask questions about his identity.
- Jesus encourages a shift in the woman from a *literal* understanding of water to a *symbolic* interpretation, which opens up for her a *spiritual* awareness as she comes to see that the life of God is available to her in and through Christ.

- She feels safe enough to reveal her desire for a better quality of life.
- Jesus clearly is listening to the Holy Spirit as he talks with the woman – hence his invitation to her to 'call her husband'. Although many commentators say she was a woman of questionable virtue, she may have been caught up in the lottery of levirate marriage.[13] Either way, Jesus helps her face her social isolation and praises her honesty.
- As she goes deeper in self-awareness, she begins to talk more about her faith. They begin a discussion on the *differences* in their worship practices which ends when she states her belief: 'I know that Messiah is coming . . . ' (verse 25).
- And then Jesus takes the unprecedented step of revealing his true identity to her.
- The encounter changes her. She returns to her village and is impelled to talk to those she meets, sharing the wonder of his revelation to her.

Jesus, by taking a risk, by showing acceptance, by using the ordinary as a gateway to the divine, by discussing points of difference, by gentle challenge, by wise discernment, by affirmation and by self-revelation, helped this unnamed woman pay attention, respond, grow and move out into her community in faith and wonder. This is spiritual direction in action, and a pattern we can aspire to as we companion others.

But, unlike the single encounter that Jesus had with the Samaritan woman, and the other biblical examples we have looked at, spiritual direction undertaken by fallible human beings – both director and directee – is generally a slower, unfolding process which can take different forms depending on the model of spiritual direction which is being practised as we shall see in the next section.

✠

Reflection questions

⚲ Choose either passage and make some notes about how Jesus related to the person concerned and what we can learn about spiritual direction from his example:

Zaccheus: Luke 19.1–10

The lawyer: Luke 10.25–37.

⚲ Referring back to the table, make a list of the common threads and the differences in the way Jesus offers spiritual direction to:

Nicodemus: John 3.1–21

---

13 For a less disparaging view of the Samaritan woman, see for example Newsom, Carol A. and Ringe, Sharon H. (eds), *Women's Bible Commentary*, Louisville, KY: Westminster John Knox Press, 1998, p. 384.

The rich young man: Mark 10.17–22

The disciples on the road to Emmaus: Luke 24.13–35.

What would you like to incorporate in your own practice of spiritual direction?

♦ If you have some experience of seeing a spiritual director, compare the way Jesus offered spiritual direction with the way you have experienced it so far.

1.6 Contemporary models of spiritual direction

Evelyn Underhill, who has already been mentioned briefly, was not averse to expressing disapproval of the clergy's inability to provide spiritual direction, as an extract from her letter to the Archbishop of Canterbury before the Lambeth Conference in 1930 demonstrates:

> All who do personal religious work know that the real hunger among the laity is not for halting attempts to reconcile theology and physical science but for the deep things of the spirit . . .
>
> We look to the clergy to help and direct our spiritual growth. We are seldom satisfied, because with a few noble exceptions they are so lacking in spiritual realism, so ignorant of the laws and experiences of the life of prayer. Their dealings with souls are often vague and amateurish. Those needing spiritual help may find much kindliness, but seldom that firm touch and firsthand knowledge of interior ways which come only from a disciplined personal life of prayer . . .
>
> The two things the laity wants from the priesthood are spiritual realism and a genuine love of souls.[14]

In response to this need, which is still as real as when Underhill wrote her letter, spiritual direction formation has been slowly gaining ground since the 1970s. However, it is important to note that there is more than one way of being *formed* in and practising spiritual direction.

You may wonder why I have used *formed* and not *trained* in spiritual direction. This is because spiritual direction is an art, a dynamic flow of listening and responding, of questions and wonderings, of encouragement, of silence, all in the context of prayer. Although people can be exposed to a body of spiritual direction principles, practices and attitudes, the actual application of these is dependent upon the relationships between the directee and God, the director and God, and the director and the directee. This book encourages substantial personal reflection because spiritual direction education at its best seeks to be *formative*, to provide

---

14 Ball, *Journey into Truth*, pp. 52–3, from a typescript copy of Underhill's letter.

a *process* in which the spiritual director develops personally and spiritually, while gaining the knowledge and practical skills related to a particular model of spiritual direction.

A spiritual direction 'model' relates to a set of underlying principles, core practices, content and attitudes which together form a coherent and consistent way of working with directees. In each case, the theoretical background gives rise to a particular style of interaction between director and directee, and a way of viewing their respective roles and responsibilities. While in the early stages of formation in this ministry emphasis may clearly be given to one particular model, in contemporary spiritual direction experienced directors may occasionally draw from a variety of models. Keeping that in mind, we will look briefly at several contemporary models of spiritual direction and will then explore in more depth the model on which this book is based: contemplative, incarnational spiritual direction.

Institutional spiritual direction

The institutional model of spiritual direction has commonly been associated with religious seminaries and residential theological colleges. Often the person responsible for the spiritual development of novices has to manage several tasks:

- Instruct the novice in the *charism* of the particular order's leader and what was expected in terms of being a member of this part of the Church, for example a Jesuit brother or priest would become familiar with St Ignatius' life and works and the order's reputation for intellectual excellence.
- Guide the development of the novice's spiritual life in ways that were appropriate for that particular order, institution and denomination, with little variation for the individual.
- Maintain orthodoxy of belief and adherence to the practices and dogma which were central to the preservation of the particular denomination.
- In many cases, be the person to whom novices would make their confession.

Someone who has experienced this model might understand spiritual direction mainly in terms of passing on a body of knowledge, hearing confession, guarding orthodoxy and encouraging the individual to abide by the institutional norms. This is the sort of spiritual direction which is described in Mother Teresa of Calcutta's letters.[15]

---

15 Mother Teresa, *Come be my Light*, Brian Kolodiejchuk (ed.), New York: Doubleday, 2007.

Sacramental spiritual direction

Closely linked to the institutional model is the model of sacramental spiritual direction, which is predominantly expressed through the ministry of Confession and Absolution (more likely called the ministry of reconciliation nowadays). In this form of spiritual direction, the priest or minister is the confessor and the directee is the penitent who comes to speak honestly about the shortcomings in his or her life and to hear the forgiveness of God pronounced by a person assigned this responsibility by the Church. The dynamic between the director and directee is that of one being the agent of God's forgiveness to the other, and so the focus is on those areas of the directee's life where there has been a falling short of godly standards of behaviour and attitudes – in other words, sin. However, this focus means that other areas of the person's life, including their spiritual experience, may not be given specific attention.

Ignatian spiritual direction

As the name suggests, this model of spiritual direction is based on the teaching of St Ignatius of Loyola, founder of the Jesuits and the author of the *Spiritual Exercises*. Spiritual directors formed in this tradition will be guided by Ignatius' ideas about discernment, encouraging the directee to notice interior movements, feelings of 'consolation' and 'desolation'. Attention will be paid to the value of meditating on scripture particularly using the imagination to enter into the scene as completely as possible. The practice of the *Examen* – an evening recollection of the day's events and personal behaviour – is also recommended.

Interpersonal spiritual direction

Following the Celtic tradition of the soul-friend (*anam cara*) and other examples of spiritual friendship between director and directee, this model has become more widely promoted, especially among those in the evangelical movement who are familiar with the Prayer Partner concept and who seek the benefits of one-to-one spiritual direction. David Benner in *Sacred Companions*[16] writes helpfully of the ideals of spiritual friendship and the possibility of spiritual direction between friends – even between marriage partners.

However, one disadvantage of giving and receiving spiritual direction in this model is the risk of losing one's ability to be objective and, if necessary, confrontational, 'speaking the truth in love' in the interests of the other person's spiritual growth. Mutual spiritual direction can certainly work for mature Christians able

---

16 Benner, David G., *Sacred Companions*, Downers Grove, IL: InterVarsity Press, 2002.

to maintain good boundaries, but may be less appropriate for those new to either giving or receiving spiritual direction.

Psychotherapeutic spiritual direction

Some spiritual directors work from a theoretical base which draws heavily on psychotherapeutic practices or psychological principles; for example, considerable attention may be given to inner-child work or psychosexual integration, all with the worthwhile intention of bringing healing and freeing the person from past trauma. It is possible, however, that their focus may be more on the individuation process from a psychological perspective than on the directee's experience of God and how that might be moving the directee towards spiritual and psychological maturity.

Interfaith spiritual direction

This is a form of spiritual direction that is gradually emerging as interfaith dialogue gathers momentum in various parts of the world. While some would shy away from the idea that a Christian spiritual director could, with integrity, accompany a Muslim directee for example, there are some directors who choose to make themselves available to people of a faith tradition different from their own. This is particularly true for ministers who work in chaplaincy contexts as we shall see later.

Spiritual direction in other faith traditions

There have always been people in other faith traditions who have been available to help their members grow. Over the past ten years, some people from other faith traditions have participated in Christian-based spiritual direction formation programmes, but more recently dedicated formation programmes for other faiths have begun to emerge, for example a group of Jewish spiritual directors has been formed in the USA and acts as a focus, education provider and support for other Jews offering spiritual direction ministry elsewhere.

Contemplative, incarnational spiritual direction

Two rather long words describe the model of spiritual direction on which this book is based. In terms of spiritual direction *incarnational* recognizes that God is at work within the directee and the director and that both bring their full personhood to the task of spiritual direction. God finds a way *into* our lives through our physical, emotional, rational, relational and spiritual selves, and the way we use them in all our relationships. And God engages with the world *through* our embodied selves as Teresa of Avila reminds us: 'Christ has no body now but yours, no hands, no feet on earth but yours. Yours are the eyes through which He looks compassion on this world.'[17] God's Holy Spirit informs our thinking, strengthens our will, guides our decision-making, and enlivens our prayer – and enables us to be present to another person in the compassionate listening which is at the heart of spiritual direction.

The other word, *contemplative*, links spiritual direction with a particular tradition in the Christian Church and with a model of spiritual direction which has re-emerged over the last 30 years. Initially described by Sandra Schneiders, Madeline Birmingham, William Barry and Bill Connolly, this model has been the basis for many formation programmes in spiritual direction around the world. It describes spiritual direction as enabling a person (the directee) to:

- pay attention to God's personal communication to him or her;
- respond to this personally communicating God;
- grow in intimacy with this God; and
- live out the consequences of the relationship.[18]

How do *you* understand the term 'contemplation'? You may like to consider not only the Christian context but how the term is used among the general population. Again, once you have made some notes, compare them to what is written below and note any questions which arise.

✠

Walter Burghardt defines 'contemplation' as 'taking a long loving look at the real'.[19] Contemplation from this perspective means that we take time to stop and pay attention to *anything in our experience which attracts our attention*. We engage in a form of 'concentrated looking' which allows us time to see below the surface to a deeper level of meaning, or beyond the literal to the symbolic. So we might, for example, take 'a long loving look at' a mother pushing a pram; a youngster with ear and nose piercings playing a guitar in the shopping centre; an old man walking with the aid of a stick; or an urban fox moving like a mist through the garden.

---

17 Teresa of Avila – widely quoted.

18 Barry, William A. and Connolly, William A., *The Practice of Spiritual Direction*, San Francisco: HarperCollins, 1982.

19 Burghardt, Walter J., 'Contemplation: A Long Loving Look at the Real', in *Church*, Winter 1989. Quotation accessed at website <http://www.shalem.org/resources/quotations>, 3 December 2006.

Or we might pay attention to our inner reaction, for example the deep joy after a friend's phone call; or our surprising sense of loss when a child leaves for a well-planned and anticipated 'gap' year.

If we expand this idea of *concentrated looking* to include things we think of as belonging to our spiritual life such as our reading of scripture or singing of a hymn or our prayer, we can see that contemplation simply means stopping and paying loving attention to God who comes to meet us in the midst of everyday events or places. It means allowing ourselves to be caught up, however momentarily, in the reality of Jesus as Emmanuel, God with us.

There is a second way of using the word 'contemplation'. In the sixth century, Gregory of Nyssa described contemplation as 'the knowledge of God impregnated with love . . . the *fruit* of reflection on the word of God in scripture and at the same time a *gift* of God . . . *resting* in God . . .'[20]

For many centuries, reflecting on the word of God was a common method of prayer, and in essence means *paying loving attention* to a small daily portion of the word of God. Traditionally called *lectio divina*, or sacred reading, the dynamic process is well described by Dom Marmion: 'We read under the eye of God, until the heart is touched and leaps to flame.'[21] The process involves four elements which weave together like a braided river to connect us with God:

Lectio	Slow, reflective reading aloud of a few verses of scripture or other spiritual literature.
Meditatio	A thoughtful consideration of how these words relate to our current circumstances.
Oratio	Discoveries, emotional responses, movements of the heart and will, questions or doubts are shared with God.
Contemplatio	The person at prayer stills his or her activity and 'contemplates'.

This second use of the word 'contemplation' relates then to a state of resting in God, all our striving set aside, allowing ourselves to be open to meeting the One who created us. Contemplation from this perspective is a gift of grace to a heart and spirit open to the wonder of the love of God. And most importantly, this form of Christian contemplation, rather than being considered as the preserve of a spiritual élite, is for *any* Christian who wants to respond to the Spirit-initiated desire for more of God, and who is willing to be moved from word-filled activity to wordless receptivity.

---

20 Keating, Thomas, *Foundations for Centring Prayer and the Christian Contemplative Life*, London: Continuum, 2004, p. 20. Italics mine.

21 Hall, Thelma, *Too Deep for Words: Rediscovering Lectio Divina*, New York: Paulist Press, 1988, p. 44.

As we shall see later, the term 'contemplation' is significant in the writings of spiritual teachers such as St Teresa of Avila and St John of the Cross. In their descriptions of growth in prayer, 'contemplation' occurs when all our customary images, words, meditations and effort in prayer are replaced by a grace-full and loving God's self-communication.

Contemplation and action

There is a common misconception that contemplation takes us away from the struggles of 'the real world'. But Catherine of Siena reminded the Church of the true relationship between action and contemplation when she wrote: 'The secret of Christian contemplation is that it faces us with Jesus Christ *toward* our suffering world in loving service and just action.'[22] To be able to bring touches of healing, reconciliation, encouragement, challenge and consolation to those we meet in our parishes, chaplaincies and wider circles, we need time apart with God so that we may be filled regularly by the Spirit's love and wisdom, listen to God so we can make good choices, and so we may know, right in the core of our being, that we are beloved of God, so that when we fail or falter, as we most likely will, we can still trust the reality of the solid ground of grace beneath us. And that knowledge comes as we listen deeply to God in contemplative prayer. If we engage in action without contemplation we run the risk of:

- expending our resources of time, money and people-power on things that may not really further the kingdom;
- failing to consider the real motives that lie behind our actions;
- not noticing Spirit-inspired ways of handling a project or solving a problem;
- falling into the trap of thinking that everything depends on us, not on God.

However, if our action is informed by our contemplative practices, we are spiritually and personally equipped at a deep level to do what God calls us to do. Jesus modelled this balance for us as he regularly sought places of solitude where he could spend time in prayer to his Father (for example Luke 5.15–16; Mark 6.46). Once renewed in spirit, he would return to the demands of the day, to the people pressing in on him, looking for miracles and mercy wherever he went.

Mother Teresa of Calcutta spent her life on the hard edge of world poverty and disease. Each morning, she and her group of Sisters would spend substantial time in contemplative prayer, drawing strength from God for the demands of the day ahead with its relentless stream of desperately needy people seeking a place

---

22 Shalem Institute, <http://www.shalem.org/resources/quotations>, accessed 3 December 2006.

of sanctuary away from the impersonal Calcutta streets. One of her prayers helps us appreciate the grace-filled movement from contemplation to action, as God resources our service and brings peace:

The fruit of silence is prayer
The fruit of prayer is faith
The fruit of faith is love
The fruit of love is service
The fruit of service is peace.[23]

In contemplative, incarnational spiritual direction, we depend on the Holy Spirit to guide our thinking, warm our compassion, inspire our discernment and help us assist our directees to:

- explore their experience of God, whether in prayer, through traditional vehicles of scripture and creation, or through daily life events or symbols which attract the directee's attention;
- grow in their ability to rest in God;
- express their emotions as well as their thoughts;
- begin to believe they are loved and allow more of God into more of their lives;
- let the changes in them become visible in their outer world, i.e. increasingly behaving in ways that promote justice, care for creation and encourage reconciliation, and in Foster's words, develop 'a holy habit of contemplative love that leads us forth in partnership with God into creative and redeeming work'.[24]

✠

Reflection questions

- Which models of spiritual direction have you already come across in your own experience or from your reading or conversations with others?
- If you were looking for a new spiritual director, what questions would you want to ask that person before making a decision about whether or not you could work together?
- Think back over your experience as a member of a faith community.
  To what extent does that church or group demonstrate or teach a balance between contemplation and action? Who do you know whose life reveals such a balance?

23 In Vardey, Lucinda (compiler), *A Simple Path: Mother Teresa*, widely available on websites, e.g. <www.soulbusiness.com>.
24 Foster, Richard, *Streams of Living Water*, London: HarperCollins, 1998, p. 58.

🕯 Spend a few minutes with Mother Teresa's prayer – make a note of your response to the order:
silence, prayer, faith, love, service and finally peace.
What might this prayer have to say to you?

1.7 What does spiritual direction look like in practice?

Spiritual direction conversations can take place anywhere. As I think back over the past month, while mostly I have seen people in my study, some brief but valuable conversations have happened in unexpected places: sitting beside a stranger in a plane, stopping among the vegetables in the supermarket and, after a funeral, standing talking to a person deeply troubled by the premature death of her friend. Spiritual direction can look like two people sitting together in a corner of the garden where they won't be disturbed, or slowly walking along a quiet path, or leaning against a warm wall facing the sea – or it can look like two people in an office somewhere in a church building or in a set-apart space at the director's home or in a retreat house. No matter where we may meet, director and directee meet for the same purpose – to help the directee attend to God.

Two contemporary metaphors will help us deepen our understanding of the process of spiritual direction. Margaret Guenther, an Episcopalian priest, spiritual director and writer, offers us the first metaphor, that of the spiritual director as 'midwife to the soul'. Scripture is full of accounts of birth and struggle, new life and opportunity, so the metaphor is well connected to the Christian tradition. Whether or not we are parents, we can appreciate the comfort which a midwife's familiarity with the process of bringing new life to birth provides for expectant parents.

However, her[25] role is *not* to do the work for the mother-to-be – that is of course impossible – but to encourage and inform, to build confidence, monitor movement and discern potential danger. The midwife also holds the focus of the task when pressure is mounting and fear threatens, and shares in the celebration of new life. At times too, the midwife needs to support and stand alongside a family when things go wrong, when expectations are not met, or when death or disappointment shatter hopes into a thousand empty pieces.

Margaret Guenther believes that the spiritual director works in a similar way:

- staying beside the soul in labour;
- helping people recognize the signs of God at work;

---

25 I've used the feminine pronoun here but I do acknowledge that there are male midwives!

- watching for the shy indications of conception, pregnancy, movement and growth;
- being alert for those factors which might harm or hinder the birthing process; and
- helping celebrate new life even if it emerges from the death of our expectations or previously cherished images of God.

Alongside Guenther's feminine and familiar image is a second metaphor from Simon Brown, a New Zealand pastor, spiritual director and storyteller who writes:

> The task of the spiritual director is to be positioned, like a campfire in the wilderness, welcoming sojourners from all corners of life to stop, relax and yarn for a while. A place where tired bodies and spirits are warmed by the fire and refreshed. A friendly atmosphere where stories of the road are shared amongst travellers. The job of the spiritual director is to keep the fire burning because one never knows when a traveller will come to sit. It doesn't matter where on the journey the traveller has been exploring, or how long they have been walking, if they come in peace to sit on a log by the campfire, they are welcome.[26]

Two points are worth noting from Brown's metaphor. First, he talks about the task of the spiritual director being to 'keep the fire burning'. In doing so he draws our attention to the essential work of a spiritual director – maintaining our own relationship with God. We cannot offer hospitality to another seeker if our own 'fire' has been allowed to dwindle to nothing.

Second, the radical availability suggested by Brown's metaphor presupposes a theological position that believes God is already at work in all people, constantly inviting, drawing, encouraging folk to come home – not home to a building or a set of dogmatic statements, but home to the One who creates us and loves us beyond our wildest imagination. The hospitality offered is safe, simple and warm, emerging from *a deep confidence in God* and a healthy awareness of our own poverty. It is offered in the recognition that we are only one part of the network of people and opportunities which God might use to reach out to those on the spiritual journey.

Although spiritual direction can take place in any setting and in a group context (and we shall look at that in Chapter 6), this book specifically explores regular, intentional one-to-one spiritual direction where the focus is on the directee's experience of God in the context of normal life-events. Such committed, focused attention to God's activity often emerges out of everyday pastoral conversations

---

26 Brown, Simon, *Mission and the Art of Spiritual Direction*, © Spiritual Growth Ministries Trust (New Zealand), available on website <www.sgm.org.nz>. Used by permission.

and social interactions such as those listed in the imaginary compilation of people which follows, whom we will meet again in Chapter 5. As you read through this list, imagine that you are the minister listening with your spiritual director's 'antennae' up and note your initial responses.

Alex   Recently widowed, Alex is finding it hard to think about arrangements for the interment of his wife's ashes. During the course of the conversation with you, he comments that he's afraid he's lost God as well as his wife.

Beth   A priest and chaplain, who, after recent cancer surgery, tells you that she is fine and plans to return to work shortly because she doesn't want to let people down.

Charles A layman, he comes to talk to you about his sense of being drawn towards ordination. As he talks, he refers to some difficulties in his marriage.

Derek   A faithful priest from another denomination whom you have met a few times at ministers' gatherings comes to see you. He says he is too embarrassed to let his colleagues know that his prayer life is 'drying up'.

Evan   An unmarried man of 35 in your Bible study group shyly talks about struggling with loneliness, and mentions that he has met a 'nice woman' on the internet.

Marie   Widowed two years ago, this articulate woman has had six, monthly meetings with you to talk about her faith and life. She does not seem to be 'getting anywhere'.

Henry   The 18-year-old son of your neighbour, a regular communicant. He trusts you and reveals that he thinks he might be gay.

Iain   A farmer in your neighbourhood, he rings up and asks to see you. After a bit of social chat, he tells you that he thinks Someone has met him in the middle of the cow-shed and asks you, 'Am I going mad?'

Jenny   You call in to see a terminally ill parishioner and are introduced to his daughter, recently returned from overseas. Over a cup of tea she tells you that she has just spent a year in a Buddhist monastery.

Kelly   The middle-aged wife of a choir member, she is clearing up with you after the service. She is talking about her family, and then suddenly blurts out, 'There must be more to God than this!'

Tom   You met this lively 82-year-old recently on a retreat in daily life and were delighted when he finally found that God *loved him*. Now he wants to come and talk to you, and you wonder if all is well.

Reflection questions

☖ Read through the list of 'directees'. Draw up a table with *two* columns: in one, write the names of those whose situation you would feel relatively comfortable listening to, and in the other write the names of those whose situation would provoke a sense of discomfort, or possibly even panic! Then choose *one* from each list and answer the following:
  - What would you be listening for as you help each one talk about their situation?
  - What stories from scripture might relate to what each one is experiencing at the present?

☺ If you have the opportunity to work with others, you may like to role-play the first meeting with each of the *two* directees you have chosen and get feedback about what others observed!

☖ 'Brown's metaphor presupposes a theological position that believes God is already at work in all people, constantly inviting, drawing, encouraging folk to come home.'
The traditional term defining this concept is the 'doctrine of prevenient grace'. How do you respond to the idea that God is already at work in everyone, before you or I or any other minister might 'bring them the Gospel'?

1.8 What makes a good spiritual director?

As you have been reading this first section about the history and nature of spiritual direction, you may also have begun to think about your capacity for this type of ministry. Fr Reginald Ward reminds us that: 'the task of the Spiritual Director . . . is not that he should be a judge or a dictator issuing commands, but that he should be a physician of the soul whose main work is to diagnose the ills of the soul and the hindrances to its contact with God; and to find, as far as he is given grace, a cure for them.'[27]

☖ What characteristics would *you* look for in a spiritual director?

✠

Kenneth Leech suggests the following:

- The first and essential quality of the spiritual guide is *holiness of life*, closeness to God.

---

27 Ward, Reginald Somerset, *A Guide for Spiritual Directors*, London: Mowbray, 1957, p. 7.

- Second, the spiritual director is a person of *experience*, someone who has struggled with the realities of prayer and life.
- Third, the spiritual director is a person of *learning*.
- Fourth, the spiritual director is a person of *discernment*, perception and insight.
- Fifth, a spiritual director *gives way to the Holy Spirit*.[28]

The term 'holiness' may lead you to imagine an old man or woman of faith whose demeanour and wisdom emerge from a lifetime of paying attention to God. People like Simeon and Anna come to mind (Luke 2). But the term 'holy' can be applied to *any* Christian, for 'holiness' is about being committed to God, to following Jesus, to prayer and self-discipline, to sharing of resources, to upright behaviour and just action in the service of others. People look for these qualities in the person with whom they will share their innermost stories, shames and longings.

What about experience? Certainly having been through similar life experiences as our directees gives us potential for more empathy, but sometimes our experience can hinder their growth in God if we get caught up in comparisons or offer our solutions to the issues they are facing, instead of helping them listen to God for the best way forward.

It *does* help our directees if we have some knowledge and experience of the dynamics of prayer, the patterns and the pitfalls of growth in the spiritual life, and the perceived absence of God. It also helps if we have done our own work, if we have explored the 'big' questions, such as suffering and the death of innocents. This doesn't mean that we have to have answers, but rather that we are aware of some of the struggles which such questions can evoke in terms of how we look at God and how we understand ourselves.

'People' may say that spiritual direction can only realistically be offered by those who are in the second half of life. True, the majority of spiritual directors are over 40, but this does not preclude younger people from being able to serve more than adequately as spiritual directors, particularly if their life circumstances have caused them to examine their own faith, struggle with prayer and grapple with some of life's mystery.

What you take from this book will make up part of the resources you will use in spiritual direction practice. Added to those resources will be your own formal or experiential learnings, about God, about scripture, creation, people, about faith. Part of the learnings too will relate to your experience of discernment – finding out, often by trial and error, how to work out whether desires and thoughts are coming from God, from yourselves or from another source which is not of God.

If we offer our learnings and experience, however meagre, to God, if we are aware of the gaps in our knowledge and sensitivities and take steps to learn more,

---

28 Leech, *Soul Friend*, pp. 84–5.

if we know our own poverty of heart, then we are more likely to depend on God for guidance and wisdom as we companion others. This is as it should be, because, as has been mentioned earlier, the real 'director' is God the Holy Spirit. We lay aside our ideas about what might be best and instead follow the Holy Spirit's agenda for the directee, knowing that God will continue to guide the directee once the spiritual direction session concludes.

There are two other things I would like to emphasize before we draw this chapter to a close.

First, all the learning and skills in the world won't be much use if we don't have *compassion* for our directees. We pray for them, we long for them to know the reality of God's love for them, we want their highest good – that is the sort of soul friendship we offer, not a mutual chat over coffee in a social setting, valuable though that might be at times, but a committed, prayerful hopefulness and encouragement on their journey.

Second, to do the work of spiritual direction we need to be in spiritual direction ourselves. It is vital that we are paying attention to our own experiences of God in our prayer, study, relationships, ministry, recreation, in the whole of life. Working with a competent, compassionate spiritual director ourselves means we can share our discoveries, our disappointments or doubts, and can, in safety, explore theological questions, our unfolding understanding of the Christian life and its implications for our own pattern of service, all in an atmosphere of prayer.

If you need to find a spiritual director, starting points could be to ask friends, fellow ministers, your vicar or tutor if they know of anyone who might be suitable; to contact your denominational or diocesan spirituality adviser or ministry educator; or to get in touch with the National Retreat Association, email: <info@ retreats.org.uk> or visit their website, <www.retreats.org.uk>. If living outside the UK, you could contact Spiritual Directors International, an American-based network which has a global membership of people interested in spiritual direction. Email: <info@sdiworld.org> or website: <www.sdiworld.org> to help you connect with spiritual directors in your own country.

Before we move into the rest of the book, it is appropriate to offer a few words of caution. In his introduction to the revised edition of *Soul Friend*, Leech raises some concerns about trends in spiritual direction which have emerged over the last 20 years. Although I have hinted at these in earlier sections, it does no harm for us to be reminded of their reality as we prepare to move into the sections which deal with spiritual direction practice in more detail. Leech particularly warns against spiritual direction:

- being turned into another therapeutic intervention, like counselling or psychotherapy;

- being used to promote a view of spirituality which reinforces individualism and privatization of religion at the expense of community;
- becoming over-professionalized to the point where directors assume more importance than is appropriate.[29]

Bakke, spiritual director and author of *Holy Invitations*, comments on the need for us as spiritual directors to keep our sense of perspective. She specifically writes of the risk of directors:

- thinking that 'spiritual direction is the only way' in which people may deepen their relationship with God;
- thinking that 'we are the primary cause of spiritual growth', when of course we know full well that growth in faith is a God-given gift; and
- taking ourselves too seriously![30]

✠

Reflection questions

⚮ Look back over the list of attributes of a spiritual director, and then consider how you understand each one. Note the things that you pull back from or can't imagine, and the things that you can honestly recognize are in process in you.

⚮ Are there any attributes of a spiritual director which are not mentioned here, which you consider to be important?

⚮ Look at the list of 'warnings' which Leech and Bakke have raised.
Have you encountered any of these attitudes or behaviours in yourself or in others offering spiritual direction? If so, how was the process of spiritual direction affected?

⚮ Choose one of the metaphors for spiritual direction which have been mentioned already, for example the bridge-builder, the midwife, the tender of the campfire or any other helpful metaphor you know, and write your own poem or make a collage to illustrate something of the relationship between the director, directee and God.

---

29 Leech, *Soul Friend,* pp. xiii–xix.
30 Bakke, Jeannette, *Holy Invitations*, Grand Rapids, MI: Baker Books, 2000, pp. 57–8.

Suggestions for further reading

Spiritual direction

Bakke, Jeannette A., *Holy Invitations*, Grand Rapids, MI: Baker Books, 2000.

Ball, Peter, *Journey into Truth: Spiritual Direction in the Anglican Tradition*, London: Mowbray, 1996.

Barry, William A. and Connolly, William A., *The Practice of Spiritual Direction*, San Francisco: HarperCollins, 1982.

Benner, David G., *Sacred Companions*, Downers Grove, IL: InterVarsity Press, 2002.

Guenther, Margaret, *Holy Listening: The Art of Spiritual Direction*, Boston: Cowley, 1992.

Leech, Kenneth, *Soul Friend: Spiritual Direction in the Modern World* (revised edition), Harrisburg, PA: Morehouse, 2001.

Long, Anne, *Approaches to Spiritual Direction* (third edition), Cambridge: Grove Books, 1998.

Listening

Hedahl, Susan K., *Listening Ministry: Rethinking Pastoral Leadership*, Minneapolis: Fortress Press, 2001.

Huggett, Joyce, *Listening to God*, London: Hodder & Stoughton, 1986.

Long, Anne, *Listening*, London: Darton, Longman and Todd, 1990.

Drawing on the treasures of the Christian tradition

Julian of Norwich, *Revelations of Divine Love*, trans. A. C. Spearing, Penguin Classics Series, London: Penguin, 1999.

Simpson, Ray, *Exploring Celtic Spirituality: Historic Roots for our Future*, Suffolk: Kevin Mayhew, 2004.

Williams, Rowan, *Silence and Honey Cakes: The Wisdom of the Desert*, Oxford: Lion, 2003.

The contemporary scene and the emerging Church

Church of England's Mission and Public Affairs Council, *The Mission-shaped Church*, Willow Publishing, Australia under licence from Church House Publishing, 2005.

Fresh Expressions of Church website: <www.freshexpressions.org.uk>.

Riddell, Mike, *Threshold of the Future*, London: SPCK, 1998.

Tacey, David, *The Spirituality Revolution: The Emergence of Contemporary Spirituality*, Sydney: HarperCollins, 2003.

Taylor, Steve, *The Out of Bounds Church: Learning to Create a Community of Faith in a Culture of Change*, Zondervan (Youth Specialties), 2005.

Introduction to Chapters 2 and 3: Listening and Responding to God

In remote parts of New Zealand there remain very small populations of an endangered, flightless parrot called the kakapo. These appealing birds have a curious mating habit: the male bird digs out a series of trails leading to a 'bowl', a hollow in the earth in which he sits. Once settled, he starts a unique, sustained vocal performance called 'booming', a sound like the rolling of distant thunder or even the rhythmical beating of the heart. Audible for miles, the call is made hundreds of times an hour, six to seven hours each night for a three or four month period. This heroic behaviour is not without cost, for a kakapo male loses half of his body weight with the effort needed to maintain this continuity of call. Even with all this exertion, there is no guarantee that there will be any response, as females are few and scattered widely. Yet season after season the male will return to reissue his poignant invitation, 'booming' into the darkness of the southern night, hopefully calling for a partner to join him in procreation.

The kakapo's call is a tiny reflection of the persistent, sacrificial call of God echoing down the ages to the lost and the lonely, the powerful and the poor, constantly reissuing the invitation to participate in God's ongoing creativity wherever we find ourselves.

Scripture reminds us of the dynamic mutuality of this relationship in the stories of people who have listened to God and responded in obedience – sometimes with joy, often with reluctance and struggle, as the following few examples show:

- Samuel responded with fear when asked to find the Lord's anointed, but listened to God's instructions and considered all of Jesse's sons, including the one they had to fetch from the fields – David (1 Samuel 16).
- Gideon asked for proof before acting (the dry and wet fleeces: Judges 6.36–40) but then co-operated as God reduced his army from 32,000 to 300 (Judges 7.1–23).
- Simeon listened with joy as the Spirit revealed the identity of Jesus (Luke 2.25–35) and responded with thanksgiving and an acceptance of the completion of his earthly task.

- Jesus called his disciples from their livelihoods and homes – a response that would result in the birth of the Christian Church and would ultimately cost most of them their lives.
- In Gethsemane, Jesus himself struggled with the call to walk the way of the cross (Matthew 26.36–46) but responded in obedience to the will of the Father.

Perhaps you know people who think that today God would speak only to 'special' people such as clergy or church leaders! Unaware of their own value as children of God, they don't expect God to be interested in their concerns and so they don't recognize God's activity.

You will have your own listening/responding history. There may have been times of absolute clarity and joyful, prompt response, as well as times of uncertainty, stabbing in the dark to get an answer, times of apparent silence from God, times of action based solely on trust and the teeth-gritting reality of knowing only 'one step at a time'.

You will have discovered that the process of listening and responding to God is not straightforward, and in the early stages of your faith journey you may not have even realized that God was at work. A personal story may illustrate the point.

In my mid-thirties and married for four years, I hadn't been able to conceive, and became anxious and depressed. I went to talk to a friend whom I'll call Helen. Without judgement she listened to me with her heart and skill before saying, 'The only answer I can offer you is Jesus Christ.'

I remember that moment as a turning point in my life, for something in me recognized the truth of what Helen had said. I went and spoke to the local vicar and joined a Life in the Spirit seminar, which was about to begin. However, after the second week's session I was struggling with whether or not God actually existed. The issue was so pressing that I went to the quiet church alone one afternoon and poured out my questions and doubts before the altar. I can still clearly recall offering to God, as fully as I could, the little part of myself that really wanted to believe. As I drove home that same afternoon I started to sing – in tongues! God had listened and had answered in a way that bypassed my analytical preference, recognized (before I did!) the importance of singing as prayer, and began to build up my fragile spirit. I started to talk and listen to God intentionally; I read and reflected on the Gospels and joined a small group where I could hear others' experience and learn more about God. I continued to meet each month with the vicar to reflect on what God was doing in my life, my first experience of regular spiritual direction.

God's action in me was initially unrecognized, although now, knowing more about God, I can see that it was God who prompted me to go and see Helen, to return to the church when I was wondering about God's reality, and to continue with the journey. It was God who prompted Helen to verbalize God's invitation through Christ to come close for healing and resourcing.

Since that turning point there has been a series of calls and responses – to chaplaincy, to priesthood, to spiritual direction, to leadership, to writing – all of them emerging as I have spent time paying attention to God and discerning the way forward.

As spiritual directors, we listen and watch for this sort of divine weaving of listening and response in the experience of those we companion, alert for anything that hints at a movement of the Spirit in the life of the individual.

      Reflect on a significant time of listening and responding to God in your own life. Consider the extent to which you recognised that God was at work.

✠

Before we move into the next four chapters of this book I want to comment briefly on the centrality of listening in the ministry of spiritual direction. The reality for those in ministry is that much day-to-day work revolves around *talking* – leading intercessory prayer and worship, preaching, teaching small groups, chairing meetings and pastoral visiting. Initially it can be a struggle to restrain our tongues when engaged in spiritual direction, particularly if those we meet want quick answers, or we want to cover up gaps in our own knowledge or experience rather than, in humility, stopping and, together with the directee, listening to the Spirit. But as Douglas Steere comments: 'To listen another's soul into a condition of disclosure and discovery may be almost the greatest service that any human being ever performs for another . . . One can listen someone into existence.'[31]

In Acts 3.6 the apostle Peter says to a lame man, 'I have no silver or gold, but what I have I give you; in the name of Jesus Christ of Nazareth, stand up and walk.' And the lame man was healed, at once. The dynamic of 'What I have I give you' applies in spiritual direction too, but in a different way: we do not give to our directees *our* answers to life's difficult questions; we do not impose upon them *our* ways of praying or imply that *our* way of seeing or understanding God is the only way. What we do want to be able to give, to model, are:

- Our confidence that the God of grace will meet and touch people who want to find their spiritual direction.
- Our sense of being on solid ground based on our experience of encounter with the reality of God in our own lives.
- Our learnings about the territory that directees may discover as they leave familiar road maps of faith, not so we can *tell* them the way – that is the work of the Holy Spirit – but so that we can fearlessly companion them when they enter desert or darkness on their journey with and towards God.

---

31 Steere, Douglas in *Weavings*, IX(3), Nashville, TN: The Upper Room, p. 25.

• Our capacity to 'listen the directee's soul into fuller existence'.

✠

Spend a few minutes in honest appraisal of your listening skills, considering for example:

   i Which people/groups can I listen to with focus and compassion?

  ii Which people/groups do I struggle to hear?

 iii What is going on in me when I find myself mentally 'switching off'?

2

Listening to God

2.1 Who is the God we and our directees are listening to?

The enquiry Jesus made of his disciples, 'Who do you say that I am?' (Mark 8.29) is also addressed to us and to those we companion. Much of the content of spiritual direction is influenced by the way directees view God and by their struggles to allow their image of God to develop as they discover more of God's character, and experience more of God's love.

Perhaps you remember Joan Osborne's song 'One of us'? Although offensive to some, this song illustrates a continuing fascination with the nature of God's identity and relationship with humanity. As Christians, we can affirm that God uniquely became Emmanuel, 'one of us' in Jesus and that, rather than being 'slobs' as the song suggested, we are formed 'in the image of God'. Therefore, as the Catechism says, we are 'free to reflect God's own nature, to make choices: to love, to create, to reason, and to live in harmony with God and all creatures'.[32]

The term 'image of God', however, refers not only to the wonder of the divine imprint within us, but also to our particular way of viewing God and hence of relating – or not relating – to God. Our 'image of God' is crafted, often unconsciously, from a range of influences including:

- our ideas and thoughts about God, shaped for example by the teaching of a particular faith community or denomination;
- our feelings about God, for example anger at what is seen as God's 'failure' to answer prayer;
- our individual and corporate religious/spiritual experiences;
- cultural influences, for example dominance of patriarchal systems, persecution or state support;
- representations of God/Jesus in sculpture, painting, music, poetry and film;
- the names others use for God, for example the Parentless Parent, the 'guy upstairs';
- life events, especially major transitions including death, grief, immigration and birth.

---

32 *A New Zealand Prayer Book*, Auckland: Collins, 1989, p. 926.

Arguably the most significant factors in shaping our image of God are our early childhood experiences at the hands of caregivers, and the way power was exercised over us by influential adults. Two people's contrasting childhood memories illustrate this:

> My father wove the first prayer-threads into the fabric of my experience . . . not that he taught me prayers, nor that he prayed with me. Instead he taught me the value of prayer by allowing me to watch *him* at prayer . . . he would close his eyes, bow his head and bury his apple-red face in one hand . . . often I would contemplate his wavy, auburn hair and sit very still while I watched his thin lips move . . . When he lifted his head again, I would sometimes climb up on his knee, snuggle into his arms and play with his floppy ear-lobes before giving him a smacking kiss on the cheek nearest the fire: the cheek which would be warm.[33]

The second extract tells a very different story:

> At school . . . I was caned often enough . . . but I was immune to such feeble assaults for I had experienced the Wrath of God administered by the (bamboo) garden stake. There was a ritual to these punishments, which began with me being locked in my bedroom and given time to reflect on my sins. Then would come the footsteps on the stairs. My father would unlock the door, and order me to strip naked, after which he beat me in a frenzy compounded of dislike, righteous fury and despair for my soul. Afterwards, all passion spent, he would ask me to kneel and pray with him . . .
>
> At ten years old I stood outside his study . . . I could see him and he could not see me, and I watched him pray . . . He raised his arms to God, beat them on his breast, he wept, he was pleading. He was in agony, yet he had done everything right. He had succeeded in business, given his soul to Jesus, rescued five other souls from sin, and he was so angrily unhappy.[34]

Warmth and safety on one father's knee; the horror of violent physical abuse at another father's hand – both in the context of religious observance and prayer. What was the outcome for each person? Although many factors contribute to the direction that a person's faith life will take, it may come as no surprise to learn that the first person grew up to be a respected Christian writer, while the second became an atheist.

---

33 Huggett, Joyce, *Listening to God*, London: Hodder & Stoughton, 1986, pp. 17–18.

34 Cornwell, Bernard, 'Cakes and Ale', 2005, quoted in *The Week*, 9 July 2005, No. 519, London: Dennis Publishing Ltd, pp. 44–5, from *Family Wanted: Adoption Stories*, Sara Holloway (ed.), Granta Books.

This latter outcome reminds us that those who profess to be atheists must at some point have decided to reject a particular way of seeing God. The question, 'Who is the God you don't believe in?' asked in the context of open-hearted listening, can invite a re-examination of the experiences, the philosophy and beliefs, and ultimately the image of God which has culminated in the person making a choice to deny God's existence.

Metaphors

All human attempts to describe God are partial, but the metaphorical language of scripture helps us to understand a little more about who God is and about God's way of being in the world. We know that God's character and covenantal commitment to humanity are unchanging, but having access to a variety of metaphors to describe God provides us with different ways of experiencing and connecting with God; and, both as individuals and as community, helps us broaden our image of God. Individually, we can reflect, for example, on what would it be like to relate to God as:

- Potter (Jeremiah 18);
- Healer or doctor (Psalm 147.3);
- Rest giver (Matthew 11.28–30); or
- Lover (Song of Solomon).

As a community of faith, the Hebrew people knew the stories of God guiding their ancestors out of Egypt in a pillar of fire by night, a pillar of cloud by day; the psalmist used a variety of images for God, sometimes within the space of a few lines, for example 'Blessed be the Lord, my rock . . . my rock, and my fortress, my stronghold and my deliverer' (Psalm 144.1a, 2a).

Jesus himself uses a range of metaphorical language, speaking of God as Vine Grower (John 15) and as Home-maker (Luke 15.8–10); speaking of himself as the Good Shepherd (John 10), the Bread of Life (John 6), Living Water (John 4), the Bridegroom (Mark 2), the Light of the World (John 8).

We are accustomed to relating to God using metaphor or symbol as devices to help us access and appropriate more of the truth about God's nature, but these metaphors or symbols may change over time as we and our directees pray, deepen our engagement with scripture, and pay attention to the world around us, alert for God's personal communication.

Sometimes we add *unconventional contemporary images* to the gallery of 'God-portraits' we have gathered over the years. After I had been in England studying some years ago, I returned to New Zealand and attended the Diocesan Synod at an Anglican boys' school. I went to sit in the chapel and, feeling unsettled, was contemplating one of the windows depicting a teenage Jesus. The shape and colour of the halo around his head reminded me of a lifebuoy – the ring thrown to support a drowning person – and suddenly I knew that Jesus was my *life-boy*! This unexpected image of God in Jesus became an ongoing support for me, helping to 'keep me afloat' as I adjusted to being back 'home'.

With plenty of urban or other contemporary examples to choose from, we would expect that directees may want to talk about unusual or unconventional images of God, such as the Tandem Sky-diving instructor, the Mountain Guide, or the Quilt-maker. These new symbols often highlight particular godly attributes which are relevant to the directee's life at that time. As we help directees describe their discovery, we'll be watching for signs of what this new way of seeing God does for their relationship with God, encouraging them to set their new image of God alongside tested reference points.

Gender issues and image of God

Sometimes a change in our image of God will be in the form of an expansion of our storehouse of biblical metaphors for God, including an introduction to some of the *feminine images* for God buried in the text and not often recognized:

- the woman in labour (Isaiah 42.14);
- the mother (Psalm 131.2; Isaiah 66.13);
- the midwife (Psalm 22.9–10);
- the mother eagle (Deuteronomy 32.10-12);
- the nursing mother (Isaiah 49.15);
- the mother hen (Matthew 23.37); and
- in Hosea 13.8, the terrifying mother bear robbed of her cubs!

Feminine metaphors for God can be especially valuable if our directees are struggling with the often patriarchal structures of the institutional Church or are working through the distress of abuse by a male perpetrator, perhaps even their father. However, we cannot make assumptions about what will be appropriate for any given directee; while one directee who was abused by her father may recoil from 'Father God' because that image of God reminds her too painfully of the failure of fathering she has experienced, another abused directee may find enormous comfort in Father God, the perfect parent who wants only her highest good.

Men too may find in the feminine images of God some respite from 'warrior' or 'king' imagery with which they may never have felt comfortable. For them, these images bring a balance to their way of seeing God and reinforce the nurturing, compassionate side of themselves which may have been submerged in a 'macho' culture.

46

Trinity

Traditionally, Christians affirm that God is Three in One – the doctrine and truth of the Trinity. Often, however, we relate more to one member of the Trinity, and the others will be less in focus. Yet, if we look back into the Celtic Christian tradition for example, we find that it was intensely Trinitarian, prayers being offered for every activity, every life passage, always with confidence in the Trinity's comprehensive enfolding. For those early Christians, God as Three Persons was woven into the whole of life. St Patrick's Breastplate speaks of Christ within, behind, before, beside, beneath and above each one of us: a Christ who wins, comforts, restores us; a Christ who is present in all aspects of life. The doxology reads:

> I bind unto myself the name,
> The strong name of the Trinity,
> By invocation of the same,
> The Three in One and One in Three,
> Of whom all nature hath creation,
> Eternal Father, Spirit, Word.
> Praise to the Lord of my salvation:
> Salvation is of Christ the Lord.[35]

As we talk with our directees, we notice which member of the Trinity has special significance, arising out of their understanding of Christian teachings and scripture, their actual experience of God, and the stream of faith in which they are immersed.

Some of us are at home relating to God as Creator, experiencing a deep sense of connection to the natural world; some may come to God as Father or as Mother – the Parent who will never let us down or mistreat us; there are those who may prefer the less personal 'God of the universe' – a being so omnipotent, so transcendent, that the concept of a close one-to-one relationship seems irrelevant.

Jesus represents the 'human face of God', the person of the Godhead to whom many relate most naturally. In his full humanity he is indeed our 'brother' – growing up in an ordinary family, feeling a full range of emotions, discerning the shape of God's call on his life, interacting with those on the margins and those in authority, suffering a humiliating, horrible death at the hands of the powerful. In his full divinity he redeems us, calling us to resurrection, offering abundance of life and freedom of heart; as we get closer to Jesus over the years, we may come to see him through a variety of 'lenses': as friend, saviour, good shepherd, best mate, mentor, social activist, even as lover. But for some people, Jesus poses a challenge – his call

---

35 St Patrick, *St Patrick's Breastplate,* trans. Mrs Cecil Francis Alexander, in *Hymns Ancient and Modern Revised*, Norwich: SCM-Canterbury Press. Used with permission.

to intimacy in relationship is uncomfortable and risky, requiring us to move closer, to let ourselves be loved just as we are, and to love him in return.

For others of us, the person of the Spirit has been predominant in our experience and Christian upbringing; we relate to God through the gift of tongues, words of knowledge and wisdom, alert to the prompts of the Spirit to guide us as we move through each day. The Spirit too poses a challenge to many people, particularly if their denomination has not been accustomed to teaching about the Spirit or providing a safe context in which the gifts of the Spirit may be exercised appropriately.

Like a plait woven in three colours, the different persons of the Trinity will from time to time occupy the central position in our awareness, but we and those we companion will miss the fullness of God if we limit our focus primarily to one person of the Trinity. It is in the inter-relationship of the persons of the Trinity that we find our model for life and for love: inexhaustible love, being forever offered; vulnerable love, forever receiving and being broken open; comforting, guiding, challenging love moving among us, inspiring all humanity.

Salvation and our image of God

When we explore directees' ideas and feelings about God in spiritual direction, we find that a surprising number see God as some sort of celestial policeman, spoilsport or vengeful judge. Somehow the Good News that the God whom Jesus reveals as absolute, unconditional, grace-full Love, is undermined by a notion of God as fickle and violent, waiting to hurl thunderbolts to punish people and destroy all that they love and live for. Contributing to this way of seeing God are two factors: whether we read scriptural accounts of vengeful punishment literally or symbolically,[36] and our understanding of salvation.

Sooner or later, personally and in spiritual direction, we are going to be confronted with the question of whether or not God sends people to hell. Although our role is to help directees explore such a question for themselves, it is still vital that we have, for *ourselves*, explored the concept of salvation, have studied and prayed with the 'vengeful punishment' passages of scripture, and have seen how these stand alongside our own sense of who God is.

🯅 As a way of engaging personally with this crucial issue, read the following quote from the Doctrine Commission of the Church of England, and make some notes about how this compares with your own position:

---

36 For a readable exploration of 'vengeful punishment' in scripture see Linn, Dennis, Sheila Fabricant Linn and Matthew Linn, *Good Goats: Healing our Image of God*, New York: Paulist Press, 1994.

Although God's love goes, and has gone, to the uttermost, plumbing the depths of hell, the possibility remains for each human being of a final rejection of God, and so of eternal life. Burnaby has written:

> Dogmatic universalism contradicts the very nature of love, by claiming for it the kind of omnipotence which it refuses. Love cannot, because it will not, compel the surrender of a single heart which holds out against it . . . Love never forces and therefore there can be no certainty that it will overcome. But there may, and there must, be an unconquerable hope.[37]

Final judgement . . . remains a reality. Moral and spiritual choices are ultimate and serious choices. In the past the imagery of hell-fire and eternal torment and punishment have been used to frighten men and women into believing. Christians have professed appalling theologies which made God into a sadistic monster and left searing psychological scars on many . . .

(More recently there) . . . has been moral protest from both within and without the Christian faith against a religion of fear, and a growing sense that the picture of a God who consigned millions to eternal torment was far removed from the revelation of God's love in Christ. Nevertheless it is our conviction that the reality of hell (and indeed of heaven) is the ultimate affirmation of human freedom. Hell is not eternal torment, but it is the final and irrevocable choosing of that which is opposed to God so completely and so absolutely that the only end is total non-being . . .

If God has created us with the freedom to choose, then those who make such a final choice choose against the only source of life, and they have their reward. Whether there be any who do so choose, only God knows.[38]

Whatever our personal viewpoint regarding salvation, in spiritual direction we companion directees as *they* work through the implications of *their salvation questions*. We do not offer 'cheap grace' or minimize people's accountability for their actions, but we help them bring their uncertainty to God, we help them deepen their relationship with Jesus, we help them listen to the compassionate Spirit.

Suffering and our image of God

Sometimes tragedy forces us to re-examine our image of God and particularly what we think about God and suffering. People who have watched a loved one

---

37 Burnaby, John, *Amor Dei*, p. 318, quoted in *The Mystery of Salvation*, The Doctrine Commission of the Church of England, London: Church House Publishing, 1995, p. 198.

38 The Doctrine Commission of the Church of England, *The Mystery of Salvation*, pp. 198–9.

in pain or who are overwhelmed by tragedies in the world may find their faith undermined or even demolished when their image of God cannot be reconciled with the distress they see. How often in pastoral ministry do we encounter questions such as: 'Why did God do this to me?' or 'What has she done wrong to be punished like this?'

I vividly remember the dreadful events in March 1996 when a gunman entered a gymnasium in Dunblane, Scotland, and started firing on a class of five-year-old children. As the horror unfolded, like many I was forced to face the gulf between my concept of a God who literally protected people from harm, and the awful reality of the death of innocent children and their teacher. Theodicy – reconciling the power and goodness of God with the reality of evil and suffering – demanded my attention.

This question has vexed theologians and philosophers throughout history. We cannot go into detail here about the various attempts made to address the apparent paradox of a God of love creating a world in which 'bad things happen to good people'. What we can do, if we haven't already done so, is to begin to think the matter through for ourselves, wrestling and reflecting, so when the question emerges in spiritual direction, as it likely will with the next major tragedy, we can be in a better position to companion others in their own exploration of the issue.

Rowan Williams, writing in the aftermath of the Boxing Day tsunami of 2004, revealed something of his own process of thinking about this question:

> In 1966, when the Aberfan disaster struck, I was a sixth former beginning to think about studying theology at university. I remember watching a television discussion about God and suffering that weekend, with disbelief and astonishment at the vacuous words pouring out about the nature of God's power or control, or about the consolations of belief in an afterlife or whatever.
>
> The only words that made any sense came from the then Archbishop of Wales . . . What he said was roughly this: 'I can only dare to speak about this because I once lost a child. I have nothing to say that will make sense of this horror today. All I know is that the words in my Bible about God's promise to be alongside us have never lost their meaning for me. And now we have to work in God's name for the future.'

Archbishop Williams continued by noting how often people of faith stand up for the value of individual human life. It is this very attitude which makes the losses suffered in any disaster so hard to bear and the desire to do our best for those who are affected so strong, even while we may be wrestling with the 'big' philosophical or theological questions. He continues:

The odd thing is that those who are most deeply involved, both as sufferers and as helpers, are so often the ones who spend least energy in raging over the lack of explanation. Somehow, they are most aware of two things: a kind of strength and vision just to go on; and a sense of the imperative for practical service and love. Somehow in all of this, God simply emerges for them as a faithful presence. Arguments 'for and against' have to be put in the context of that awkward, stubborn persistence.

What can be said with authority about these terrible matters can finally be said only by those closest to the cost. The rest of us need to listen; and then to work and – as best we can manage it – pray.[39]

✠

In spiritual direction we walk alongside those who are grappling with the theological, relational, communal and personal implications of a changing view of God and how God works in the world. We hear people saying things like:

- How could God have let this happen?
- What I've been taught about hell and heaven no longer makes sense compared to my experience and understanding of God's grace and mercy. Where to from here?
- How do I relate to a God who delights in me like a lover?
- How can I stay in my church when the view of God I hear from the leadership no longer fits with how I see God?
- What if there are treasures in other faiths? How can I express the uniqueness of Jesus when people say 'all paths lead to God'?
- I am coming to realize the vulnerability of Jesus – God made powerless – and I don't know if I can cope with a God like that.

We are of little use to others if we have not done our own work here, if we are not able to sit with directees and acknowledge with them the mysteries of life and death. We are at risk of responding with platitudes when these and other questions are raised, if we have not engaged at depth and at cost, with the seeming enigma of a God of love and a world of suffering; if we have not found for ourselves the truth of the God who is present – seen or unseen – even in the midst of chaos and tragedy

✠

---

39 Rowan Williams, <http://www.telegraph.co.uk/opinion/main.jhtml?xml=/opinion/2005/01/02/do0201.xml>, accessed 19 August 2007.

Reflection questions

⚬ Divide a page into segments to represent your life for example 0–10, 11–20, 21–30 etc. In each segment, write or draw a symbol to indicate what your primary image of God was during each period.
How has your image of God changed, and what factors have promoted that change?

⚬ What name/s do you currently use to address God when you pray?
Which member of the Trinity do you relate to most easily? Least comfortably?
What unconventional images of God have you encountered personally or in others' journeys?

☺ Discuss the following quote from Alan Jones, spiritual director and dean of a large cathedral:

> Christian orthodoxy requires that I believe in the logical possibility of hell (utter lostness and damnation). It does not require that I believe anyone is there. There is nothing to prevent my hoping that hell is empty.[40]

⚬ Chart your own thinking around the questions of God and suffering and God's place in the deaths of innocents. Spend some time talking and listening to God about how you might be a helpful presence to those engaging with this question.

2.2 Why listen to God?

Old Testament prophets frequently bore God's words to an inattentive and disobedient people:

> Return, faithless Israel, says the LORD.
> I will not look on you in anger,
> for I am merciful, says the LORD.
> I will not be angry for ever.
> Only acknowledge your guilt,
> that you have rebelled against the LORD your God,
> and scattered your favours among strangers under every green tree,
> and have not obeyed my voice, says the LORD. (Jeremiah 3.12b–13)

---

40 Jones, Alan, *Soul-Making: The Desert Way of Spirituality*, San Francisco: HarperCollins, 1989, p. 172.

In the New Testament, the parable of the sower (Mark 4.1–9, 14–20) reveals various patterns of attention and response: some people hear the word but choose not to obey; others hear and start to respond but give up at the first hurdle; others hear but are 'too busy', distracted by worldly concerns or the love of money. Only a few choose to listen to the word and respond willingly to the seed that God sows in their hearts.

So why should we listen to God? Because:

- listening is central to the development of any lasting relationship. Listening to God helps build bonds of love between ourselves and God, and helps us receive God's love deep within our spirits;
- God tells us to: 'This is my Son, the Beloved; with him I am well pleased; *listen* to him!' (Matthew 17.5b). We are called to imitate Christ, who listened to the Father, withdrawing regularly into solitude so he could be still and silent enough to hear clearly;
- by listening to God we acknowledge our creature-hood; God sees the bigger picture whereas we see only a part. We don't always know the answers or what is best for us, but God does;
- listening helps us to co-operate with God in furthering the work of the kingdom; as we listen, options for service are explored; relationships are healed; choices are discerned; ways forward for wise use of resources and time are found;
- other people receive the help they need as we attend to the promptings of the Holy Spirit;
- listening to God can help keep us out of trouble, for example Joseph's warning dream to take Jesus to safety in Egypt (Matthew 2.13–15).
- listening to God helps us learn about ourselves: we are encouraged, in the safety of God's acceptance and love, to face our frailty and to develop our potential; gradually the fruit of the Spirit grows in our lives. The more we listen and respond, the deeper the cycle of disclosure and intimacy between ourselves and God and the deeper the level of trust.

✠

The following dialogue illustrates what can happen in the life of someone who has begun to listen and respond deeply to God. During a retreat in daily life,[41] 'Tom', an elderly man, discovered that God loved *him* as he spent time listening to God through the words of Herbert's poem 'Love bade me welcome'. With this and the other dialogues which follow later, put yourself in the minister's place and take time to consider your feelings and thoughts as you read or role-play the script:

---

41 'Retreat in daily life' is the name given to a range of inexpensive, flexible, non-residential retreats of varying lengths. Full details for running such retreats can be found on <http://spiritualorientations.com/bob/retreat.htm>, accessed 8 May 2007.

Mary   Hello Tom, It's good to see you again! How are you?

Tom   I'm doing very well thank you. *(They chat a little . . .)*

Mary   How are things with you and God?

Tom   That's what I wanted to talk to you about. You know that poem that was so helpful . . . ?

Mary   The George Herbert one – about Love welcoming you?

Tom   That's the one – and you know at the retreat that I said I'd been reading it the whole week and it was like he, Jesus, actually wanted me to have dinner with him . . .

Mary   Yes I remember that very clearly –

Tom   Well, I've been doing that – some nights I don't have my meal in front of TV any more. I set the table for two and I say grace and I light the candle in his place. Sometimes I put on some old hymns or talk about the day and I ask for help for the night-time because that's been the hardest time for me in the past you know, since Betty died . . . but most of the time I just sit quietly and listen.

Mary   And what are you noticing as you sit and listen?

Tom   It's amazing really, but I don't feel lonely any more . . . I feel sort of . . . cosy.

Mary   Cosy?

Tom   Mmm . . . Yes that's the word . . . *(he pauses for a moment, smiling)* . . . cosy . . . that was one of Betty's favourite words – cosy. But what I really came to tell you was that I've taken a big step –

Mary   That sounds intriguing . . .

Tom   Last week I asked my neighbour Stan if he'd like to have a meal with me. He's a widower too. We haven't had much to do with each other before, just said hello and that's about all. But when I was sitting quietly with Jesus at dinner a couple of weeks ago, the thought came into my mind to ask Stan round. It took me a while to get up the courage to do it, but the idea didn't go away and so I asked him and he accepted. So we had a meal together on Saturday and began to get to know each other a little bit. He's lonely too, his family lives overseas like mine.

Mary   So the idea came to mind when you were listening to Jesus, and it wouldn't go away and you found the courage to act on it?

Tom   Yes. And I'm so glad I did because . . . well, the funniest thing happened . . .

Mary   What was it?

Tom   Just as we were finishing dinner, before we watched the football, he smiled at me and said, 'This is an answer to prayer, Tom.'

Mary   What was that like for you – to hear Stan say that?

Tom   Well . . . it means that he knows about Jesus too . . . and . . . it means that I'm an OK person . . . in spite of what I've done . . .

⚜ What can we learn about spiritual direction from this dialogue?

✠

You may have noticed some of the following:

- Very early in the session, Mary gives Tom the opportunity to talk about God.
- Mary creates a safe environment with no sign of impatience or scepticism.
- Mary helps Tom talk about his experience by asking *open-ended* questions:
    'What did you notice . . . ?'
    'What was that like for you . . . ?'
- By simply restating all or part of Tom's words, Mary helps Tom unfold his story.

This portion of Tom's story illustrates the way God can enter someone's life and bring fresh hope and peace even in old age. Tom listened deeply over the several days of the retreat, and as he has continued to listen and to respond to God, his life is slowly beginning to change – instead of being socially isolated he finds courage to reach out to another lonely person, following the prompt of the Holy Spirit. He is beginning to experience the truth of the scripture: 'Listen carefully to me, and eat what is good, and delight yourself in rich food. Incline your ear to me, and come to me; *listen, so that you may live*' (Isaiah 55.2b–3a).

✠

Reflection questions

⚜ Think back to your own spiritual journey. Which of the reasons for listening to God seem to apply to you at the start of your faith walk? Now?

⚜ Look back at the dialogue between Mary and Tom.
    What surprised you? What didn't you like?
    What might you have said or done differently, and why?

⚜ What key/potent words did you notice in this dialogue – words that say something about the inner life of the directee or of his experience of God?

⚜ What issue/s does this dialogue raise for you?

2.3 How does God communicate with us?

In scripture God is revealed as *relational*, not remote, addressing people by name, using the emotionally rich and personally revealing language of authentic relationship. We see this language for example:

- in the call of prophet Jeremiah: 'Before I formed you in the womb, I knew you, and before you were born, I consecrated you; I appointed you a prophet to the nations' (Jeremiah 1.4–5);
- in God's uncompromising words spoken by Nathan to David, chastising him for his adultery with Bathsheba and for arranging the murder of her husband Uriah (2 Samuel 12);
- in God's affirmation of Solomon's unselfish prayer (1 Kings 3.5–15);
- in the intimate exchange between Jesus and Peter at the foot-washing (John 13).

God can 'speak' or enter a person's life in a whole variety of ways. In spiritual direction, if we are aware of this diversity we are better placed to help directees pay attention to God, so let's consider some common communication channels.

Scripture

People who read the Bible regularly are building up an awareness of God's nature and dealings with humanity, and the ways and work of Jesus and the Holy Spirit. They are being exposed to major theological themes such as creation and redemption, and are becoming familiar with the stories of countless ordinary people whose lives and struggles remain surprisingly relevant in our contemporary context. They are also 'banking' a range of scripture verses in their minds, verses which the Holy Spirit can bring to a person's recall at appropriate times.

But as we see people for spiritual direction, we come to realize that directees bring a wide range of *experience* of interacting with scripture. Some directees may not have opened a Bible for months or even years; others may faithfully read daily Bible passages, perhaps with the aid of Bible-reading notes; licensed lay people may have gone deeper into more formal study of scripture. Some directees will be used to relating scripture to their lives, while others may find, after years of reading, that scripture has 'dried up'; for others, perhaps stung by spiritual abuse, the perceived patriarchal milieu of scripture only causes them further pain.

In addition to differing experience of scripture, directees can also hold different *attitudes* towards the authority of scripture, seeing it variously as:

- the word of God to be taken literally, no questions asked;
- a God-inspired set of principles for living well;

- an interesting historical document with little contemporary or personal relevance;
- a set of stories of people's encounters with the living God, which resonate with our own stories;
- a powerful living text, a vehicle of God's contemporary communication and continuing self-revelation.

As spiritual directors we may find ourselves viewing the Bible differently from our directees. One particular director, for example, may consider that evolution is a perfectly possible mechanism through which the creative Spirit of God shaped and continues to shape life on earth, while a directee may hold to a more literal understanding of the opening chapters of Genesis. A director may believe that in the feeding of the five thousand, Jesus was able supernaturally to override the laws of nature and matter, multiplying the meagre food supply so all were more than satisfied, while a directee might consider that the gesture of the little boy who offered a few loaves and fishes brought out the best in everyone present, so they were prepared to share what they had, and the 'miracle' was the move from selfishness to sharing.

It is not the role of the spiritual director to enter into theological debate. However, if a directee brings to spiritual direction a 'hot topic' such as homosexuality and Christian leadership, then the director's role is to listen well, before encouraging the directee to put the questions and concerns raised directly to God and to listen for God's response. As spiritual directors we do well to have done our own reflection and research on topical issues as they arise, so we are not caught 'on the hop' and in a reckless moment say something which compromises our working alliance with the directee.

Creation – 'God's other book'

There are several different ways of interacting with creation which we will consider in turn:

1 For people who have no connection with the institutional Church, the natural world may well be the primary avenue through which they will experience something of the sacred, something which may propel them into further exploration of the nature and reality of God. Many people report feeling close to 'something', somehow 'connected' when outdoors, hiking or swimming or walking on the beach or in the woods, whether they would describe that awareness in religious terms or not.
2 Christians may be accustomed to seeing in the natural world a reflection of God's beauty, grandeur or strength: 'The heavens are telling the glory of God, and the firmament proclaims his handiwork' (Psalm 19.1).

3 Some Christians may see natural events, especially the apparently increasing numbers of significant weather-related disasters worldwide, as indicators of God's displeasure or the approach of the end of the world. Whether we agree or disagree with this position, our task is to help directees listen to God for themselves, to act justly and to respond to God's invitation to serve and to share.

4 Often a metaphor or static symbol from nature helps us learn more, both about the relationship we have with God and God's character. Julian of Norwich, fourteenth century Anchoress, in one of her 'shewings' wrote:

> He showed me a little thing, the size of a hazelnut, in the palm of my hand, and it was as round as a ball. I looked at it with my mind's eye and I thought, 'What can this be?' And answer came, 'It is all that is made.' I marvelled that it could last, for I thought it might have crumbled to nothing, it was so small. And the answer came into my mind, 'It lasts and ever shall because God loves it.' And all things have being through the love of God. In this little thing I saw three truths: The first is that God made it. The second is that God loves it. The third is that God looks after it. What is he indeed that is maker and lover and keeper? I cannot find words to tell. For until I am one with him I can never know it until I am held so close to him that there is nothing in between.[42]

5 The natural world is not a static billboard advertising God's majesty but rather a synthesis of dynamic elements which can move and change in ways that surprise. Scriptural examples of the natural world being shaped by God specifically to effect a particular outcome include God using the plagues, and the parting of the Red Sea to free the Israelites from slavery under Pharaoh (Exodus 7.12, 14); the provision of quails and manna in the desert (Exodus 16); Jesus' changing of the water into wine (John 2); the calming of the storm (Matthew 8.24–27); and the raising of Lazarus (John 11).

While not on the same scale, unusual events in the natural world still catch people's attention. Bruce[43] shares the following experience:

Several years ago my wife was very ill, as she underwent a long period of chemotherapy for non-Hodgkin's lymphoma. Through the generosity of a family friend my wife and I were able to stay in their home near the beach during the last few days of each treatment cycle. During one of these restorative times I increasingly became aware of how fearful I was of death, in a very real way potentially my wife's, and in a more abstract manner, my own mortality. Thoughts of death

---

42 Julian of Norwich, *Enfolded in Love: Daily Readings with Julian of Norwich*, London: Darton, Longman and Todd, 1980, p. 3 from Julian of Norwich, *Revelations of Divine Love*, trans. Marian Glasscoe (ed.), Exeter Mediaeval Texts, Chapter 5.

43 Bruce is happy for me to use his first name.

increasingly intruded; and I began to realize that a fear of death had dogged my steps for a very long time.

One morning, while my wife rested, I walked through a woodland area on my way to the beach. I paused to watch the pirouetting flight of a monarch butterfly, with the sun reflecting on its wings in the early morning stillness. As I continued to watch, this monarch was joined by another and then another until everywhere I looked there were monarchs twisting and turning. As I continued to watch this beautiful and unusual scene, I became aware of an inner thought or voice saying, 'This is all death is, the transformation from one state to another, from the crawling caterpillar to the graceful dance of the butterfly. It is just like passing through the thinnest of veils to another, more beautiful reality.' It was as if God had provided a unique and startling metaphor from nature to answer my own personal fears. I immediately felt a tremendous sense of peace as my anxiety and fear fell off me.

From that moment on, the death of those closest to me and my own death has not disturbed me. I think that as a consequence, I have lived more boldly, more assuredly and far less fearfully in every area of my life.

And a recent personal memory: when I was beginning to write this book and had been talking to God about the enormity of the task, I went for a walk with my dog. I had only gone about 100 yards before my attention was drawn to a magnolia tree, covered in buds ready for their spring shining. *One* bud was open, revealing deep pink and purple petals; the rest were closed, waiting. And it was as if God was saying to me, 'The book you're writing is like this tree: each bud will open when the time is right. You begin with *one* chapter and the rest will follow. Trust that other chapters will blossom in their turn, you only have to make a start.' I felt immediately reassured and comforted; the memory of that moment has continued to sustain me when I have felt a bit bogged down or discouraged. I was grateful to God for a prayer answered through creation in such a clear and appropriate way.

This same process holds true for many people and can become 'food' for spiritual direction as directees speak of moments of connection with God through a natural object which symbolizes some aspect of their lives and their relationship with God. Part of the work of spiritual direction is to help people explore such incidents and observations within the context of their life experience and what is known about God's nature to see what might be learned for their own benefit and for others.

The 'still, small voice' and 'inner promptings'

In the examples listed above you may have noticed that although a natural object was the initial subject of reflection, it was in the person's thought-life that the communication with God took place. If we are expectant and still enough to hear the 'still, small voice' we may find ourselves being led by the Spirit of God working with our spirit. Dallas Willard puts it this way:

> God comes to us precisely in and through our thoughts, perceptions and experiences, and can approach our conscious life *only* through them, for they are the substance of our lives. We are, therefore, to be transformed by the *renewing of our minds* (Romans 12.2). God's gracious incursions into our soul can make our thoughts his thoughts. He will help us learn to distinguish when the thought is ours alone and when it is also his.[44]

The book of Acts is full of the Holy Spirit leading people who were ready to listen, for example Philip was given specific instructions to meet the Ethiopian eunuch on the road to Gaza, share the scriptures and baptize him (Acts 8.29–38); and Ananias was prompted to restore Paul's sight (Acts 9.10–19).

If we recognize the truth that God is both transcendent (far greater than anything we could even begin to imagine) and immanent (at the heart of each one of us) then it should not surprise us that through the Holy Spirit, God can put ideas into our heads, words into our mouths, invite action, remind us when we fall short, reassure us of forgiveness and reveal the limitlessness of grace. Our responsibility is to maintain an inner attentiveness so we are able to hear the 'still, small voice' of the Spirit of God guiding us through the events of the day or helping us in our decision-making.

Christians today know that the Holy Spirit still prompts them to act; in spiritual direction we help directees reflect on their response – or lack of response – to the 'nudges' of God. I still recall being strongly nudged by the Spirit to go back to my mother's hospital room the day before her hip surgery to give her another hug. I went back, but when I saw her chatting to the nurse and saw the notice on the door 'Isolation – surgery tomorrow', I allowed my tendency not to intrude to overpower the Spirit's prompt, and turned away. Mum died the next day. How easier my grieving would have been had I been brave enough to obey God and discount hospital protocol and my natural reticence.

Dreams and visions

The Bible refers to dreams being used to warn, inform, encourage and guide. While generally biblical dreams are unambiguous, occasionally help is sought in

---

44 Willard, Dallas, *Hearing God*, London: HarperCollins, 1999, p. 93.

interpretation, for example Joseph is called upon to interpret Pharaoh's dream (Genesis 41). Matthew's Gospel records several dreams (1.20; 2.12–13; 2.19; 2.22) relating to the birth of Jesus, showing God's intervention, guidance and protection. Much later, Cornelius and Peter in deep prayer receive visions which open the way for the gospel to be taken to the Gentiles (Acts 10). We should not be surprised if, from time to time, directees want to talk about a timely, frightening or puzzling dream. While only the dreamer can make true sense of his or her own dreams, we can offer simple ways of working with dreams either in the direction session or between sessions – see Chapter 4.

Other people – their conversations with us, or what we happen to overhear may provide the 'right word in season'; people's generosity, or help in times of crisis, model God's care and love; children remind us of joy and simplicity, and of Jesus' welcoming acceptance; practical help when resources are stretched are part of God's provision.

Hymn and song lyrics – we can be touched by lyrics when reading, listening, singing or writing; particular words or verses reach into our lives to nourish or console us as the melody replays in our minds.

Other elements of institutional church life – many faithful Christians find that the Eucharist, the Liturgy, the prayers of the people, the seasons of the church year, the commemoration of Saints' Days, corporate or choral singing, sermons, multimedia presentations, may be instruments of God's grace and personal communication to them.

An unexpected invitation or opportunity or financial provision – can often act as confirmation of a way forward when we are trying to sort out what to do; or may come 'out of the blue' when we have made a gesture of opening ourselves to God's will more fully.

Directly through the senses – some directees may report hearing an audible voice; feeling a sensation of warmth (as when John Wesley's heart 'was strangely warmed'), experiencing a light touch on the shoulder, or smelling a sweet fragrance.

The creative arts – God can reach us through literature, film, music, drama, dance, painting, sculpture, etc. and through architecture such as cathedrals, bridges, buildings and the interplay of space and light.

Last, but by no means least, God communicates through *silence*, doing a deep work in our spirit without words or analysis. We may not be able to name what is happening, but something is rearranged in our psyche and we are moved towards wholeness as we set aside our words and open ourselves as fully as we can to God.

We all have our own particular combination of ways of hearing from God, so it should come as no surprise if in spiritual direction we meet people who have a totally different 'profile'. However, if we are not careful we may unconsciously discount the person's story simply because it does not match our experience. In the next section we will look at religious experience in more detail and consider how we might begin to discern whether a directee's experience might or might not be of God.

✠

Reflection questions

- ⚱ Take a few minutes to write down the ways in which God has communicated with you, apart from through creation.
- ⚱ Look again at the section on interacting with creation. How has the natural world been a vehicle of God's communication to you?

- ☺ In a small group, take a large sheet of paper and brainstorm ways in which God met people in the scriptures. Then discuss how your own experience relates to the scriptural stories.

- ⚱ How do you view scripture?
  What would you find difficult if a directee viewed scripture differently from you?
- ⚱ When have you been conscious of an inner prompting to do something or go somewhere?
  What were the outcomes for you and for anyone else involved?

2.4 Religious experience

As the model of spiritual direction we are working with involves paying close attention to the directee's religious experience, it is important for us to have some understanding of what constitutes such experience, and how to discern its authenticity and origin.

Since the start of the twentieth century there has been a growing interest in 'religious experience',[45] not only in theology but in disciplines such as philosophy and psychiatry in such contributions as the following:

---

45 Because this book is set in a Christian context I will continue to use the phrase 'religious experience'. However, if you are working with people for whom Christianity is unfamiliar, using the term 'spiritual experiences' may be more appropriate.

- *The Varieties of Religious Experience* by William James was published after he gave the material as the Gifford Lectures in Edinburgh in 1901–2.
- Carl Jung explored the role of religious experience in the lives of those who entered psychoanalysis and commented: 'Among all my patients in the second half of life – that is to say over 35 years of age – there has not been one whose problem, in the last resort, was not that of finding a religious outlook on life.'[46]
- Rudolph Otto's *The Idea of the Holy*, published in 1950, introduced the concept of the 'numinous' and the *'mysterium tremendum et fascinans'*, a term which attempts to describe the awesome 'otherness' of God, a mystery at once appealing and disturbing in its power.[47]

To help us establish what constitutes a genuine religious experience, first we will look to scripture which is full of such accounts. Many of the relationships between God and people described in the Bible begin with a single, striking moment of encounter and then develop into an ongoing relationship as the person's capacity to 'keep company' with God and participate in God's work grows.

☺ Look at the scriptural stories in the table below, and note their characteristics. From your discussion draw up a list of common elements and then highlight those which you think are *reliable* indicators of an *authentic* religious experience.

Person	Initial encounter	Characteristics	Common elements
Moses: Exodus 3	The burning bush and voice of God.		
Mary: Luke 1	The angelic visitation.		
Elizabeth: Luke 1	John leaping in the womb; acknowledgement of Mary as God-bearer.		
Saul/Paul: Acts 9	The Damascus road blinding and voice of Jesus.		

---

46 Jung, C. G., *Modern Man in Search of a Soul*, London: Keegan Paul, 1933.

47 More recently the disciplines of quantum theology and neurotheology have opened up whole new ways of looking at the nature of the divine and our response. A web search on these topics will prove fascinating.

Now compare your response with the suggestions in the table below and with the list of possible indicators of religious experience:

Person	Initial encounter	Characteristics
Moses: Exodus 3	The burning bush and voice of God.	Unexpected; unusual, natural event attracted Moses' attention when he was alone; sense of the 'holy'; fear; conversation; audible voice of God; led to Moses agreeing to lead Israel out of Egypt.
Mary: Luke 1	The angelic visitation.	Unexpected; Mary was alone; reassuring; conversation with visible angelic presence giving message from God; led to the birth of Jesus Christ and the salvation of the world.
Elizabeth: Luke 1	John leaping in the womb; acknowledgement of Mary as God-bearer.	Unexpected; delight-full; affirming Mary's call; deep sharing of the experience; felt and spoken; led to a shared time of preparation and quiet strengthening.
Saul/Paul: Acts 9	The Damascus road blinding and voice of Jesus.	Unexpected, frightening, strong physical impact; audible voice experienced by others, not just Saul; conversation with Jesus; led to Saul's conversion and, as Paul, the spread of the Gospel.

You may have included some of the following characteristics of religious experience in your list:

- Unexpected, often happens when the person is alone.
- The person has not planned or manipulated events to make the experience happen.
- Difficult to describe to others.
- A quality to it that is more 'real' than normal reality.
- Personal even if others are present.
- Associated with a wide range of feelings, from fear to joy.
- May come in a range of forms, for example an inner voice, an angelic vision, a movement of the spirit.
- Two-way communication may take place during the experience.
- There is a felt experience of the holiness or power or mystery of God.
- The outcome of the encounter brings good or growth for the person and for others.

You may be thinking, 'That's all very well, but these events happened thousands of years ago – what about now? Surely these sorts of experiences don't still occur?' Let's consider the story of a young university student whose study challenged his previously held belief system, and brought him to a place of relativism and agnosticism – until something happened:

> In the late spring of 1974, at the beginning of a long university summer holiday, David was working at a local freezing works. He was bottom of the pecking order: a blood sweeper and brisket puncher. This particular day he'd returned to his parents' home after work, showered, and gone out to water their garden. It was near sunset, with the scent of jasmine hanging heavy in the air. He remembers:
>
> 'I could see my parents inside the kitchen. They'd just switched the light on. I turned away – and suddenly I had this overwhelming sense of the presence of God. In me, and around me, and in Creation. It was unexpected, totally uninvited . . . and truly unmistakable. My whole being felt it. It was an extraordinary feeling . . . It wasn't in a church service, or because of a church service. It was, nevertheless, an overwhelming sense of God in the world, and God in people.
>
> 'I think I stood there for about 20 minutes. I suppose I could have seen it as a rush of blood, or a bit of romantic imagery of some sort. But the feeling didn't go away. When I went back inside, I still felt it. I felt it for days . . . and the lovely thing, which I'm still so grateful for, is that it happens a lot. Even now. Again, unexpectedly.'
>
> The experience in the garden stood the young man's world on its ear. 'I immediately found', he says, 'that God was more important than anything else.'[48]

§ Re-read this description and note your responses and questions.
Then look again at the list of biblically based criteria for helping assess the validity of 'religious experience' and see what points of similarity/difference you note.

One of the ways of 'testing' religious experience is by looking at its fruit. The young man in the above story offered all his gifts to the service of God, applied and was accepted for ordination in the Anglican Church and now, just over 30 years later, David Moxon is one of the Co-Presiding Archbishops of the Anglican Church in Aotearoa, New Zealand and Polynesia, modelling a sharing of leadership in the multicultural context of a three-stranded Church: Pakeha,[49] Maori and Pasifika.

---

48 Adapted from an article by Lloyd Ashton, 'A Man for all seasons', in *Anglican Taonga*, 22, Spring 2006, pp. 9–10.

49 *Pakeha* is the Maori word for light-skinned people, those of Caucasian ethnicity.

Research into religious experience

Comprehensive research into religious experience reveals that such events are not isolated, nor something reserved for those destined for leadership in the Church. Starting in the 1960s, British marine biologist Sir Alister Hardy began testing the hypothesis that people had an inbuilt religious potential or awareness, asking people a single question: 'Have you ever had a religious experience or felt a presence or power, whether you call it God or not, which is different from your everyday life?'

Hardy set up the Religious Experience Research Centre at Oxford (now relocated to the University of Lampeter in Wales) and, as a good scientist, sorted the 3,000 responses to his initial enquiry into categories. Dr David Hay and others continued this research in the latter decades of the twentieth century, and new research in China is nearing completion. The eight categories of religious experience originally drawn up by Hardy are:

1 *Synchronicity and the patterning of events* – for example 'coincidence', 'things falling into place' or 'working out', unexpected but timely opportunities or meetings with people.
2 *The presence of God* – may be described as a 'felt' presence, warmth, light, deep intimate silence, the inner voice of the Holy Spirit.
3 *A sense of prayers being answered* – much mystery surrounds answered prayer, but there is no doubt that people experience their prayers being answered in ways that defy logic or circumstance.
4 *A presence not called God* – those who reported this were positive about the 'Other' but did not necessarily want to name that person as 'God' – they were not assigning a 'religious' label.
5 *A sacred presence in nature* – may be associated with, but not limited to, indigenous spiritualities For example Australian Aboriginal, New Zealand Maori or North American Indian.
6 *Experiencing that 'all things are one'* – such experiences occur when a person, even for a split second, has a deep awareness of being at one with the whole of creation, and everything that defines the self as separate is momentarily suspended.
7 *The presence of the dead* – this does not mean praying to the dead or anything associated with séances or the activities of mediums, but rather being aware of a person who has died, often in an unexpected brief moment of farewell or encouragement. Occasionally this will include an uninvited and unwelcome presence in a building or place.
8 *The presence of evil* – not all spiritual experiences are from God, and we have to be alert to the possibility that a person may have been touched by some force opposed to God.

To Hardy's original eight categories, experienced psychiatrist and spiritual director Gerald May adds spiritual experiences such as visions, intentional imagining, or gaining a sudden intellectual insight; extrasensory experiences such as seeing auras, and classic Christian charismatic experiences which include healing, speaking in tongues and prophecy.[50]

A comparison of survey results about 'religious experience' in Britain[51] shows an intriguing increase:

Nature of survey	Year of publication of survey results	% of people reporting a spiritual or religious experience
Gallup National Survey: sample size 985[52]	1987	48
Repeat survey done in conjunction with the BBC series Soul of Britain[53]	2000	76

David Hay and Kate Hunt,[54] who conducted this Soul of Britain study in 2000, attribute this rise in reporting to 'people's sense of the degree of social permission for such experience. Somehow or other (perhaps through the influence of postmodernism) there is a growing feeling that it is acceptable to admit to such awareness, though it is still something that most people feel quite deeply embarrassed about.'[55]

To this we can add the work of Paul Hawker, who not only described his own 40-day spiritual pilgrimage in the Tararua Ranges[56] of New Zealand but, using the Hardy categories as his frame of reference, has also recorded 'stories' of many people's spiritual or religious experience in an Australasian setting.[57]

When we put all of this alongside the growing interest in spirituality which was noted in Chapter 1, we see that, particularly for those who do not have any definite

---

50 May, Gerald, Care of Mind, Care of Spirit, New York: HarperCollins, 1992, p. 38.

51 See Hay, Religious Experience Today, 1990, p. 79 for a summary of research results conducted in the UK, the USA and Australia between 1962 and 1987.

52 Hay, David, Religious Experience Today: Studying the Facts, London: Mowbray, pp. 83–5.

53 Hay, David, The Spirituality of the Unchurched, conference paper for British and Irish Mission Association, 2000, p. 1. Full text available on <www.martynmission.cam.ac.uk/BIAMSHay.htm>, accessed 11 December 2007. From research undertaken by Hay, D. and Hunt, K., Understanding the Spirituality of People Who Don't Go to Church, Centre for the Study of Human Relations, University of Nottingham, 2000.

54 Hay and Hunt, Understanding the Spirituality.

55 Hay, The Spirituality of the Unchurched, p. 2.

56 Hawker, Paul, Soul Survivor, Canada: Northstone, 1998. (Republished as Soul Quest, Canada: Wood Lake Publishing, 2007.)

57 Hawker, Paul, Secret Affairs of the Soul, Canada: Northstone, 2000.

religious reference points, the possibilities for dialogue about spiritual experience are exciting. Hardy's original question, or our own version of it, can provide an entry point into spiritual conversations with people in every walk of life and may even be a catalyst for people moving towards a deeper connection with God.

However, there is a caution about actively seeking such experiences or paying too much attention to the experience itself. Religious experiences can be powerful, even life-changing, but they are not in themselves the goal of Christian life. Growing into the likeness of Christ, following the way, the truth and the life and living out the consequences of that choice in service to others – these are the focus of the spiritual quest. In spiritual direction we certainly help directees to explore their experience, and what it might teach them about God and about themselves, but we also invite them to hold such experiences lightly, as May writes:

> . . . in the early phases of spiritual growth . . . experiences are very important as sources of motivation, energy and aspiration. To deny their value would in most cases constitute a rejection of the directee's humanity, and in some instances it would amount to an attack on the directee's faith . . . Gentle and prayerful attention combined with good common sense and classic discernment methods are sufficient for most discriminations that need to be made regarding spiritual experiences.[58]

If we have concerns that a directee's 'experience' may be emerging from his or her own unmet needs, psychological vulnerabilities or neuroses, Lovinger[59] suggests being alert for signs of:

* shallowness in the experience;
* a narcissistic display of the directee's self, their piety or their good deeds (*showing off*);
* an inappropriate effort to keep 'parental' approval (with the director *in loco parentis*);
* bargaining with God or the expectation of reward;
* excessive dependence on an outside authority (i.e. on the director) *to validate the experience.*

And we can ask questions and be observant about the following areas:

* How does the experience described by the directee compare with any others which the directee knows are from God?

---

58 May, *Care of Mind*, p. 43.

59 Lovinger, Robert J., *Working with Religious Issues in Therapy*, New York: Jason Aronson Inc., 1984, p. 186. (Italics mine.)

- What are the effects of the experience on the directee's communication with God, i.e. does the dialogue become more real and alive; is there a greater sense of desire to talk *and* listen to God, or is the directee closing down?
- What does the experience reveal about God? About the directee?
- Is the directee moving towards God or further away; towards greater connectedness with other people, or is there a withdrawal from reality?
- Are there signs of greater self-awareness and the development of the fruits of the Spirit: love, joy, peace, patience, kindness, generosity, faithfulness, gentleness and self-control? (Galatians 5.22–23).

For someone who has a background in the faith, 'religious experience' can be significant in re-connecting them with God. Similarly a 'spiritual experience' can be the triggering event which turns a person without any particular faith tradition towards the One who is greater than themselves. In either case, the true test of the authenticity of their experience of the 'Other' is determined by the outcomes over a longer period. Spiritual direction can help directees work out where their experience comes from, but is more focused on where it might be leading them, whether towards God or away, as we shall see in the section on discernment. Such experience, if genuine, will not then be an isolated event but a springboard for the development of a conscious, ongoing personal relationship with God, and an ability to see God in the midst of the everyday.

Hardy's and Hay's research provides us with the encouragement to trust that there is a very good chance that people we meet – whether casually, in our community or in our congregations – will have had some sort of spiritual experience which can be a starting point for further exploration as relationships are built. As Hay comments:

God the Holy Spirit communicates with all of Creation. From this perspective one might see the mission of the Church as to be alert to – and be in tune with – the ways in which God is *already in touch with everybody, inside or outside the Church*.[60]

✠

Reflection questions

⚱ Those whom we meet in casual conversation or those whom we see for spiritual direction may talk about *any* of Hardy's categories of religious/spiritual experience:
  - synchronicity and patterning of events;

---

60 Hay, *The Spirituality of the Unchurched*, p. 2. Italics mine.

- presence of God;
- answered prayer;
- presence not called God;
- sacred presence in nature;
- experiencing that 'all things are one';
- presence of the dead;
- presence of evil.

Which of these have I experienced in my own spiritual journey?

With which of these do I feel comfortable? Do I struggle?

From my responses, what might I take to prayer, to spiritual direction, or to supervision?

Now consider the sorts of spiritual experiences mentioned by Gerald May: visions, intentional imagining (as in praying imaginatively with scripture), gaining a sudden intellectual insight, extrasensory experiences such as seeing auras, and classic Christian charismatic experiences which include healing, speaking in tongues and prophecy.

What is your personal experience of any of the above?

Which have you encountered in the experience of other people?

Which of these experiences raise questions for you? How might you address those questions?

How do you respond to Hay's perspective that 'the mission of the Church is to be alert to – and be in tune with – the ways in which God is already in touch with everybody, inside or outside the Church'?

☺ Next time you are with friends, try asking the contemporary version of Hardy's question:

'Have you ever had an awareness of a power or presence different from your everyday life?'

2.5 God in the everyday: learning to pay attention

For those who have been Christians for some time, experience of God may have been present but the chance to explore or receive it more fully may not have arisen. As we, and our directees, begin to develop an awareness that God can be found in the midst of ordinary routines, and as we realize that *any* aspect of daily life can be used to aid reflection and connection with God, life becomes a real adventure. We become aware of the unexpected moments through which the Holy Spirit may touch and teach us, using the most common symbols or the simplest events.

This is what Jesus helped his followers to do: he used pieces of everyday experience and familiar objects to help people connect with God and discover more about themselves. Old and new wineskins; houses built on rock or sand; a fallen sparrow; light hidden or revealed; oil saved or squandered; seed scattered on paths, rocky ground, among thorns or in good soil – the stuff of everyday experience became the symbols Jesus used to reveal more about the reality of God's invitation to abundant life:

> Consider the lilies of the field, how they grow; they neither toil nor spin, yet I tell you, even Solomon in all his glory was not clothed like one of these. But if God so clothes the grass of the field, which is alive today and tomorrow is thrown into the oven, will he not much more clothe you – you of little faith? Therefore, do not worry . . . seek first the kingdom of God. (Matthew 6.28–33)

Let's see what Jesus is doing here:

- First of all, Jesus *draws people's attention* to something that was commonplace, inviting them to stop and take a good look, in essence encouraging them to 'consider', i.e. 'take a long, loving look at the real'.
- He then helps people start to make connections with something from their own sphere of knowledge/experience, in this case from their faith tradition, as he talks about Solomon.
- Then Jesus asks them to make another connection – this time with what this example might say to them about their relationship with God . . . and he encourages a response to the God who cares for them.
- And finally Jesus invites them to make their relationship with God their priority, to find rest in the care of the God who loves them beyond all reason.

In section 2.3 ('How does God communicate with us?'), examples were given of natural objects and events being used as symbols or metaphors to help us connect more deeply with ourselves and with God. But symbols need not be solely from the natural world; those of us who live in cities have another whole set of potential symbols available to us. When something catches our attention and we stop long enough to take that 'long, loving look', God can 'speak' to us in the midst of an ordinary urban context:

- Perhaps you have tripped and stumbled going down some stairs. Shocked, you have taken a few moments to recover, and in that silent space you have wondered if your life is 'off balance'. With this recognition you resolve to bring that question to prayer as soon as you get home.
- Perhaps the freshness of the aroma from the local bakery has stopped us for a few moments and reminded us of childhood. If we give God space, the Spirit may move us to consider our need for spiritual nourishment. 'Our Father . . . give us

this day our daily bread' might come to mind and our need to ask God for what we need for the day.

When we begin to explore those *simple moments which attract our attention*, we are building the bridge towards God. We are shifting our perspective from a literal understanding to a symbolic 'reading' of a man-made or natural object and a common event. Frederick Buechner expresses it beautifully when he invites us to:

> listen to your life. See it for the fathomless mystery that it is. In the boredom and the pain of it no less than in the excitement and gladness, touch, taste and smell your way to the holy and hidden heart of it because in the last analysis all moments are key moments, and life itself is grace.[61]

Many of these 'key moments' involve other people: family, colleagues, friends and those whom we might meet but once in a lifetime. As we relate or react to others we are given glimpses into our own functioning and can learn more about how we hinder or aid others' growth. We can also gain insights into how God reaches us through others. Teresa of Avila reminds us of God in others, God in us:

> Christ has no body but yours, no hands, no feet on earth but yours,
> Yours are the eyes with which he looks compassion on this world,
> Yours are the feet with which he walks to do good,
> Yours are the hands, with which he blesses all the world.
> Yours are the hands, yours are the feet, yours are the eyes, you are his body . . .
> Christ has no body now on earth but yours.[62]

When we sit in silence beside a grieving friend we are bearers of God's consolation; when someone does the same for us, we know that God is reaching out to sustain us in our sadness. We can help directees pay attention to key moments of graced encounter, knowing that God will unfold for them the truth of the ancient Christian text: *Ubi caritas et amor, deus ibi est* – 'Where true love and charity are, God is there.'

Other key moments may relate to our response to profound beauty. Inspired by the passage from Philippians 4.8, we can be alert for God's imprint in ' . . . whatever is true, whatever is honourable, whatever is just, whatever is pure, whatever is pleasing, whatever is commendable' and 'if there is any excellence, if there is anything worthy of praise, [we can] think about these things'.

More commonly though, what prove to be key moments emerge from bits and

---

61 Buechner, Frederick, *Listening to Your Life*, SanFrancisco: HarperOne, 1992, p. 2.

62 Teresa of Avila, see e.g. <http://www.calvin.edu/faith/worship/chapel/prayer-series/sample-prayers.htm>, accessed 11 December 2007.

pieces of life experience, so ordinary they could be overlooked or so frightening that we would prefer not to dwell on them. Several years ago I had to drive 200 miles home after facilitating a workshop. I was very tired and made an error of judgement, overtaking on a narrow bridge and barely missing a head-on collision with a fully laden milk tanker. Two days later, as I was walking to the park, my attention was taken by two butterflies. I watched them dancing in the air across the road and then, to my horror, saw them smashed against the grille of an approaching car. As I walked on, feeling a bit shocked by their abrupt and messy end, the thought suddenly came to me that that could have been me two days ago – all my potential and creativity and joy wiped out in a split second. I thought I had a glimpse of how God might feel – the deep sadness at the wrong choice which could have led to disaster. I found out the next day that two of the people attending the workshop who had driven home ahead of me had suddenly felt that they were to pray for me while on the journey.

8 If you were my spiritual director, what questions would be raised for you about what I described? What thoughts and feelings were you aware of as you read the story?

✠

When I went to spiritual direction, a few things unfolded:

- As we explored the context of the 'near miss', I recognized that I had not only been tired but also was a bit 'full of myself', congratulating myself for having finished a major project the day before the workshop – pride was (and remains) a weakness which could be exploited (by ego-inflation or forces opposed to God).
- I had to admit that I had grieved God by my foolishness and thoughtless risk-taking.
- I was challenged to think about how prayer 'worked' – for I was in no doubt that the prayers of my friends had something to do with my survival. It encouraged me to approach intercessory prayer with more hope.
- I wasn't used to people praying for me – it invited humility and gratitude.

The focus on this 'key moment' during spiritual direction enabled me to face part of my 'shadow' as well as acknowledging other, more 'acceptable' parts of my self; in spiritual direction I was able to articulate my need of grace, to find a way forward that was appropriate, and to draw nearer to God. The 'key moment' also propelled me into a deeper exploration of prayer and a greater commitment to praying for others as they are brought to mind by the Holy Spirit.

In practice, if we want to help people 'listen to their lives' we can encourage them to apply the *lectio divina* model prayerfully to the key moments of their daily experience. As with anything we might offer to those we companion, we do so in response to their journey's movement and having spent some time with this model ourselves, so we are not simply presenting something theoretical but something we know will work. Using *lectio divina* to engage with a key moment looks like this:

Lectio	'Reading' the event or contemporary image that has taken our attention, taking time to explore our initial response to the 'key moment'.
Meditatio	Thinking, reflecting, exploring, making connections, for example with scripture, with what we know of God through our experience or through what we have been taught or seen in others, with our own situations including our questions, struggles and joys. We listen for the inner promptings of the Holy Spirit who knows what we need to be asking ourselves!
Oratio	'Talking' to God about what we are discovering about God and about ourselves through this event/image/'key moment'; responding to God with our whole selves, our feelings and our imagination, our bodies and our minds.
Contemplatio	Resting in the love of God, letting ourselves open to the Love which waits to enfold us, consenting to the work of the Holy Spirit within us.

As directees get used to working with 'key moments' of their lives, instead of experience of God being thought of as a major – or isolated – event, directees start to see the whole of life as an adventure with God, a journey that maximizes the directees' potential, enables them to cope with the variable circumstances of living and which helps them move out in loving service to others as God leads.

✠

Reflection questions

- In your own spiritual journey so far, what experience have you had of 'seeing God in the midst of ordinary life'?
- What symbols (from creation or man-made) have been part of your learning about God and about yourself?
- What 'key moment' would you choose to explore using the suggested fourfold *lectio divina* process?
  If you can, try helping one another use this process to explore a piece of your experience/a key moment, taking turns to be director and directee.

🕯 When have other people been Christ's body/eyes/hands or compassion for you?

When have you been Christ's body/eyes/hands or compassion for another?

What is it like for you now, as you reflect on being a receiver or bearer of God's grace?

2.6 Discernment: how do we know it is God?

In the Christian tradition, the word 'discernment' refers to the process of:

* determining what God is asking of us; and
* deciding whether our spiritual experience is actually from God, from our own imaginings or compulsions, or from some negative force.

The process of discernment is more an art than an exact science, and the results often more tentative than precise. At the heart of the process must be our deep desire to do the will of God, for there can be no Godly discernment if we have our fingers crossed behind our backs, hoping God won't ask us to do something inconvenient or costly.

In line with contemporary expectations of 'instant everything', from soup mixes to global communication, when faced with the need to make choices, we expect quick answers. When we unconsciously transfer this attitude to matters of faith, we can be left wondering why we haven't 'heard' from God as soon as we bring God our needs or our requests. God, however, works to a different schedule, and spiritual direction helps directees to adjust their pace, to develop patience and a willingness to wait as complex factors are explored. It also allows time for directees to examine their heart's attitude towards God, their desire for God and gives them time to begin to discover more about the nature of God – not as a volatile 'spoilsport' but as the One who desires their highest good as individuals and, ultimately, in community.

The process of discernment can be like trying to put together a jigsaw puzzle with no corners, turning over one apparently random puzzle piece after another, while working from a plain box that simply says 'FOLLOW ME'! Fortunately in our Christian tradition there are tested guidelines to help people notice a growing sense of direction as, through prayer and perseverance, various puzzle pieces come together and begin to shape a possible path. Dreams and discussion; community and chaos; logic and list-making; instinct and information; risk and responsibility – these may all contribute to the discernment process. However, key 'pieces' to look for when trying to make a decision include:

- What scripture is saying to the directee, in terms of principles, i.e. is what is being considered in line with scriptural principles of 'doing justice, loving kindness, and walking humbly with God'? (Micah 6.8); *and* what is emerging as the directee engages with scripture in prayer and reflection?
- Circumstances – how does the directee's current situation help or hinder what God may be calling the directee to? What doors are 'opening' or 'closing' in the person's life?
- Common sense – is the new call something that is within the directee's abilities (although it may s-t-r-e-t-c-h them beyond their comfort zones!)? Might it be unhelpfully disruptive to existing primary relationships or stage of family life? Does it seem 'timely' at this point?
- Other people's perception – what do the directee's mature Christian friends have to say about the possibility the directee is considering?
- Sense of leading of the Holy Spirit – how does the directee sense the Holy Spirit at work in this discernment process? What inner prompts/words/pictures/ themes are forming for the directee? Is there an inner sense of enthusiasm or peace as the path unfolds?

While all of the above are clearly relevant, it would be wrong to ignore another valuable source of information – our feelings. We all know that feelings can be fickle and transitory when linked to such simple triggers as winning a football game or being let down by a friend. But feelings are an integral part of being human and, when reflected on in prayer, can be valuable indicators of our spiritual well-being and our orientation in relation to God. However, many people have been taught to distrust or discount their feelings and, as we shall see later in Chapter 5, it takes time for directees to develop a ready awareness of their feelings as they arise.

Ignatius of Loyola knew this and his *Spiritual Exercises* are designed to help people develop an awareness of their inner life; in essence, *a discerning heart.* Space does not permit a full discussion of Ignatian discernment principles here but, in brief, the process invites us to notice our interior emotional movements in response to prayer and external life events. Do these feelings draw us closer to God and the greater freedom inherent in God's kingdom, or drive us further away from God into the confined empire of self-interest? Ignatius uses the terms 'consolation' and 'desolation' to help us recognize the different feelings which are the result of turning either towards God or away from God. David Benner writes:

Desolation is spiritual turbulence. Although we are highly adept at ignoring it, if we learn to become spiritually attentive and discerning, we notice that we feel churned up from time to time. These are the times when we have taken our eyes off God and turned our backs towards God. In contrast, when we turn towards God in a posture of surrender, we feel instantaneous spiritual peace and consolation. This sense of well-being is much deeper than happiness. One can be happy but in a state of desolation when superficial pleasant feelings block out the dis-ease of a soul in turbulence. But equally important, one can be unhappy yet in a state of profound consolation that offers deep assurance of God's presence in the midst of distress.[63]

Some examples may help illustrate what Ignatius and Benner mean by 'consolation'.

Recently Barbara was a passenger on a cruise liner which struck severe gales and huge waves, putting the vessel at risk. Wondering if she would survive, she had prayed all night and had held tight to a little toy dog, a symbol for her of God's faithful companionship. Talking to me about it later, she said that, in spite of her fear, somewhere deep inside her she knew that everything was all right – even if the ship were to founder and her life be lost. She knew consolation in the midst of distress and found that Julian of Norwich's 'all shall be well, and all manner of things shall be well' resonated with her own experience.

When my husband John was undergoing coronary bypass surgery, we were hundreds of miles away from our home. Although it was a deeply stressful time, I knew consolation as God cared for us through skilled medical care, friends' texts and phone calls, flowers, visits by cousins who drove for hours, and a kingfisher's bright company on a walk – a symbol for me of the presence of God.

Christians are meant to live 'in consolation' – with a sense of the strong foundation of our relationship with God supporting us, no matter what the circumstances. This sense of consolation even in the midst of feelings of anxiety and stress is one of the gifts of the Christian faith, made possible by our Lord's work on the cross as he entered fully into human reality with all its pain, transforming our narrow, fear-frozen vision into the assurance of new life in the kingdom of God.

When engaged in a major discernment process or even in the midst of ordinary life choices, we can often feel afraid and anxious, with doubts and questions about the way forward. How might we discern whether something is clearly of God or coming from our own ego, unmet needs or 'old tapes' from significant others in our lives, past or present? What do we do if inner 'messages' or experiences are from a source that, depending on our (and our directees') theology, might variously be labelled as 'negative', 'evil' or 'demonic' – some force that is working against human well-being and growth in God?

We cannot simply ascribe unsettling feelings to 'evil' or peaceful feelings to God. First, we need to see where these feelings are leading us: if they prompt us to consider our possible choices more seriously, and to be open to recognizing a deeper invitation from God, our heart's desire, then we can be more confident that these

---

63 Benner, David, *Desiring God's Will: Aligning Our Hearts with the Heart of God*, Downers Grove, IL: InterVarsity Press, 2005, p. 115.

movements come from the 'good spirit' (from God); although initially unnerving, these feelings ultimately lead us towards our highest potential.

If, on the other hand, in a person who is not depressed or neurotic, these worrying feelings lead only to a vicious cycle of self-doubt, deepening fear and confusion, loss of confidence and a sorry spiral of negative self-talk with no sense of light or hope or possibility, it is likely that the 'evil spirit', a force opposed to God's good activity in us, is at work. There are clear biblical principles available to us in such cases, for example we can put on the 'whole armour of God', in particular using the 'sword of the Spirit . . . the Word of God' (Ephesians 6) to resist the adversary's attempts to undermine our spiritual well-being. Being honest with God in prayer, seeking the prayer support of trusted friends and anchoring ourselves in scripture are also important.

What are the pointers to help us tell when a thought or 'inner prompting' comes from God? As we gain experience of listening to God (as Paul Hawker did on his 40-day pilgrimage) we begin to recognize the particular qualities of God's communication. We recognize that God's 'voice' is:

- consistent with what we know of God, particularly God as revealed in Jesus, in scripture;
- encouraging and helpful;
- relevant to our situation – like an answer to an unspoken prayer;
- patient and loving, even in reproof;
- sometimes surprising and challenging in a way that deepens our character and commitment;
- practical and relevant to our situation;
- open to reflection and scrutiny;
- not generally needing to be acted on right away (unless in times of imminent danger).

By contrast, the interior voice of our own personality and ego can be discerned when it has the qualities of:

- a thought-through process, resulting from applying logic and reasoning to a situation;
- making us feel good about ourselves, i.e. appeals to the ego;
- varying, depending on what information we receive and the outer circumstances;
- helping us to 'save face' in front of others or to look good;
- positive or negative 'self-talk' – our interior conversation with ourselves;
- a replay of 'old messages' from parents or significant adults, which we still use as reference points, and which may contain criticism that as adults we have yet to set aside;

'Voices' that may be from a spiritual source that is not of God tend to be:

- accusing, nasty, putting us down, playing on our vulnerabilities;
- causing confusion, promoting fear, panic, anxiety and guilt;
- disturbing our peace, unsettling us;
- misrepresenting God's character;
- undermining our faith;
- attacking our confidence in God;
- 'pushy', insistent, trying to compel a sudden reaction.[64]

✠

However, considering the origin of our thoughts should not distract us from paying attention to the implications of following a particular path. Are we drawn towards God or driven further away? Are we moving towards wholeness or regressing into dependency and anxiety? Are we going to become more fully ourselves or become boxed in and restricted? If we make choice X and not choice Y, will our life be used in service to others or will it be self-serving? As Jesus reminds us, again using a symbol from nature: 'No good tree bears bad fruit, nor again does a bad tree bear good fruit; *for each tree is known by its own fruit.* Figs are not gathered from thorns, nor are grapes picked from a bramble bush' (Luke 6.43–44).

Common discernment issues and questions which arise in spiritual direction include:

- How do I know if this is God's 'perfect plan' for me?
- What if I make a wrong choice?
- Will God expect me to do something I really don't want to do?
- How will I know that this is God's leading and not just my own idea of what I'd like to do?
- Am I supposed to be a missionary? Celibate? A teacher?
- How do I use the gifts that God has given me?

These are all legitimate and important questions which need to be addressed, but they often mask not only a particular theological position and a particular way of looking at God, but also an underlying anxiety. There is a great deal of difference between approaching discernment fearfully, trying hard to 'get it right', and approaching discernment from a position of confident expectation that God wants our highest good.

---

64 This list is based on a summary made by Paul Hawker following his pilgrimage, as documented in his book, *Soul Survivor*, pp. 213–15.

Fear-based attempts at discernment may be constrained by our own, sometimes neurotic needs, by our incomplete understanding of who God is and who we are in Christ. We are more focused on self than on a God of infinite mercy, grace and hope.

A love-based approach to discernment, however, is founded on an established *relationship* with God who knows us to the very core of our being. We bring to such a process not only a realistic sense of who we are, our strengths and our vulnerabilities, but also a deep, heart-level trust in God. Thomas Merton, Trappist monk and social activist, expressed something of this when he wrote this revealing passage in *Thoughts in Solitude*:

> My Lord God, I have no idea where I am going. I cannot see the road ahead of me. I cannot know for certain where it will end. Nor do I really know myself, and the fact that I think I am following your will does not mean that I am actually doing so. But, I believe that the desire to please you does in fact please you. And I hope I have that desire in all that I am doing. I hope that I will never do anything apart from that desire. And I know that if I do this you will lead me by the right road, though I may know nothing about it. Therefore I will trust you always though I may seem to be lost and in the shadow of death. I will not fear, for you are ever with me and you will never leave me to face my perils alone.[65]

Ultimately God invites us to an increasing sense of freedom to be who we are. If we are being fully ourselves, using our gifts and enjoying God, we are expressing God's image in us as much as we can . . . moving closer towards fulfilling Jesus' seemingly unattainable command: 'Be perfect [complete] therefore, as your heavenly Father is perfect' (Matthew 5.48).

Let us turn now to Charles, who is keen to talk to his spiritual director, Martin, a layman in a neighbouring town, about his sense of being drawn deeper in his faith. As you did with the earlier dialogue, try to put yourself in the director's place and note your responses to what Charles has to say:

Charles I hope you don't mind my making an extra appointment, Martin – I know we're not scheduled to meet for another fortnight but I wanted to talk something through . . .

Martin No problem. I'm just going to make a coffee – want one? *(. . . they settle down in the study)*

Martin You said you wanted to talk something through?

Charles Yes, and it's not the sort of thing that I want to discuss with Sally – at least not yet.

---

65 Merton, Thomas, *Thoughts in Solitude*, Boston: Shambala, 1993, p. 55.

Martin   Okay . . . well you know that of course I won't say anything to anyone about our conversation.

Charles   Thank you – well, it's just that for a few months now . . . and I haven't mentioned it to you before . . . but I've sort of . . . had this feeling that God wants more of me . . .

Martin   In what way?

Charles   Well, you know that I'm a lay reader at St Mark's, and I really enjoy that – have done for the last three years – but it seems that God might be asking me to work for him full time in some way, perhaps even . . . perhaps even to work as a priest somewhere.

Martin   What makes you think that God might be calling you to a deeper level of commitment?

Charles   Well, about three months ago I was reading the daily scriptures – I usually do that on my way to work in the train – and I got so drawn into the story of Simon Peter being called by Jesus that I almost missed my stop. I mean, I've read that story many times, but for some reason I found myself in Simon Peter's place as I read it.

Martin   It really came alive for you . . .

Charles   Yes it did, and I've been thinking about it ever since. And then I went to the cathedral the other day, just for the mid-day Communion service – I try to do that at least once a week. I was sitting there quietly just listening and watching as the priest was saying the prayer of Great Thanksgiving and suddenly it was as if there was a voice in my mind saying to me, 'Will you feed my sheep, Charles?' It was as clear as anything.

Martin   You were watching the priest and in your mind you clearly heard this voice?

Charles   Yes, it came out of the blue – until the Simon Peter reading I'd never thought of myself in that sort of nurturing or shepherding role before, never imagined God might want that of me – and it really scares me.

Martin   Scares you?

Charles   Yes, because – and this is really difficult to say and I don't want you to think that I don't love Sally because I do, but I don't know how she would react if I told her – she's pretty marginal as it is when it comes to church. I take the girls to Sunday school without her most Sundays – and to be honest, Martin, she seems to have no interest in growing in her faith – she says one religious nut in the family is enough.

  What's going through your mind as you read this dialogue? Notice how you are *feeling*, and what you are *thinking*.

  What discernment issues or questions are already surfacing – remembering that spiritual direction is all about the relationship between God and the directee and working out how that relationship is lived out day by day in the midst of family, work and leisure?

✠

Issues/questions for discernment may include:

- The two 'religious experiences' which Charles reports – are they authentic or wishful thinking? How might you help him explore these experiences more deeply?
- Sally and her attitude to church and to Charles. For example, is the term 'religious nut' her language or his, was it said in love or with derision? What's their relationship really like – could it stand the rigours of Charles 'going into the Church'?
- Is Charles trying to immerse himself in spiritual practices in order to avoid emotional intimacy with his wife?
- Would Charles be wise to consider marriage guidance? How might a referral be made?
- Charles seems serious about his Christian faith – how might you help him explore the possibility of offering more of himself to God?

Martin may hold the middle three questions in the back of his mind as he begins to help Charles reconnect with his two religious experiences and how they might affect the question of further ministry.

We know that discernment takes time; it is a process which unfolds in an atmosphere of love and prayer, and cannot be rushed, yet much in contemporary society works against this process. If we are offering spiritual direction to others, it is vital that we are also practising discernment about matters great and small, taking time to be with God in silence and openness, willing to bring the process of decision-making to our own spiritual director and to wait for the many pieces of the puzzle to come together in God's good time.

✠

Reflection questions

🕯 Think back to a major decision you have made which proved to be life-giving to you and to others. Trace the process you used to discern your path. How did this process compare with the guidelines available in the Christian tradition?

🕯 Recall a decision you made which subsequently turned out to be ill-advised.

Think back to the extent to which God was – or was not – part of that decision. Talk to God about any regrets you have – and, if appropriate, arrange to meet with a priest or minister for the sacrament of reconciliation or restoration of a penitent/confession.

§ How do you respond to the concept that your feelings are potentially valuable raw material for the development of your relationship with God?
How aware are you of your feelings as you go through each day?
What has been your own experience of 'desolation' and 'consolation'?

§ Look back through the list, giving some suggestions about how to recognize 'voices' from different sources. Consider how this list lines up with your own experience. What might you want to add, debate or remove?

§ Have you ever had to deal with something that is clearly from a source other than God, for example a house in which strange things are happening?
What or who are you aware of in your own network or denomination which would help you respond to such a situation?

§ Re-read the quote from Thomas Merton.
How do you respond to the sentiments expressed?
How would you describe the God that Merton believes in?
How does Merton's way of seeing himself and God relate to your own experience?

To begin to bring this all together, we turn now to another dialogue. One of our fictional directees, Iain, has come to see the minister Stephen because of something that happened one day on his farm:

Stephen   Hello Iain, it's good to see you.
Iain   Well, I wasn't sure I should come – I don't want to bother you when you've got all the parish stuff and the AGM's coming up ... (*a few more general sentences are exchanged before ...*)
Stephen   You mentioned that there was something you wanted to talk about?
Iain   I don't really know where to begin ... you're going to think I'm a bit odd ...
Stephen   Just take your time.
Iain   It was a week ago you see. I was just milking like I always do – just the usual morning milking on my own. The girls were good as gold – nothing seemed different ... (*Iain is clearly struggling ...*)
Stephen   (*Stays quiet but nods encouragingly*)
Iain   Well ... I don't know how to put it ... it was just that ... well, somehow out of the blue. There was a sort of a – a person ... (*there is a long pause*)

Stephen	Someone you knew popped in unexpectedly?
Iain	*(Chuckles and relaxes a bit)* . . . I suppose you could say that . . . but – it wasn't a person I could actually see . . . it was more like a feeling that someone was there *(there is a pause . . .)* someone sort of special.
Stephen	Someone special?
Iain	Someone who knows me through and through. *(Another thoughtful pause . . . Stephen stays silent, waiting and eventually Iain says very quietly)* . . . I sort of felt it was Him . . .
Stephen	Him?
Iain	You know – Him – God – Jesus – Him.

🕯 What's going through your mind so far ?

Your response could range from thinking, 'Oh dear, we've got a right one here!' to offering an immediate enthusiastic agreement that Jesus had indeed met Iain in the milking shed. A middle path might be wise – taking time to find out more about Iain and about the 'religious experience'. Let's continue:

Stephen	So you're in the milking shed, on an ordinary morning, and unexpectedly you have this sense that someone is with you – someone who knows you better than you know yourself, someone that you think might be God or Jesus?
Iain	Exactly . . . *(looking worried . . .)* You don't think I've lost the plot, do you?
Stephen	Has anything like this ever happened to you before?
Iain	No – I've always had my feet on the ground, I'm a down-to-earth bloke really.
Stephen	Can you go back to that experience and say a bit more about what it was like – after you had the idea that it might be, as you put it, Him?
Iain	Well . . . *(taking time to think)* . . . it was sort of very calm, and . . . things seemed to stop for a moment. I don't remember hearing the milking machines or the generator or anything – it was like being caught up in a moment in time that was different, and I just felt . . . *(he smiles)*, I just felt as if everything was OK – like I used to feel when I was a kid and my dad would give me a hug or swing me up in his arms – like that . . .
Stephen	Sort of safe . . .
Iain	Safe – yes, that's what it was – and fun. Like we could do all sorts of great things together . . .

From this portion of the conversation, we see that the spiritual director, Stephen:

- is welcoming and helps Iain get to the point;
- listens carefully without rushing;
- takes Iain seriously, doesn't make fun of him;
- doesn't answer Iain's direct question: 'You don't think I've lost the plot do you?'
- uses a closed question to check out Iain's history: 'Has anything like this ever happened before?'
- summarizes the story to make sure he has heard correctly;
- gives Iain space by leaving silences unfilled;
- invites Iain to re-enter the experience more fully;
- doesn't pass judgement on the authenticity of the experience but listens to the story.

You will probably have noticed that Iain was very tentative in his approach to Stephen. In spite of Hay's comment on the latest research, people still find it difficult to risk talking about their spiritual experiences for fear of being ridiculed or thought mad.

But Stephen too is tentative, staying alert to his own inner responses (whether of longing, or interest or scepticism) while weighing up in his mind how this experience stacks up against what he knows of Iain and of God. He is well aware of the risk of jumping to conclusions about the origin of the experience, but is conscious of the huge step Iain has taken in coming to talk about it. At the very least, Iain has shown courage and a longing for God which is precious and to be handled with care.

- How does Iain's experience measure up against the characteristics of biblical religious experience discussed earlier in this section?
- What questions arise in you from your observation of Stephen's handling of this encounter?
What would you have found difficult?

Suggestions for further reading

Discernment

Benner, David, *Desiring God's Will: Aligning Our Hearts with the Heart of God*, Downers Grove, IL: InterVarsity Press, 2005.
Green, Thomas, *Weeds Among the Wheat*, Notre Dame, IN: Ave Maria Press, 1984.
Lewis, C. S., *The Screwtape Letters*, a widely available classic.
Silf, Margaret, *Landmarks*, London: Darton, Longman and Todd, 1998.

Image of God

Linn, Dennis, Sheila Fabricant Linn and Matthew Linn, *Good Goats: Healing our Image of God*, New York: Paulist Press, 1994.

Thomas, Carolyn, *Will the Real God Please Stand Up*, New York: Paulist Press, 1991.

Religious experience

Barry, William, *Spiritual Direction and the Encounter with God*, New Jersey: Paulist Press, 1992.

Hardy, Alistair (research centre) – now located at the University of Wales in Lampeter as the Religious Experience Research Centre, see <www.alisterhardytrust.org.uk>; <www.lamp.ac.uk>.

Hawker, Paul, *Soul Survivor*, Canada: Northstone, 1998. (Republished as *Soul Quest*, Canada: Wood Lake Publishing, 2007.)

—— *Secret Affairs of the Soul*, Canada: Northstone, 2000.

Hay, David, *Religious Experience Today: Studying the Facts*, London: Mowbray, 1990.

James, William, *The Varieties of Religious Experience: A Study in Human Nature*, Edinburgh: Gifford Lectures, 1901–2.

3

Responding to God

'We love because God first loved us . . . '(1 John 4.19). We respond to God be-cause God initiates communication, igniting the fire of love in our lives, whether or not we recognize that dynamic. In spiritual direction we help directees nurture their response to God in ways that are authentic for them, that emerge from their own context, perhaps in the midst of pain or doubt, or in the joy of celebration. We help directees approach the passionate God who calls us all to intimacy, and invites us to listen *and to respond* to God's voice as we try to live a spiritual life.

3.1 Praying

We all have our favourite ways of thinking about prayer and of actually praying – and so will the people whom we see in spiritual direction. Some directees will have a background in the faith and will have been taught ways of praying as part of their tradition; familiar patterns such as ACTS – adoration, confession, thanks-giving and supplication for example. Others will 'chatter to God all day' or have a regular 'quiet time'. In terms of praying with others, some will be familiar with liturgical prayers, others will be suspicious of formal written prayers, believing they lack spontaneity. Some may be wary of free vocal prayer, while others will relish the flexibility and immediacy of spontaneous intercession or thanksgiving. Some people naturally 'feel' connected to God as they pray, while others may 'feel' little.

However, prayer is not so much about feelings as about faithfulness – God's total, enduring commitment to us and our embryonic, often conditional, com-mitment to God. It is not so much about doing more, but about doing less and trusting more – for God is constantly moving us into broader spaces, enlarging our vision and capacity for risking more of ourselves for God and the kingdom.

Whatever a person's experience and understanding of prayer, in spiritual direc-tion we meet directees where they are, and help them grow in their prayer. 'When God's word touches our heart, responses are many and varied. It is important to recognize them all as prayer.'[66]

---

66 Pritchard, Sheila, *The Lost Art of Meditation: Deepening Your Prayer Life*, London: Scripture Union, 2002, p. 30.

Nearly 30 years ago, when I first began my journey back to God, my view of prayer would have been restricted to using the Prayer Book liturgy, praying for those I loved, and sending 'arrow prayers' to God when I really needed something. Then I was sharing only a relatively small portion of my life with God, and although the Anglican Catechism clearly states, 'Prayer is our response to God's love . . . ',[67] the rich potential of that definition would have completely eluded my early understanding. Now, when I think about my own prayer as it has changed over the years, I recognize that talking *and* listening, dancing, grumbling, singing, focusing attention, arguing, note-making, imagining, tongues, weeping, journalling, silence, noting distractions, longing, mystery, discipline, struggle, more silence, simply being, love and surrender – all these weave in and out of my prayer as I try to live my life turned towards God like a satellite dish, 'tuned in' and receptive.

In the early sessions of spiritual direction we encourage directees to explore their experience and understanding of prayer, using the sorts of questions you will find in the 'Reflection' section. When we ask directees, 'What is prayer for you?' a frequent reply is: 'Prayer is "talking to God".' It is no surprise to see that the emphasis is on the directee's side of the equation, rather than on two-way communication. We are habitually self-focused, yet the irony is that, as we shall see later, when directees talk about issues of concern, and their directors ask them, 'How are you praying about that?' nine times out of ten directees will answer, with a look of surprise, 'Well, I haven't actually prayed about it at all!'

God 'speaks straight' to us and wants us to respond with similar honesty. However, instead of trusting God with the whole of our lives, we all too often hide from God the real truth about our situation, we sanitize the feelings we reveal to God, we suppress the 'un-Christian' thoughts that surface as we deal with life's hard issues. As a result, our communication with God can lack the reality, the heart and the immediacy of genuine conversation. Compare these prayers by Pete's partner, Joy:

Dear Lord, I pray for Pete's surgery today. I pray for wisdom and skill for the surgeon and for attentiveness and competence for the anaesthetist. Pete's been so patient waiting for this operation and he really wants to get back to his job. Please guide all who will be in theatre and taking care of him. Through Jesus Christ, Amen.

Dear Lord, Pete is having surgery today. You know I was absolutely furious when he got bumped off the waiting list last month, but now the operation's today, I feel really anxious. I am afraid of something happening during the operation like it did when Dad died so suddenly . . . I know I shouldn't worry but I can't help it. *(Silence . . .)*
Thank you Lord for reminding me that

---

67 Catechism, *A New Zealand Prayer Book*, London: Collins, 1989, p. 934.

you were with me when Dad died and
you are with me now. Please help me to
entrust Pete to you. Thank you, Jesus.
Amen.

§ What do you notice about these two prayers – apart from the difference in
length?
Which prayer helped the relationship between Joy and God to grow? How?

Simple prayer

The second prayer above is an example of what Richard Foster calls 'simple
prayer', prayer in which:

> . . . we bring ourselves before God, just as we are, warts and all. Like children
> before a loving Father we open our hearts and make our requests. We simply
> and unpretentiously share our concerns and our petitions. There is no pretence
> in Simple Prayer . . . We do not attempt to conceal our conflicting and contra-
> dictory motives from God – or ourselves . . . When we pray, genuinely pray,
> the real condition of our heart is revealed . . . This is when God truly begins to
> work in us.[68]

Although 'simple', this way of prayer is foundational and will probably always
form part of our communication with God, no matter how 'far' we may go in the
spiritual life. Simple prayer can be prayed *anywhere*, *any time*; including while
someone is walking to work, preparing a sermon, or sitting by the bed of a sick
child. Simple prayer encourages us to verbalize what is really going on; to involve
God in the daily detail; to invite Jesus into the heart of our pain or our joy; to ask
the Holy Spirit to help us persevere or relinquish, discern and decide. But directees
often raise barriers to such radical simplicity and honesty in prayer:

1 *'God's got better things to do than listen to my little worries!'*
This comment may stem from the directee's image of God as remote and uncaring;
we are less likely to want to be honest with a God we don't trust or know very well.
But it may be that the directee genuinely has a low opinion of herself and cannot
imagine God, or anyone in 'authority', noticing or caring for her. Or directees
may simply not believe that God could be interested in what seems trivial – the

---

68 Foster, Richard, *Prayer: Finding the Heart's True Home*, London: Hodder & Stoughton,
1992, pp. 9–13.

petty disappointments, the small sadnesses, the little lifts of the heart, the modest hopes.

2 *'Why tell God what God already knows!'*

Of course God knows everything about us,[69] but the point of talking to God about our reality is twofold: first, to hear ourselves fully acknowledge what is going on for us; and second, to build our relationship with the God who cares for us – just as children feel closer to parents who, despite sensing what the problem might be, still listen patiently, holding their children close in love when the telling is over.

3 *'What's the point – nothing's going to change!'*

Philip Yancey's book *Prayer: Does it Make Any Difference?* addresses this and other awkward questions about prayer. We may not know *how* prayer works; we may not understand why some prayers are answered and others seemingly ignored. What we do know is that scripture reminds us that prayer made a difference to our forebears in the faith: to Hannah, praying for a child; to David, singing his psalms; to Elizabeth and to Mary in celebration of new life; to Jesus alone on the mountain or abandoned by his friends in Gethsemane; to Paul and Peter and countless others through the ages. Prayer changed them and will change us: in the process of praying we learn how to pray.[70]

In spiritual direction our concern, then, is to help directees discover, with God's guidance, ways of praying that are appropriate, taking into account such variables as their circumstances, degree of familiarity with Christianity, their personality, etc. In the establishment of any relationship, the early stages can be a bit tentative and awkward, but 'simple prayer' provides a universal starting point as directees 'simply' put into words their thoughts and feelings as they talk with God (the Holy One/the Sacred Other). They don't have to have any theological background, attend any courses or make a commitment; they are simply encouraged to 'respond'. If we return to Stephen and Iain's dialogue, we can see this process unfolding:

Stephen So you have this sense of connection with Someone who makes you feel safe and happy, like a dad with his son – enjoying being together.

Iain Absolutely – I haven't felt like that for years, completely secure and accepted. I mean Elly loves me – I know that – but this has a different feel to it somehow.

Stephen A different feel?

---

69 See Psalm 139.

70 Adapted from Sheila Pritchard, *Prayer* (Module 4, Spiritual Directors' Formation Programme), New Zealand: Spiritual Growth Ministries Trust, 2007, pp. 9–12.

Iain	Yes. I just felt that everything was somehow OK.
Stephen	What's happening now as you talk about this?
Iain	There's a . . . feeling of . . . I guess I just wish He'd stayed longer!
Stephen	You'd like to stay in touch?
Iain	That's a funny question – how can I stay in touch with Someone who's invisible?
Stephen	*(Smiling)* Well, I suppose you could describe prayer that way.
Iain	Hmmh . . . I don't see myself as a 'down-on-your-knees-beside-the-bed-gentle-Jesus- meek-and-mild' sort of person.
Stephen	There are all sorts of ways to pray, and people pray in all sorts of places.
Iain	Even cowsheds?
Stephen	Seems an ideal spot – no one's going to disturb you. What do you think about talking to that Someone – God or Jesus – imagine He's there and talk to Him just like you'd talk to your dad if he'd called in to see you while you're milking?
Iain	What would I say?
Stephen	I don't know – whatever comes to mind – what's going on in your life – there's no right or wrong way to begin.
Iain	Sounds a bit weird – this whole thing's a bit weird. But . . . there's something going on . . . inside me . . . I haven't been able to stop thinking about it. So I guess I'll give it a go and see what happens.
Stephen	Would you like to come back and talk to me about what does or doesn't happen?
Iain	*(Clearly relieved)* That'd be good! I don't want anyone else to know – not yet.
Stephen	You just ring me when you're ready – it's your call. Shall we pray now before you go?
Iain	*(Iain nods and bows his head)*
Stephen	Thank you God for this time together. Thank you for Iain's courage in coming to talk about this experience. Be with us both until we meet again. Help us 'see you more clearly, follow you more nearly and love you more dearly, day by day'. In Jesus' name and love, Amen.

⚬ What did you notice about Stephen's handling of this portion of the session?

What questions arise for you?

What might you have done differently?

What does Stephen 'teach' Iain about prayer?

Praying with scripture

For directees from an evangelical tradition, praying with scripture can expand their practice of prayer and encourage their honest communication with God. Even for those directees who have no scriptural background, if they are willing to consider that the characters and stories in scripture may inform their own experiences, praying with scripture can help forge a strong relationship with the One who inhabits those pages and the lives of us all.

Some directees may think they are being presumptuous by imaginatively putting themselves into a Gospel passage, but for directees who want to get to know Jesus, nothing emphasizes his humanity more than for them to realize that he felt as we feel, knew celebration and betrayal, delight and disappointment, frustration and fellowship. Similarly, directees will be helped to engage more fully with the divinity of Christ if they place themselves in the crowd, watching as the loaves and fishes feed thousands, or as Jesus stops and touches a blind man, restoring his sight and his life.

When my 18-year-old son left home to go to university, I can remember praying with two passages: Matthew 4.21–22 in which Zebedee watches his adult sons, James and John, leave everything and follow Jesus, and Luke 2.41–52 which describes the boy Jesus' choice to follow his own path, remaining in the temple while his parents began their journey home after celebrating the Passover. As I let myself go deeper in each passage, the pain of separation was met by a developing sense of rightness, even joy, at the way in which James, John and the 12-year-old Jesus followed their hearts, their vocation, God's call; I was enabled to pray for that same freedom and joy for my son as he left our home.

Directees are frequently used to studying scripture but may not know how to pray with scripture, so here are three possibilities from which they can choose:

1 Lectio divina *or sacred reading* – sometimes called Benedictine prayer. This process of praying with a small portion of scripture is suitable for directees of any temperament. Mentioned briefly in Chapter 1 (section 1.6) it can further be described in the words of a twelfth-century Carthusian monk:

> *Reading* seeks for the sweetness of the blessed life,
> *meditation* perceives it,
> *prayer* asks for it,
> *contemplation* tastes it.

> *Reading*, as it were, puts food whole into the mouth,
> *meditation* chews it and breaks it up,
> *prayer* extracts its flavour,
> *contemplation* is the sweetness itself which gladdens and refreshes.[71]

---

71 Guigo II, quoted in Jeannette A. Bakke, *Holy Invitations: Exploring Spiritual Direction*, Grand Rapids, MI: Baker Books, 2000, p. 201.

If we read scripture or any suitable spiritual material *really slowly (lectio) and* allow time for thought and making connections with various aspects of our life (*meditatio*) *and* time for making our reply to God (*oratio*), this interwoven pattern of listening and response will lead naturally into deeper and deeper relationship with God – into contemplation, the prayer of openness to God.

Directees who regularly practise *lectio divina* begin to slow down, to look more closely, to see how the words or phrases connect with their circumstances, to share their discoveries with God, and to cease striving. While the first three stages may be familiar, it is the *fourth* stage which brings us to a place of stillness and silence before God. This silence is itself an act of worship because in it:

- we are making a choice to set aside our ego's agenda;
- we are recognizing that God alone knows what is best;
- we are co-operating with God's work in the depths of our spirit;
- we are admitting our poverty of heart and mind; and
- we are following the example of our brother Jesus, coming to the heart of God in trust and with confidence.

If people are struggling with the fourth stage of *lectio,* the letting go of 'doing' and the movement into 'being', it can be helpful to introduce 'Centring Prayer'[72] to aid this transition into contemplation in which we rest in God. In Centring Prayer the healing love of God meets our frailty as we acknowledge and consent to the work that God is already doing in us. Gently repeating a sacred word (such as Abba, Jesus, Spirit, Love) as an anchor point, we sit quietly and let God work in us. When distractions come, rather than being distressed by them we simply turn our thoughts back to the sacred word, reaffirming our choice to be united with God. It's good to know that if we are distracted 50 times during our 20 minutes of prayer, we can make 50 choices to return to God!

2 *Ignatian or imaginative prayer* encourages us to put our mind's creativity to Godly use, as we engage with stories of personal encounter with Jesus or God. We choose a scene from the Gospels for example, and visualize the surroundings of first-century Palestine, hear the sounds, get a sense of the smells and tastes – we see Jesus and those around him and, with the guidance and grace of the Holy Spirit, we inhabit the passage and encounter Christ in his own context.

3 *Augustinian prayer* is somewhat similar, but this time we transpose the key features from the Gospels into our current setting – twenty-first-century rural or

---

72 As taught by Benedictine, Fr Thomas Keating. See <www.centeringprayer.com> for further resources. While Centring Prayer is devotional in its intention, it also has an effect on the psychological well-being of the practitioner as it releases repressed emotions and material from the unconscious.

urban life. What would it be like, for example, to imagine Jesus walking with several disciples (including you!) through the streets of your town, stopping to talk and heal the people whom you see on the margins? Or Jesus meeting you at a favourite café and ordering a cappuccino and a brownie as he sits down to talk to you about what truly satisfies? I recently led a Quiet Day for primary state school chaplains and saw how much they valued imagining Jesus walking with them into the school they served – entering corridors and classrooms, sitting in the lunch area with the children, or playing with them on the fields. For some, this changed their sense of isolation, to one of being 'partnered with Jesus' as they did their faithful visiting week in, week out.

Whichever type of prayer fits for our directees, we invite them to think of appropriate scriptures *themselves* if they can, or we silently ask the Holy Spirit to draw our attention to relevant Gospel passages from which they can choose. For example, for a directee who has been let down or who has failed someone badly, praying with Psalm 55, or Peter's denial of Christ in Mark 14, may help develop a deeper relationship with Jesus and an awareness of the magnitude of God's grace and forgiveness; for a person who is seeking liberation from painful habits or a restricting relationship, the raising of Lazarus in John 11, or Isaiah 61's 'release the captives' might be helpful.

Most Bibles have a list of Jesus' miracles and significant acts in his ministry, and these can be a helpful starting point. Also useful will be your own imaginative prayer with scripture, for then you will have experienced at first hand the benefits of this way of praying.

Two words of caution though: first, not everyone will find it easy to use their imagination in this way. Some people form an inner 'impression' rather than being able to 'see' something as clearly as a clip from a movie. Others simply cannot work this way and therefore would find *lectio divina* more appropriate. Second, avoid offering a particular passage of scripture to a directee just because that passage has been powerful for you. Always encourage directees to choose for themselves.[73]

The more familiar we are with the stories of scripture ourselves, the more we have read, studied and prayed with scripture, the better equipped we will be to encourage praying with scripture when it seems the right option for our directees.

Movements in prayer: changes in the way we respond to God

Spiritual direction from a contemplative stance watches for the Holy Spirit's invitation to directees to *move* in prayer as they are freed to experience more of God. This movement is not tidy or sequential but is fluid, responsive both to God and

---

73 As described in Michael, Chester P. and Norrisey, Marie C., *Prayer and Temperament: Different Prayer Forms for Different Personality Types*, Virginia: The Open Door, 1991.

to the situation in which directees find themselves. Nor is there a 'right' or 'wrong' path: directees may at times return to earlier ways of praying or find that several of these movements are occurring concurrently. Thus, over the years, we and our directees may experience changes in our prayer:

- From bodily passivity to letting our bodies help us express our prayers, for example through dance and movement, the shaken fist in rage, the prostration of the body in devotion and humility.
- From dependence on the prayers of others to being free to write or offer our own prayers and psalms.
- From a variety of prayers to a simple few, for example the Jesus Prayer: 'Jesus Christ, Son of God, have mercy on me, a sinner', which expresses our longing for more of God and our awareness of our poverty of heart.
- From occasional haphazard prayer to frequent prayer, for example using a single verse of scripture as a breath prayer for reassurance or strength, accompanying a directee as they walk or work, for example 'The Lord is my strength', 'Be strong, take heart', 'Bless the Lord my soul'.
- From prayer supported or stimulated by words and ideas, and sensory response to objects, for example creation, paintings, icons, the rosary (*Kataphatic*) to prayer without any words, images or stimuli from the natural world (*Apophatic*).
- From prayer once a week at church to prayer that welcomes each morning, enfolds each hour and all whom we love, gathers up the day's events each night, and moves through our minds and hearts and onto our lips even in sleep.
- From activity and busyness, to longer periods of receptivity and stillness, from verbal prayer and meditation to contemplative or 'listening' prayer.

In spiritual direction, then, initially we help directees notice their own patterns of personal prayer, develop the ability to share honestly with God, and try new ways of verbal and meditative praying as they are led by the Spirit. Over time a miraculous change takes place, as Foster writes:

In the beginning we are indeed the subject and the centre of our prayers. But in God's time and in God's way a Copernican revolution takes place in our heart. Slowly, almost imperceptibly, there is a shift in our centre of gravity. We pass from thinking that God is part of our life to the realization that we are part of his life. Wondrously and mysteriously God moves from the periphery of our prayer experience to the centre. A conversion of the heart takes place, a transformation of the spirit . . . a wonderful work of Divine Grace . . .[74]

---

74 Foster, *Prayer: Finding the Heart's True Home*, pp. 15–16.

To help us understand this process we turn to two classical descriptions of growth in prayer:

1 The 'Three Ways' of purgation, illumination and union. Although described differently through the ages,[75] for the purpose of clarity we will consider only the 'Three Ways' as described by John of the Cross. His description is based on Evagrius (d. 399) for whom the *active* life of prayer related to the Purgative Way and the two degrees of the *contemplative* life of prayer corresponded to the Illuminative and Unitive Ways. (In Chapter 1, section 1.6, contemplation as part of the *lectio divina* process, and contemplation as radically opening ourselves to God's self-communication, were introduced.)

2 Teresa of Avila's *Interior Castle*, which describes the soul's journey through seven 'dwellings' to the centre where the soul is united with God.

Teresa of Avila's *Interior Castle*[76]	The Three Ways
i The first of these 'mansions' is about self-discovery and self-knowledge. The soul becomes alert to the possibility of interior journeying, towards the core of our being.	Purgative (the degree of the beginner)
ii To realize this is to come to the second mansion, to be lit up by the desire for prayer and conversation with God. This means a kind of conversion. We begin to face inwards rather than outwards. Christ is revealed to us, leading us towards . . .	The early stage of the spiritual life when we become aware of our shortcomings, and try to purify our life from sin and its effects, and establish virtuous habits. Prayer is primarily verbal, actively using our mind and senses to help us connect with God. Gradually our prayer life becomes simpler and includes more of our feelings.
iii The third mansion where we are called to a life of virtue. Many people live their entire spiritual lives at this point, and can become complacent, failing to take the risk of another journey . . .	Biblically, this way corresponds to repentance and the putting on of the new humanity in Christ (e.g. Col. 3.1–10). If responsive to God's continuing invitation we enter the Dark Night of the Senses in which the soul is purified of its attachment to sensual things.

75 To read about these different ways of understanding the three ways of growth in prayer, see Ernest E. Larkin, *The Three Spiritual Ways*, available on <http://carmelnet.org/larkin/larkin081.pdf>, accessed January 2008.

76 Summarized from Byrne, Lavinia, *The Life and Wisdom of Teresa of Avila*, London: Hodder & Stoughton, 1998, pp. 50–3.

iv The fourth mansion is a place of transition: human effort becomes transformed by God's grace. God takes over the life of the soul . . . the prayerful person now moves from a spiritual life based on effort and action to one based on receptivity. Prayer becomes more passive: God's work, not our own.	Illuminative (the degree of the proficient) We are increasingly restored to the life of grace. At our core, we know both the reality of our selfish nature *and* the love and grace of God which constantly enfold us.
v In the fifth mansion the soul feels as though it is asleep, enjoying the prayer of passive recollection, a sweet openness to the will of God and tender rest. There is a death of understanding which now surrenders itself into the understanding of God.	Prayer of the heart (honest sharing with God) and a growing desire to be quiet with God are typical of the Illuminative Way. As a precursor to the Unitive Way, we enter the Cloud of Unknowing, the Dark Night of the Soul or Spirit in which the soul submits itself to God's purifying action, and is stripped of all its remaining attachments.
vi In the sixth mansion, the will lets go and the soul is besieged by raptures, ecstasies and trances. Teresa writes from her own experience as she tries to reassure the prayerful person that these spiritual phenomena, while unusual, are not totally terrifying. She teaches discernment . . .	
vii All is gift and grace as the soul approaches the innermost mansion of all, the place of true encounter and union with God. Here in the seventh mansion . . . the death or release of memory secures the presence of the soul in God, God in the soul.	Unitive (the degree of the perfect) The stage where the soul regains its original state as intended by God and is united with God in love. According to Bernard, 'we will experience the joy of the Lord and be forgetful of ourselves in a wonderful way. We are, for those moments, one mind and one spirit with God.'[77]

It is useful to know that not everyone who enters the Unitive Way has an intense *experience* of union such as that described by Teresa or implied by Bernard of Clairvaux. According to O'Hare,

God – dwelling in love in our souls, accepting and embracing all of who we are, working in and through us – brings us into union with God's own life in the normal events of our everyday existence. The experience of union manifests itself in our desires as we come to want what God wants. Surrendering with

---

77 Adapted from Pritchard, Andrew, Module 6, Spiritual Directors' Formation Programme, New Zealand: Spiritual Growth Ministries.

trust and freedom to a merciful, loving God, caring only that we serve Him in all things, we become receptacles of, and channels for, God's love.[78]

As with any model, the transitions between 'stages' or 'ways' are not usually clear cut. We can have a moment of spiritual awakening or illumination while still in the midst of working to eradicate unholy habits. We can find ourselves struggling to understand our pettiness or greed even though we have had moments of deep connection with God.

✠

Reflection questions

⚱ Before we can companion others we need to consider our own prayer practice. Spend a few minutes making some notes about your prayer history, based on the following:
How did I pray when I was a child? How has my prayer changed over the years?
How do I *actually* pray now? What happens? What doesn't happen?
Where is God when I pray? What is God's name for me?
⚱ Think of one situation which you are currently facing, and, if you haven't done so already, bring this to God using 'simple prayer'.
⚱ What is your experience to date of praying with scripture?
What have you been taught about using the imagination?
How does that affect your attitude towards using this faculty in your prayer?
⚱ Re-read the two classical descriptions of growth in prayer.
Which of the two models resonates more closely with your experience?
Think of someone whose spiritual journey you know well – and reflect on what you see in these classical descriptions that matches this person's prayer and life.

3.2 Keeping a spiritual journal

Some of the richest and most helpful resources for our spiritual journey come to us from the writings of those who have kept a record of their stumbling, frustrating

---

78 O'Hare, Breige, 'Opening to Love: A Paradigm for Growth in Relationship with God', in *Presence: An International Journal of Spiritual Direction*, 10(2), June 2004, pp. 27–36, drawing on Ignatius of Loyola, *The Spiritual Exercises*, New York: Doubleday, 1964, p. 233.

and fulfilling experiences, the twists and turns of the path to and with God. Such accounts reveal the inner realities of spiritual life with all its light and darkness and provide solidarity and encouragement, food for our own sometimes halting journey towards God.

As a literary category, 'spiritual autobiography' could be said to have started with the early fourth-century *Confessions* of Augustine of Hippo. It flourished in the seventeenth century, particularly within Protestant circles; John Bunyan's fictionalized description of the spiritual life, *The Pilgrim's Progress*, is still read today. More recent nineteenth- and twentieth-century examples include Georges Bernanos' *The Diary of a Country Priest*, Dag Hammarskjöld's *Markings*, and Pope John XXIII's *Journal of a Soul*. Here is a portion of the entry that John XXIII made in his journal in August 1961, nearly three years after being elected Pope:

> As my retreat draws to an end, I see very clearly the substance of the task which Jesus in his Providence has allowed to be entrusted to me. 'Vicar of Christ?' Ah, I am not worthy of this name. I, the humble child of Battista and Marianna Roncalli, two good Christians to be sure, but so modest and humble! Yet that is what I must be: the Vicar of Christ. 'Priest and victim'; the priesthood fills me with joy, but the sacrifice implied in the priesthood makes me tremble. Blessed Jesus, God and man! I renew the consecration of myself to you, for life, for death, for eternity.[79]

In a few short lines we get a glimpse of the heart of a person we have never met. We can recognize the humanity of John's struggle with the role of 'Vicar of Christ' and we can see the movement from sharing his inner feelings with his Lord, to recommitting himself to Jesus. Although a short passage, it reminds readers of the interior struggle to respond to Jesus' invitation to live fully and freely, and the cost of the calling which brings both sacrifice and joy.

More recently has been the publication of *Come Be My Light*,[80] letters of Mother Teresa to her spiritual directors over her lifetime, letters which reveal her deep interior darkness as she followed Jesus' invitation to be his light in the hovels and holes of the poor.

Of course it is unlikely that our own attempts at documenting our spiritual highs and lows, our encounters with love and tragedy, will ever reach a wide audience. Nor would that be an appropriate reason for keeping a spiritual journal. Such a journal is first and foremost an intensely private communication, a matter for us and God alone.

---

79 Pope John XXIII, *Journal of a Soul*, London: Four Square Books (The New English Library Ltd), 1966, p. 382.

80 Mother Teresa, *Come Be My Light*, Brian Kolodiejchuk (ed.), New York: Doubleday, 2007.

Keeping a journal is a spiritual practice which acts as a doorway into our interior landscape and helps us maintain a contemplative stance as we regularly set aside time for reflection. Rather than being a simple written record of daily activities, its focus is on our response to God in the details of our lives, including where we find or don't find God. As such it is a tool for deepening our capacity to engage with ourselves and with God.

In our journal we can reflect on a key moment; we can explore a scripture passage to see what it might have to say about our current circumstances; we can track our path through grief or transition and name the signposts of grace which emerge from the darkness of such times; we can cover a page with question marks or sketch a rainbow of 'Thank-you's'; we can write a psalm of lament, or wound the page with slashes of red in anger; we can find ourselves filled with unexpected joy as we discover a fresh truth in a familiar Gospel or in the lyrics of an old hymn. Small wonder then that the act of keeping a spiritual journal (or 'journalling' as it is often called) can be likened to prayer for, in the process of engaging at depth with elements of our daily experience, we reveal more of the truth of who we are to ourselves, and bring that truth to the God who knows us intimately.

In practical terms, a spiritual journal:

- provides a private, sacred place in which to vent a full range of feelings and deepen our thinking;
- allows us to ask God questions and listen;
- includes our response to scripture passages and our developing understanding of God;
- may be in a variety of formats, from an inexpensive exercise book or scrap-book, hard-backed journal or loose-leafed folder, to a file on our computer;
- can include photos or pictures; symbols that have personal meaning; our responses to significant events; our own or others' poetry; an exploration of significant dreams; song lyrics; diagrams and drawings; collages reduced in size to fit the journal; service sheets or programmes from art and music festivals which have touched our heart: the list is endless;
- is unique and doesn't have to conform to any particular style or pattern;
- can be full of spelling and grammatical errors and no one will know;
- can be addressed to God as we currently address God, to Jesus or the Holy Spirit;
- may be used daily or weekly – some regularity is recommended, at least in the beginning.

People's patterns of using a journal will vary. I notice that sometimes I might go for a week or two without making an entry, but will journal intensely when faced with a major issue or transition – such as my mother's unexpected death. This practice helped me to be very aware not only of my own feelings and needs, but more importantly of God's presence in the midst of loss and anxiety, a presence expressed in those small mercies which could have gone unnoticed had I not taken the time to record where God was for me in each difficult day. Going back to that journal, I see an entry dated 25 June 1995 and am at once reconnected with the sweetness of God's grace. Three weeks after Mum had died I went with my husband and son to a church concert. The programme is tucked into the journal where I had written: 'There was a real blessing in the words set to "Finlandia" – I'd always loved the music but didn't know the words – "Be still my soul, the Lord is on thy side" – they spoke exactly to my situation.' Although over ten years old, that memory remains real and nourishing. Without such a record it would have been easy to forget the ways in which I experienced God's grace at that time.

In times of stress the journal can provide a tangible reminder of God's faithfulness and care; in times of doubt we can look back and see God's provision for us; in times of emerging call, we can see the signposts already passed and gain the courage to keep on looking for the next waymarker.

As with any spiritual practice, the hardest thing is simply to settle down and start. Journalling does take time and focus, but it is worth it, for over the years a journal provides a unique record of our spiritual journey, our movement towards and away from God, our pattern of circling, approaching and wandering, and gives space to honour our emerging awareness of God's personal love for us, our developing love of God, and God's challenge to us to grow in trust and service.

However, for some of us, systematically recalling our own faith development or God's activity in our life does not fit readily with our personality or lifestyle. We may have a very busy schedule and a series of reasons for not getting round to journalling – or we may be afraid of having 'nothing to say', a fear of what might be revealed if we stop long enough to look beneath the surface of our life at matters of faith, prayer, relationships, vocation.

If directees express a desire to grow in their faith, then part of the work we do in spiritual direction is to help them explore journalling as a tool in that process. We look with them at their hopes and fears, 'oughts' and 'shoulds', and discuss their preferred way of beginning such a process. We make it clear that this is not a 'one size fits all' practice but a dynamic tool to help them respond to God, and they are free to start where it seems most inviting to them.

In those who have made the commitment to keeping a spiritual journal, there are definite benefits when the time comes for spiritual direction. Frequently I will hear a directee say, 'I knew I was coming to see you, so I looked back through my journal to see what's been happening over the past month – and what I might bring to spiritual direction today.' Out comes the journal, and the relevant memory or information is immediately accessible. This is a good example of directees being intentional about their growth in God; the regular keeping of a journal aids that commitment and provides, in a full life, a means of tracking themes in life and scripture, patterns of growth, inner movements and 'God moments'.

✠

Reflection questions

⚱ What helps or hinders you starting to keep a spiritual journal?
External factors such as time pressures or privacy or . . . ?
Internal factors like fear of exposure, or emptiness, of letting God get too close . . . ?

⚱ If you already keep a journal, what have you found beneficial? Less useful? What do you notice about your pattern of writing?

⚱ As you look back over the past few months, what stands out in your life of faith?
How might you record those events/discoveries/questions/experiences so they are accessible as sources of encouragement/illumination in the future?

⚱ If you have not yet read anyone else's spiritual autobiography, you may like to go to the library and see what you can find. You may also find 'spiritual' material in 'ordinary autobiographies', for example Jane Goodall's *Reason for Hope*.

3.3 Working with symbols

Christianity is packed with symbols: the cross, bread and wine, the Light of the World, to anchor us in Jesus' life and work; rock, fortress, stronghold, to speak of God's strength; a dove to represent the presence of Spirit; a potter and the clay to help us appreciate the tender yet firm touch with which God shapes our lives and character. For some of our directees, these powerful symbols convey rich meaning shaped by the teaching and tradition of the Church. This meaning can be deepened as directees explore these symbols and discover a set of personal meanings that emerge from their experience and questions.

To be able to work with a symbol though, directees need to be able to make the sort of transition we have already seen in John 3.1–12, in which Nicodemus wrestles with the shift from a literal understanding of being 'born again' to a symbolic understanding *which gives access to a spiritual truth*.

For directees with a faith background and a strong biblical knowledge, it is natural to work with scriptural symbols. However, for others *any* symbol which has caught the directee's attention can be explored and provide 'food for the journey', as this example illustrates:

Dulcie was attending a course where a 'warm-up' exercise asked those present to think of an animal or bird to represent themselves. Dulcie initially struggled but came up with 'a turtle', telling others it was because she could carry her home on her back and 'pull her head in' when she felt she needed to. She forgot about the 'turtle' until three days later pieces of a child's jigsaw puzzle were handed around the group. Dulcie turned her puzzle piece over and found that it had a turtle on it! She was catapulted back to the first day's opening exercise and realized that this synchronicity or 'God-incidence' was inviting her to 'pay attention'. She decided she would take this experience to spiritual direction.

If we were companioning Dulcie we could use some of the following approaches to help her explore the 'turtle' symbol:

- Help Dulcie re-visit the 'religious experience', the 'synchronicity' she has noticed. Describing in detail what she thought and felt as she initially chose the turtle symbol, shared her understanding of it with others, and then turned over the puzzle-piece three days later, will make room for insights and awareness to deepen.
- Offer paper and crayons so Dulcie can draw her 'turtle', perhaps with ' head extended' and 'head pulled in' and write down some of the feelings that accompany each state. Open-ended questions could follow, for example 'What does this turtle need?', 'Where is God in this picture?' or 'Where might God like to be in this picture?'
- Encourage her to bring any major issue to prayer, honestly sharing her feelings and thoughts, asking God for the particular grace she needs, for example if she identified a tendency to withdraw when anxious, she could ask God for courage, for confidence or peace of mind.
- Invite Dulcie to imagine her turtle in the presence of Jesus – what would it be like for her if Jesus sat beside her with his hand on her shell?
- Making a collage is a contemplative activity in which Dulcie could not only put her 'turtle' on the page, but could, for example, shape its surroundings and the journey it has taken from the sea. We could wonder together what has contributed to her being 'high and dry' and away from the environment in which she had moved easily and fearlessly, i.e. 'with her head out'.
- Dulcie could even engage in an imaginary dialogue with the 'turtle' – getting to know that part of herself which gets frightened, feels overwhelmed, or struggles with change.

The second appearance of the 'turtle' symbol caught Dulcie's attention and challenged her to look at her reality. In the safe, accepting context of spiritual direction, she was able to access her feelings and admit how fed up she was with the constant moving for work; she realized she wanted to share her feelings with God and ask for God's help to come out of her shell, slowly and safely – and that is what she has done.

Working with symbols can also help those who prefer to use analysis and reasoning to make sense of the world, to gain access to their feelings. Because our conversations are often punctuated by similes, vivid phrases and allusions, by noticing metaphorical language we can help directees connect not only with their thinking but also with their emotional life; and we can wonder together where God might be in the midst of their circumstances.

For example, if a directee talks about his difficulties with a major project, we can ask him directly: 'What sort of image comes to mind when you think about this project?' He might respond with something like, 'Banging my head against a brick wall' – a vivid image which lends itself to further exploration. But if he doesn't come up with anything, we simply continue the conversation and listen closely for evocative phrases, for example 'I'm just going round in circles' or 'It's like I've been backed into a corner'. We then hold out that phrase for the directee to notice and explore, using some of the following:

• Ask open-ended questions: 'What's it like for you to be going round in circles?' (elicits both feeling *and* thinking responses) or 'What does it feel like to be going round in circles?' (concentrates on the feeling responses).

• Using paper and crayons, invite the directee to put something on the page to represent 'being backed into a corner' and to write a word or two about how that feels, what it's like.

• Help the directee notice any feeling words which surface, 'dizzy', 'trapped', and then invite them to say what it's like to be 'dizzy' or 'trapped', exploring more feelings or questions as they arise, for example 'What happens when you are dizzy?'

• At some point it is appropriate to offer a question that explores *relationship*, phrasing it in a way that is respectful of the directee's spiritual journey: 'Who is there to keep you safe, offer advice?'; 'Where is God/Jesus/Spirit in this situation?'; 'What do you need from God/Jesus at the moment?'; 'What might the Spirit want to say to you?'

Symbols also help us begin to engage with dream material, as we consider what the symbols in the dream might represent to the dreamer over a period of time. Josephine,[81] a pastor, attending a seven-day silent retreat, writes:

On the third night of the retreat a bright green gecko ran screaming through my dreams. With my director I endeavoured to unpack the gift of the sudden appearance of this normally shy little creature . . . I began to understand that beauty so rare is not discovered by crashing through undergrowth but by sitting quietly, watching for signs of its emergence.

---

81 Not her real name. 'Josephine' is one of a dozen 'voices' of colleagues in the ministry of spiritual direction who have contributed some of their experiences to this book.

Now, a year later, I am reflecting again on the significance of this encounter to the work of pastoral ministry. The appearance of the gecko in my dream has awakened me to something of the mystery of this God who withholds himself from us for our own sakes.

I have also recognized my gecko's scream as one of self-defence; she is telling me to beware. In heeding her warning I am learning that, in turn, my ministry need not be less effective in my absence. Submitting an apology for a meeting or making a phone call to someone instead of a personal visit is a necessary component of my own self-care and need not lessen God's ability to effect inner transformation in those I bear concern for – and may even enhance it.

Helping our directees use their imagination to unpack the levels of meaning contained in a symbol is exciting work. Whether emerging from daily life, scripture or a dream, symbols can help directees access feelings and deeper truths about themselves, can continue to reveal their meaning long after they first become significant, and can add yet another dimension to their growing relationship with God.

✠

Reflection questions

- 🕯 Make a list of your favourite symbols from scripture. Choose one and see if it has not only a traditional meaning but also some personal connection or application.
- 🕯 How comfortable are you with using symbols as part of your own spiritual journey?
- 🕯 What symbols from your tradition have helped you learn more about yourself? About God?
- 🕯 What symbols from dreams have you worked with? What did you discover?
- 🕯 Take an everyday item such as a cup or a toothbrush and, using paper and crayons, put it on the page and start to work with it, seeing how the process of reflection, noticing feelings, writing down powerful words or phrases, wondering where the holy/God/Jesus/Spirit might be, unfolds.

3.4 Making space, in solitude and silence

Space

As we become more accustomed to listening to God and more intentional about responding to God, we discover the value of periodically withdrawing from the busy routines of life. This drawing apart, this making of space, will take different forms depending on our life circumstances. Few of us would take the path of the fourth-century Desert Fathers and Mothers who sought the spacious confinement of the simple cell in which to wrestle with God and with themselves. Some of us may have the luxury of a room set aside solely for prayer and reflection, a room in which we can light a candle, read and ponder, pray aloud without embarrassment, keep our journal in privacy, dance and cry and sing without interruption. But others of us – and many directees – have to make do with shared space: a corner of a bedroom, a particular chair in the lounge, a park bench on the way to work, a restful spot in a church, a sunny doorstep, or a sheltered place in a garden.

We may be committed to an ideal regular 'time out' with God and diligently diary an hour a day, a full day each month, a week each year, specifically to attend to our relationship with God. But others – and many directees – make do with snatches of 'time out': a few minutes while waiting to collect a child from a music lesson, ten minutes while the baby is asleep before we do the chores, a sleepy half-hour at day's end when the house is quiet, or a 'not-quite-awake' prayer before the day rushes in on us.

Sometimes directees will bemoan their lack of dedicated space and use that lack to explain why their prayer life is 'not happening'. They clearly have not heard the story of Susanna Wesley, busy mother of numerous children including John and Charles, who would sit in her kitchen chair with her apron over her head in order to create a space for prayer. Her children knew not to disturb her until the apron was lowered!

In spiritual direction, exploring some of the following with directees might help them claim a space for themselves so they can listen and respond freely to God:

- Invite them to talk to God about their desire for a special 'Godspace' and to listen for God's response – then or later, it will come.
- In an urban context, some directees' only truly private space is in their car. Through music, through conversation and listening to God, through repetition of a 'breath prayer' or the 'Jesus prayer' as they drive, their car becomes a place of connection with God.
- For those on the move a lot, MP3 downloads from websites such as 'pray-as-you-go'[82] provide ten minutes of music and reading of scripture, with guided re-flection questions designed to help a person interact with the Bible in a personal way and experience a small oasis of prayer.
- At the office computer, using a prayer site such as 'Sacred Space'[83] connects directees with imaginative prayer with scripture for a ten-minute reflection and creates a little solitude.

---

82 <www.pray-as-you-go.com>, a Jesuit initiative, based on Ignatian spiritual practices.

83 <www.sacredspace.ie>, a website run by Irish Jesuits, also drawing on Ignatian spirituality.

- Talking about what you need with other members of the household so that they can help you find space can work well – if you will also help them take time for something special.

Solitude

Finding a suitable space is one thing. Regularly *going there* to be alone with God is another, and for some directees this constitutes a very big hurdle. Some will have little experience of solitude and silence, life as they live it being filled from waking to sleeping with the presence of other people, and with noise – the external noise of machinery and city life, the visual 'noise' of cluttered environments, or the interior noise of our thought life and self-talk.

Some may equate solitude with loneliness, and be fearful of being left by themselves, unaware of the gift which time spent without people can bring. Jesus knew the benefits of 'fasting' from social interaction, regularly 'retreating' into solitude so he could be renewed by contact with the source of all love, his Father.

Others may be afraid of what might happen if they start to look within, to begin to allow God access to the 'inner rooms' of their souls. It is very easy to hide from God in the midst of a routine of pastoral care or chaplaincy rounds, social events, cooking, washing and cleaning, even in the reciting of corporate prayers. Regularly taking time to be alone confronts us with ourselves, but the good news is that God who waits for us in the solitude *already* knows *and* loves us, just as we are.

Silence

We may have found our space; we may have chosen solitude. We want to respond to the divine invitation to 'be still and know that I am God' (Psalm 46.10); we want to adopt the receptive stance inherent in the words 'For God alone my soul waits in silence' (Psalm 62.1).

But before we or our directees do so, it can be helpful to take time to check out our 'silence' history – how we have experienced silence, the context of it, and our feelings and thinking around it. Some reflection questions for you to try for yourself and to use in spiritual direction are provided at the end of this section. If, on reflection, we become aware of some resistance to silence, some fear or pain from the past, then that is where we begin our prayer. We talk to God about our desire to come to God in silence; we share with God our feelings of uncertainty; we invite Jesus into the bad memory of silence being used to control and punish. We bring to prayer anything that gets in the way, and we ask for the grace to be silent with God.

We and our directees usually find that our attempts to become still or maintain an inner attitude of openness to God are met by *distractions*. As mentioned earlier, one helpful way of 'dealing with' distractions is to use 'Centring Prayer' to anchor the soul. Thus whenever the mind wanders off, as soon as we notice the movement away, instead of berating ourselves for our lack of attention, we gently repeat the sacred word and turn back to God.

If, however, we find the same issue or person popping into our minds whenever we settle down to spending time with God in silence, this may be an indicator that we are being invited to *notice* something that we have not attended to earlier. We can then either ask God how we should be praying about the issue or we can jot down the name of the person or issue raised so we can attend to it in some practical way once our prayer time is over.

As best we can, we attend to God, setting aside our ego's chatter, dispensing with all the words that gather our needs and wants, our fears and anxieties, our hopes for others, even our prayers for the world. This withdrawal from words is necessary because, as Rowan Williams comments: 'Our words help to strengthen the illusions with which we surround, protect and comfort ourselves; without silence, we shan't get any closer to knowing who we are before God.'[84] As we and our directees begin to move more resolutely into regular times of solitude with God, we move more deeply into interior silence, into what Thomas Keating would describe as 'The quieting of the imagination, feelings and rational faculties in the process of recollection; the general loving attentiveness to God in pure faith.'[85]

In this place of silent availability to the Spirit, God transforms and heals us.

✠

Reflection questions

⦿ Where do you pray? What sort of 'sacred space' do you have or would you like?

⦿ What part did silence play in your childhood and adolescence?
If you were ever silenced against your will, how might you bring that pain to God?

⦿ What part do silence and solitude play in your life now?

⦿ Why is it so important to 'fast' from speaking?

---

84 Williams, Rowan, *Silence and Honey Cakes: The Wisdom of the Desert*, Oxford: Lion, 2003, p. 45.

85 Keating, Thomas, *Open Heart: The Contemplative Dimension of the Gospel*, New York: Continuum, 2002, p. 146.

3.5 Growing

Spiritual growth: the metaphor of the journey

The metaphor of 'journey' aptly describes the process of spiritual growth and has been popping up throughout this book. In spiritual direction we help directees notice the signposts on the way, and make choices at a crossroads. We sit with them, tending the campfire, when they are stuck; we celebrate when 'arrivals' of some sort offer a chance of rest and refreshment, and encourage them when God interrupts their complacency and invites them out on the road again.

Although some models of spiritual growth use the term 'stages' as if 'progress' were strictly linear, we know from our own experience that spiritual growth does not happen neatly or sequentially. Nor can models of spiritual growth do justice to the unique combinations of graced invitation and resistance, questions and life-events which precipitate our exploration, but they *can* help us understand the process and, perhaps more importantly, can remind us that we are not alone. If those we meet in spiritual direction can recognize something of their own journey, and find another language for their searching, they can begin to engage with their journey more hopefully, with the beginnings of a map for the territory they are exploring.

We have already seen growth in prayer described through the writings of John of the Cross and Teresa of Avila. We turn now to two contemporary writers, James Fowler and Breige O'Hare, who highlight the dynamics of the spiritual growth process and those difficult transitions in which spiritual direction is *particularly* valuable.

Fowler's 'Stages of Faith' material has been used by others, notably Alan Jamieson,[86] to help us understand why many very committed people, especially those from Evangelical, Pentecostal and Charismatic (EPC) churches, leave the church physically, or disengage from it emotionally or intellectually. Nicola Slee responded to Fowler's work by looking specifically at women's experience of faith transitions, highlighting the value of intuitive and imaginative elements and the more complex cycles of movement than are suggested by Fowler's more linear model. Fowler uses the word 'faith' in its original sense of 'making a commitment'; he emphasizes that no one stage of faith is 'better' than another, nor do people necessarily make their transitions in the age group associated with each stage.

The first of his two stages are omitted here as they are concerned primarily with childhood. For ease of comparison, Fowler's material which helps us recognize the *all-encompassing* nature of adult transitions in faith is set alongside O'Hare's three-phase model[87] which is particularly helpful in understanding the changes in *relationship* with oneself, with others and with God.

---

86 For details of books by Jamieson and Slee, refer to the Further Reading section.
87 O'Hare, 'Opening to Love', pp. 29, 31, 34. Used with the author's permission.

Fowler	O'Hare
Stage 3 Synthetic-Conventional Faith *Adolescence* *'The Loyalist'*[88]	*Characteristics of Phase I:* *Certainty* (Typified by deference to a higher authority and following a well-defined system of rules)
Security in being part of a community – being part of a group inevitably means conforming to a set of beliefs, values and behaviours which are held out by the leadership to be appropriate. '. . . may hold deep convictions and are often very committed workers . . . they have typically not examined their beliefs and values critically. Adults at this stage tend to know what they know, but are generally unable to tell you how they know something is true without referring you to an external authority . . . such as the Bible or the Pastor . . . '[89] God is an 'external, transcendent, being'; little concept of an 'in-dwelling, immanent God'. 'Among adults, this is the stage most commonly found among church members . . . The image of the church community as a large family in which there are strong bonds and friendships is often very appealing . . . conflict and controversy are threatening to them and they will tend to work for harmony, preferring to bury conflict (rather) than allow it to surface and potentially destabilise the sense of community which is so important to them.'[90]	*Relationship with self and others* We may have difficulty knowing what's going on inside of or with others. We may be hesitant to voice uncomfortable thoughts or feelings for fear they are unacceptable to others. We may need the security of established rules and apparent facts. We may need the approval of others if we have a strong sense of being loved for who we are. *Relationship with God* We may not be aware of our lived experience of God or our true feelings toward God. We may know a lot about God but not actually know God. We may have difficulty being open and honest with God in prayer for fear of being rejected. We may think God judges us against a list of rules. We may find it hard to accept that God desires us as we are and that God's love for us is beyond our wildest imaginings.

88 The description of Fowler's Stages of Faith is based on Jamieson's understanding and uses Fowler's terms as well as titles taken from Charles R. McCollough, *Heads of Heaven, Feet of Clay*, New York: Pilgrim Press, 1983.

89 Jamieson, Alan, *Called Again – In and Beyond the Deserts of Faith*, Wellington: Philip Garside, 2004, p. 112.

90 Jamieson, *Called Again*, p. 112.

Stage 4 Individuative-Reflective Faith Young Adulthood 'The Critic'	Characteristics of Phase II Searching (Typified by adolescent or mid-life crises)
The most challenging, disorienting stage, often triggered by crisis.	*Relationship with self and others*
	We may feel different and separate from those who have a strong faith.
Involves critiquing the whole structure of one's faith: beliefs, image of God, ways of worshipping, attitudes to authority, ways of making moral choices, even hitherto strong interpersonal relationships.	We may be very aware of how we fall short of the expectations of ourselves and others.
	We realize we have not understood our own true motives and feelings, and that they are not as pure as we would like them to be.
Individuals develop '. . . a new sense of self that will take responsibility for its own actions, beliefs and values, will stand out against significant others, and . . . [can] examine objectively the beliefs, values and expectations they have received'.[91]	We may question values and beliefs we have held dearly.
	Relationship with God
'Pat' answers fail to satisfy; the image of God that may have served the person well is no longer adequate in the face of searing questions about innocent suffering, justice and pain.	We may find it difficult to trust that God is really there with us.
	We become increasingly honest with ourselves and with God, and may find it difficult to have faith in God's unconditional love for us.
Church leadership struggles to relate to someone entering, or in, this stage, who trusts their own judgement, seems self-sufficient and will no longer defer to the leadership.	We may find it difficult to trust in the transforming power of God and to believe in God's way of salvation.
This stage is potentially damaging to existing relationships within the church 'family' as one of its members seems determined to 'leave home'.	We may feel that prayer is empty or meaningless but we feel a strong desire to be with God and to please God by our actions. We are being opened to love and opened *in order* to love.

---

91 Jamieson, *Called Again*, p. 113.

Stage 5 Conjunctive Faith Middle Adulthood: 'The Seer'	Characteristics of Phase III Intimacy (Typified by relationships of greater openness and honesty)
A stage characterized by paradox – learning to love the questions and accept the 'both/and' of our lives: ageing but young in heart; male but honouring the feminine; a sinner and beloved of God. The 'firm boundaries of the previous stage become more porous. The confident self becomes humblingly aware of the depth of the unconscious and the unknown.'[92] People at this stage are less likely to label others and are genuinely open to the treasures in other faith traditions while being deeply committed to their own post-critical re-constructed faith. 'The Seer's faith . . . may be quite orthodox, deviating little, if at all, from the faith previously espoused, or it may relish aspects of faith and ideology from other perspectives. What is significant is that it is the owned and firmly rooted faith of the individual.'[93]	*Relationship with self and others* We are content to be ourselves and accept our contradictions and complexities. We are content to accept the contradictions and complexities of others and of our world. We know ourselves to be loveable just as we are.
Stage 6 Universalizing Faith *'The Saint'*	
Reached by few but typified by two major transitions: the removal of the self from centre-stage away from 'the usual human obsessions with survival, security, and significance . . . and a complete acceptance of the ultimate authority of God in all aspects of life.'[94] People such as Mother Teresa and Martin Luther King are modern examples.	*Relationship with God* We trust in God's unconditional love. We increasingly surrender to God's will and trust in God's salvation. We experience ourselves as beloved children of God without fear of punishment or rejection.

---

92 Jamieson, *Called Again*, p. 113.
93 Jamieson, *Called Again*, p. 114.
94 Jamieson, *Called Again*, p. 115.

This dismantling inherent in leaving the place of 'Certainty' or 'Loyalty' can be painful, unpleasant, disorienting and difficult, affecting the whole of the person's life. Spiritual direction can provide a safe and steady context for 'searchers' or 'critics' when everything else seems to be changing and they need a confidential, informed, compassionate companion to help them listen to themselves.

ℰ Take a few minutes to read back through the descriptions above and reflect on where you see yourself at the moment. Remember that your faith journey may have you in more than one place at a time as various elements of your spiritual life may develop at different rates.

The models we have looked at so far relate well to the contemplative, incarnational model of spiritual direction and the Christian concept of 'journey', giving us a set of descriptions and understandings to refer to when we are working with our directees. They may also resonate with our personal experience as we recognize some of the dynamics described. However, if we are working mainly with people who have little or no formal faith background, those who profess a faith other than Christianity, or those who have developed a very idiosyncratic spirituality, then the recent work of John Mabry may relate more readily.

Mabry proposes six faith 'styles': Traditional Believers, Spiritual Eclectics, Ethical Humanists, Liberal Believers, Religious Agnostics, and Jack Believers ('people who believe in a particular faith but for some reason cannot exist within it').[95] Each style Mabry believes 'carries with it certain assumptions about the Divine and the life of faith that will impact (the spiritual director's work) with one's client'.[96] He further provides a set of key questions for use in assessing 'clients', exploring their image of and relationship with the Divine; how they construct meaning; what sources of spiritual wisdom are acceptable; how they assess spiritual growth; which spiritual disciplines and practices are valued; and the advantages and disadvantages of their particular faith style.[97]

Mabry's material would provide a useful framework for those in community-facing ministry in areas with large immigrant populations, or in chaplaincies where ethnic and faith diversity is common.

The relationship between spiritual and psychological growth

Many writers have explored this relationship, but for clarity, experience, compassion and depth of description I would particularly recommend the writings

---

95 Mabry, John R., *Faith Styles: Ways People Believe*, New York: Morehouse, 2007, p. 79.
96 Mabry, *Faith Styles,* p. xiv.
97 Mabry, *Faith Styles,* p.xiv.

of Gerald May, psychiatrist and spiritual director who, until his recent death, was closely involved with spiritual directors' formation at Shalem Institute in Washington DC. (See Further Reading for details of May's writings, p. 120.)

Spiritual growth happens as we gain confidence in God's love for us, become more aware of God's holiness and call, and become freer to be honest about our responses and the true state of our inner life. Instead of having to keep up a 'front', presenting to others a 'false self' that looks capable and positive (or whatever other traits are socially expected or acceptable), we are increasingly able to see ourselves – and let others see us – as God-oriented people with a healthy acknowledgement of our strengths and a compassionate acceptance of our weaknesses.

Emerging out of the changes in prayer which were noted earlier, the 'fruit' of this deepening honesty and intimacy with God may be seen in a directee's:

- relational capacity, as in initiating reconciliation, in offering forgiveness;
- self-acceptance and self-awareness;
- creativity, whether artistic/poetic or novel solutions to problems great and small;
- deepening compassion and service;
- tolerance of uncertainty and the ability to wait;
- ever-deepening trust in God.

The goal of psychological growth is 'integration', a state in which we function well, our inner paradoxes are accepted and we are freed from the crippling effects of early trauma, anxiety and fear. Commonly, people who seek help with this process choose from a range of psychological and therapeutic models at some cost – both financial and emotional – for it is no small thing to commit oneself to the robust process of psychotherapy or analysis. For many, this route may be more about self-actualization or fulfilment rather than about being strengthened and enabled to serve others.

God calls us all 'to maturity, to the measure of the full stature of Christ' (Ephesians 4.13), inviting us to fulfil our potential as children of God, using our giftedness in service, and growing in compassion for others. The Divine Healer meets us spiritually *and* psychologically as we draw closer and closer to God. As we become silent and receptive, willing to face the parts of ourselves that have been unacknowledged, we open ourselves to comprehensive growth and healing under the guidance and protection of God. Cynthia Bourgeault, exploring the psychological implications of Keating's Centring Prayer, helps us understand the process:

Beginning in infancy (or even before) each of us, in response to our perceived threats to our well-being, develops a false self: a set of protective behaviours driven at root by a sense of need and lack. The essence of the false self is driven, addictive energy, consisting of tremendous emotional investment in compensatory 'emotional programmes for happiness', as Keating calls them . . .

It is the false self that we bring to the spiritual journey; our 'true self' lies buried beneath the accretions and defences. In all of us there is a huge amount of healing that has to take place before our deep and authentic quest for union with God – which requires tremendous courage and inner presence to sustain – escapes the gravitational pull of our psychological woundedness and self-justification. This, in essence, constitutes the spiritual journey.[98]

While Keating developed Centring Prayer with a devotional intention, it has become clear that sustained time in this form of contemplative prayer has both a spiritual *and* a psychological effect: our psyche is transformed, as God's presence warms the centre of our being, and our true selves can once more bathe in the love which we knew before birth, the love to whom we shall return. But this process is not without pain. Keating's understanding of the psychological dynamics of contemplative prayer connects with the classical descriptions of the Dark Night of the Soul and Spirit, as Bourgeault describes:

What really happens when one enters the cloud of unknowing,[99] resting in God beyond thoughts, words and feelings, is a profound healing of the emotional wounds of a lifetime. As these wounds are gradually surfaced and *released* in (contemplative) prayer, more and more the false self weakens and the true self gradually emerges. For Keating, this is the real meaning of the term *transforming union*. As he states quite clearly in *Intimacy with God*: 'We can bring the false self to liturgy and the reception of the sacraments, but we cannot bring the false self forever to contemplative prayer because it is the nature of contemplative prayer to dissolve it.'[100]

How do we know when the true self is beginning to emerge? In the intensification of the 'fruits of the Spirit' we begin to see the outworking of both spiritual *and* psychological growth. The increase in our capacity to love, to be joy-full in any situation, to be a person of peace, to be good and gentle, self-controlled and faithful, all give witness to God's healing of our spirit *and* of our psyche. In daily life we and our directees become increasingly free from having to protect our image of ourselves; we can be vulnerable before others and compassionate towards others,

---

98 Bourgeault, Cynthia, *Centring Prayer and Inner Awakening*, Cambridge, MA: Cowley, 2004, pp. 94–5.

99 Title of a book written in the fourteenth century by an unknown Christian mystic, offering guidance in contemplative prayer. See Further Reading for contemporary editions.

100 Bourgeault, *Centring Prayer*, p. 96, quoting Thomas Keating, *Intimacy with God*, New York: Crossroad, 1994, p. 98.

because we know the truth of our condition and the wonder of God's gracious love for each one of us.

In offering spiritual direction, we will also meet people whose inner peace is affected by mental illness, yet who still display a genuine willingness and capacity to respond to God. I think of a directee who struggles with severe bouts of depression but who follows her Lord faithfully as best she can. According to Gerald May,[101] unless such people are too self-preoccupied or delusional to give adequate attention to their spiritual life, psychological difficulties need not prevent them from growing in their faith.

If we find ourselves companioning people who struggle in this way, we can trust that God can still bring healing and support. We can be a part of that healing if we depend on God to guide us, if we take our difficulties to supervision, and if we are aware of the limits of our competence and the value of working alongside other health professionals.

✠

Reflection questions

- Make a diagram or time-line of your own spiritual journey, noting the moments of growth, dislocation, wandering and wondering.
- Re-read O'Hare's model and trace the way your own relationships have been affected as you have negotiated the transition between 'Certainty' and 'Searching'.
  Or – if you are still in the 'Certainty' aspect of faith, note your response to the implications of moving into 'Searching' – how it might affect your relationships and what might you fear/value?
- If you have made a difficult transition, with whom were you able to share your struggle and discoveries?
- Which of the indicators of spiritual growth listed above have you noticed in your own life?

3.6 Living out the consequences of growing in intimacy with God

Practising the presence of God

As we begin to allow more and more of God into more and more of our lives, we come to see as artificial the separation between sacred and secular. We naturally

---

101 May, Gerald, *Care of Mind, Care of Spirit: A Psychiatrist Explores Spiritual Direction*, New York: HarperCollins, 1982.

seek to integrate our beliefs and spiritual practices into the whole of our life, but how do we honour God in the middle of a meeting, supermarket shopping, or painting the neighbour's roof?

In the seventeenth century, a French lay Brother called Lawrence left behind a series of letters which, together with records of some of his conversations, give us a possible answer. Whether at work in the kitchen or sandal-making, or in formal times of prayer, he 'practised the presence of God'. By repeatedly turning his mind to God, in love, all through the day, Brother Lawrence not only deepened his own connection with God but was a vehicle of God's grace to those around him. Determined to do nothing that would displease God, Brother Lawrence gave his whole self to God, doing everything, big or small, *for the love of God*. There was no division between 'sacred' and 'secular', between leisure and work, for he did *everything* for the love of God:

> One must serve God in a holy liberty and do one's work faithfully without distress or anxiety, calling the soul gently and quietly back to God as soon as we find it drawn away from him . . . Do not be discouraged by the distaste you will feel in your human nature . . . At the onset one often feels that it is a waste of time, but you must go on, and determine to persevere therein to death in spite of all the difficulties.[102]
>
> (This practice of the presence of God . . .) must stem from the heart, from love, rather than from the understanding and speech. In the way of God, thoughts count for little. Love does everything and it is not needful to have great things to do . . . I turn my little omelette in the pan for the love of God. When it is finished, if I have nothing to do, I prostrate myself on the ground and worship my God, who gave me the grace to make it, after which I arise happier than a king . . . People look for ways of learning how to love God. They hope to attain it by I know not how many different practices . . . Is it not a shorter and more direct way to do everything for the love of God, to make use of all the tasks one's lot in life demands to show him that love, and to maintain his presence within by the communion of our heart with his? There is nothing complicated about it. One has only to turn to it honestly and simply.[103]

Life today is lived at a much faster pace than in Brother Lawrence's time. The natural rhythms of the week, including taking Sabbath time, are submerged in cultures where shopping and sport occur '24/7' and we can flick through 100 TV channels. But if we are attentive to the Spirit's leading, if we truly want to turn to God, then even in the midst of our busy lives we can practise what Brother Lawrence called

---

102 Brother Lawrence, *The Practice of the Presence of God*, trans. E. M. Blaiklock, London: Hodder & Stoughton, 1981, p. 40.

103 Brother Lawrence, *The Practice*, p. 85

the 'interior glance'. It takes only a second to bring God to mind in love over and over again as we move through our day, *whatever we are doing*.

Ethical behaviour

In section 1.8 we read Kenneth Leech's warning against spiritual direction being used to reinforce individualism and privatization of religion at the expense of community.[104] Leech is not alone in his concern. Gerard Hughes, Jesuit author of many books on spirituality and prayer,[105] had this to say at a 1998 workshop in Durham:

> God's holiness is expressed in his compassion for creation. Christians are there-fore called to live for one another, because our good is in the other. This is despite the prevailing sense in our culture that we should live for ourselves, ignoring the cost to people or others of God's creatures. So, even in develop-ing our spirituality, we should ask, 'For whose benefit is this – my own, or for others? Will it develop a growth in compassion?'[106]

In spiritual direction, while we rejoice to see our directees' personal delight in the God who is warming their hearts, part of our responsibility is also to watch for signs of a developing compassion and 'other-focus' in our directees as they learn, in Barry and Connolly's words: to *'live out the consequences of (this) relationship'*.[107]

Things change when God begins to inhabit our centre. In spiritual direction, we look for indications of 'the consequences' of this growing intimacy with God, signs not only of their growing trust in God and freedom to live less fearfully, but also evidence of a rearrangement of their priorities, a reallocation of their resources, a reduction in materialism and consumption, a restoration of relationships, and new ways of reaching out to others.

What do we do though if there appear to be no changes in the way the directee is interacting with others? To what extent may issues of justice be explored, even *initiated* by a spiritual director in the context of a spiritual direction relationship? We know that spiritual direction is *not* about being directive or telling people what to do. But spiritual direction is about helping people listen to God – who *will* be

---

104 Leech, Kenneth, *Soul Friend: Spiritual Direction in the Modern World* (revised edition), Harrisburg, PA: Morehouse, 2001, pp. xvii–xviii.

105 See for example: *God of Surprises*; *O God Why?*; *God in All things*. Details in Further Reading section.

106 <www.durham.anglican.org/reference/network/network98-3/07earth.html> (archived).

107 Barry, William A. and Connolly, William A., *The Practice of Spiritual Direction*, San Francisco: HarperCollins, 1982, p. 8.

calling them into some sort of outworking or other-focus as they grow stronger.

One way of addressing this question is to integrate it into our regular review with our directees. This review gives directors and directees the chance to talk about their relationship and offers directees space to think about the effect of their more intentional movement towards God – on them and on others in their sphere of influence. Trusting God's work in the directee, we can ask open and naïve questions: 'What has changed in your life since you started praying more often and listening to God?' or 'I wonder how are you getting on with that difficult neighbour you mentioned when you first started coming to spiritual direction?' More often than not, such questions will yield a response which reveals some growth of compassion or some insight, but it can take time for directees to realize that what might seem very small changes to them are actually indicators of God's love beginning to flow out through them into the lives of others.

Sometimes it is appropriate to offer scripture which relates to living justly. Countless Gospel stories will connect us with a justice focus, for Jesus lived out Micah's summary of the ideal human life: 'What does the LORD require of you,' writes Micah, 'but to do justice, and to love kindness, and to walk humbly with your God' (6.8). We and our directees can be encouraged to do the same in *all* aspects of our lives. Foster[108] reminds us of the three arenas in which we may exercise influence for good, each with a characteristic Christian expression:

1 *In the personal arena*: our behaviour, work practices, choices, prejudices and attitudes. *Prayer* is the most useful spiritual practice in this arena, for it is in and through prayer that we receive the enabling love of God, forgiveness and the power of the Holy Spirit to follow the 'narrow way' of Christ.[109]
2 *In the social arena*: interpersonal relationships among family, friends, co-workers, neighbours, among whom we may be agents of God's peace and reconciliation. *Christian community* provides a model of 'social life as it is meant to be lived. Communities of love and acceptance. Fellowships of freedom and liberation. Centres of hope and vision. Societies of nurture and accountability. Little pockets of life and light so stunning that a watching world will declare: "See how they love one another".'[110]
3 *In the arena of institutional structure*: By *prophetic witness* we work against commercial and political practices and values which perpetuate systemic injustice and inequality. We support institutions which promote justice, art and beauty and the care of creation.

We may companion someone who is called to a difficult, even dangerous role in the construction of a just society, perhaps joining political protests or starting a

---

108 Foster, Richard, *Streams of Living Water*, London: HarperCollins, 1998, pp. 172–3.
109 Foster, *Streams*, p. 172.
110 Foster, *Streams*, p. 173.

campaign which will prove unpopular with vested interests. Listening with the directee as he or she discerns what God is really asking becomes even more critical in these situations.

If we are serious about following Christ and helping others do the same, we should not be surprised if, as we shall see towards the end of this book, God takes us on a journey beyond our comfort zones, out into the neighbourhood to work for justice, and to empower people to re-create their lives in hope and love.

✠

Reflection questions

- How do you currently 'practise the presence of God'? What might hinder your turning repeatedly towards God as you go through each day?
- What changes in you or your behaviour have you noticed since becoming more intentional about your own spiritual journey with God?
- How able are you to speak out or act in each of Foster's three arenas of expression:
  - personal;
  - social;
  - institutional?
- What might God be calling you to notice or do in the area of social justice?

Suggestions for further reading

Growth

Burrows, Ruth, *Ascent to Love: The Spiritual Teachings of St John of the Cross*, London: Darton, Longman and Todd, 1987.
——*Interior Castle Explored*, London: Sheed and Ward, 1981.
Jamieson, Alan, *A Churchless Faith: Faith Journeys Beyond the Churches*, London: SPCK, 2002.
——*Called again – In and Beyond the Deserts of Faith*, Wellington: Philip Garside, 2004.
Mabry, John R., *Faith Styles: Ways People Believe*, New York: Morehouse, 2007.
May, Gerald, *The Dark Night of the Soul: A Psychiatrist Explores the Connection Between Darkness and Spiritual Growth*, New York: HarperCollins, 2004.
——*Addiction and Grace: Love and Spirituality in the Healing of Addictions*, New York: HarperCollins, 1991.
O'Hare, Breige, 'Opening to Love: A Paradigm for Growth in Relationship with God', in *Presence: An International Journal of Spiritual Direction*, Spiritual Directors International, 10(2), June 2004.

Slee, Nicola, *Women's Faith Development*, Ashgate, 2004.

Welch, John, *Spiritual Pilgrims: Carl Jung and Teresa of Avila*, New York: Paulist Press, 1982.

Living out the consequences of growth in intimacy with God

Brother Lawrence, *Practising the Presence of God*, trans. E. M. Blaiklock, London: Hodder & Stoughton, 1981.

Cassidy, Sheila, *Good Friday People*, London: Darton, Longman and Todd, 1991.

Hughes, Gerard W., *God of Surprises*, London: Darton, Longman and Todd, 1985 (reprinted 1992).

——*Oh God Why? A Spiritual Journey Towards Meaning, Wisdom and Strength*, Oxford: Bible Reading Fellowship, 1993.

——*God In All Things: The Sequel to God of Surprises*, London: Hodder & Stoughton, 2003.

Lentz, Robert and Gately, Edwina, *Christ in the Margins*, New York: Orbis Press, 2003.

Rohr, Richard and friends, *Contemplation in Action*, New York: Crossroad, 2006.

Steward, John, 'Drinking from the Waterfall: God Was My Companion', in *Presence: An International Journal of Spiritual Direction*, 10(1), February 2004 (reconciliation work in Rwanda).

Prayer

Foster, Richard, *Prayer: Finding the Heart's True Home*, London: Hodder & Stoughton, 1992.

Hall, Thelma, *Too Deep for Words: Rediscovering Lectio Divina*, New York: Paulist Press, 1988.

Pritchard, Sheila, *The Lost Art of Meditation: Deepening Your Prayer Life*, London: Scripture Union, 2002.

Yancey, Philip, *Prayer: Does it Make Any Difference?*, London: Hodder & Stoughton, 2006.

4

Listening and Responding to Ourselves

4.1 Self-knowledge and knowledge of God

By placing this chapter *before* 'Listening and Responding to Others', I am emphasizing the point that, unless we are intentional about developing self-knowledge,
and accepting and caring for ourselves, we risk failing those we seek to serve.
Worse still, we may put them at risk if we do not 'practise what we preach' in
terms of prayer, balance, simplicity and making our relationship with God our
first priority.

As you work through each section for yourself, you will also be picking up strategies and information which can be shared with your directees as they too come to
realize that self-knowledge and self-care are essential parts of the spiritual life.

🕯 Spend a few minutes listing your strengths and your weaknesses, then discuss the list with someone whom you trust and who knows you well.

How well *do* we know ourselves? An easy question perhaps if we answer with
a list of roles, qualifications, pleasant personality traits and family history. But
what about those parts of ourselves that are hidden, lurking somewhere in a dingy
memory, or erupting in times of stress? Teresa of Avila, in *The Interior Castle*, has
this to say about self-knowledge:

> For never, however exalted the soul may be, is anything else more fitting than
> self-knowledge . . . without it everything else goes wrong. Knowing ourselves
> is sometimes so important that I would not want any relaxation ever in this
> regard, however high you may have climbed into the heavens . . . let us strive to
> make more progress in self-knowledge . . .[111]

Why did she emphasize self-knowledge? What made Calvin, from an entirely different theological stable centuries later, say: 'There is no deep knowing of God

---

[111] Quoted in Welch, John, *Spiritual Pilgrims: Carl Jung and Teresa of Avila*, New York:
Paulist Press, 1982, p. 75.

without a deep knowing of self, and no deep knowing of self without a deep knowing of God'?[112]

Scripture gives us some clues: 'You desire truth in the inward being; therefore teach me wisdom in my secret heart.' The writer of Psalm 51.6 recognizes that God wants us to be honest with ourselves and with our Creator, so that our relationship can be deepened, our weaknesses and strengths offered to God for transformation and service. When Jesus was asked by a lawyer which was the greatest commandment, he answered: 'Love the Lord your God with all your heart, and with all your soul, and with all your strength and with all your mind; and your neighbour as yourself' (Luke 10.27).

We do our best to live out this ideal of Christian love and service, but many of us struggle with the thought of 'loving ourselves', fearing self-centredness, anxious in case introspection shifts our focus from God. However, we need not fear, for Jesus himself offers a clear invitation to self-knowledge: 'Why do you see the speck in your neighbour's eye, but do not notice the log in your own eye? . . . *first* take the log out of your own eye, and then you will see clearly to take the speck out of your neighbour's eye' (Matthew 7.3–5, emphasis mine).

In the Gospels, Jesus challenges people to examine their behaviour and motivation so they can wake up to what is holding them back from spiritual growth and service:

- The rich young man is lovingly confronted by his attachment to wealth (Mark 10.17–22).
- Simon the Pharisee is faced with his lack of hospitality (Luke 7.36–46).

God then wants us, and our directees, to face our inner reality and bring it to God in prayer, because if we deny our pain and failures, if we try to hide our anxiety or pride, if we won't face our addictions to work, pornography, substances or power, if we are out of touch with our emotional life, if we can't accept our sexuality, if we won't admit it when our spiritual life is boring and barren, we are avoiding the truth about ourselves, and denying God the chance to meet us *in our present reality*.

God will not force wisdom and transformation upon us, but waits until we acknowledge our need. Just as alcoholics cannot receive help until they face the truth about themselves and are able, publicly, to say 'I am an alcoholic', so we cannot receive God's help until we face our weaknesses and vulnerabilities and offer them to God.

But there is another aspect to self-knowledge. Jesus also *affirmed* in people many positive qualities, perhaps hitherto unacknowledged:

---

112 Calvin, John, *Institutes of the Christian Religion*, 1536 edn, trans. Ford Lewis Battles, Grand Rapids, MI: Eerdmans, 1995, p. 12.

- The woman with the haemorrhage was restored, not only to full health, but to relationship with her community as her faith and courage were acknowledged (Mark 5.25–34).
- The tenth leper – an outsider – who alone returned in gratitude, had his faith publicly commended (Luke 17.11–19).

Sometimes as Christians we can put on false modesty at the expense of truth. But God invites us to 'own' our talents and capacities, to acknowledge our giftedness. If we fail to do so, how can we offer them to God for the service of the kingdom?

Who am I?

Shortly before he was executed in 1944, Dietrich Bonhoeffer wrote a poem[113] in which he poignantly articulated something of the tension between the private self and the self that others saw. Was he the person who gave an impression of calm authority and the ability to rise above confinement and fear – or the one whose inner life was full of turmoil as he faced death and longed for freedom? Whatever he was, Bonhoeffer concluded, God alone knew, loved and accepted him in all his contradictions.

Though not in the extremity of his situation, many of us are aware of the disparity between how we appear to others and what we think of ourselves; just as Bonhoeffer did, we wonder who we really are. God invites us to find out, to learn about our functioning, our preferences and prejudices, our woundedness and giftedness. Deepening self-knowledge is necessary for our own growth, but it is also needed if we are to be effective and compassionate ministers of grace, as Rowan Williams elaborates:

> To be the means of reconciliation for another within the Body of Christ, you must be consciously yourself, knowing a bit about what has made you who you are, what your typical problems and brick walls are, what your gifts are . . . to have some kind of loving and truthful look at yourself . . . to be aware of your distinctiveness, and to be aware of it as being in the hands of God.[114]

The truth of who we are lies, then, in our relationship with Christ, who alone accepts us as we are, *and* in whom we can become who we are created to be: the 'false' self of our ego's strivings and engagement with the world is redeemed, and the true self is freed to express its uniqueness. We come to know that we are dependent on grace, are deeply loved and are met in our reality by God.

---

113 Bonhoeffer, Dietrich, 'Who am I?', *Letters and Papers from Prison*, SCM Press and Macmillan, 1971.

114 Williams, Rowan, *Silence and Honey Cakes: The Wisdom of the Desert*, Oxford: Medio Media, Lion, 2003, pp. 39–40.

How do we grow in self-knowledge, and help our directees do the same?

First, by being committed to growing in our own relationship with God. We embark on the interior journey, becoming familiar with various ways of learning about ourselves and how we 'tick'. For example, we:

- bring our desire for self-knowledge to prayer, asking for God's help;
- spend time in silence and solitude;
- pray with scripture – the most familiar piece of scripture can be personally challenging if God wants to use it to highlight an issue for us;
- regularly use a spiritual journal as an aid to reflection;
- read relevant books, find courses and workshops designed to give insight into our functioning and way of being in the world. Such opportunities help us learn about our personalities and preferences, our ego defences and those aspects of ourselves which we prefer to ignore. There is a range of assessment tools available; those often associated with spiritual growth include the Myers-Briggs Temperament Indicator (MBTI) and the Enneagram.
- ask those we live and work with for feedback about our behaviour, so long as we are able to receive it with grace and not start a fight or withdraw wounded!
- notice our strong reactions to situations or to people – more on that later!

Dreams

We can also pay attention to significant dreams, and we can stand alongside our directees as, with the Spirit's help, they find their own interpretation of what their dreams may be asking or saying. Dreams can be regarded as a tool of God to help us notice what needs attention in our inner or outer life.

A simple method to start working with dreams is TTAQ, as described by Savary, Berne and Williams in their book *Dreams and Spiritual Growth: A Judeo-Christian Approach to Dreamwork*:

Title   Give your dream a title. Let it come to you spontaneously or ask yourself, 'What title does this dream want itself to have?'

Theme   State the major themes or issues which surface in the dream. If more than one, note them in sequence.

Affect   What was the dominant feeling or emotional energy experienced during the dream? If there was a sequence of feelings, state them in sequence.

Question   What questions is the dream asking of me? What is the dream trying to help me become conscious of?[115]

115 Savary, Louis M., Berne, Patricia H. and Williams, Strephon Kaplan, *Dreams and Spiritual Growth: A Judeo-Christian Approach to Dreamwork*, New York: Paulist Press, 1984, pp. 22–5.

Savary, Berne and Williams cover over 30 further dreamwork techniques but they do not offer interpretation for, no matter what we might hear to the contrary, the dreamer is the only person who can interpret his or her own dreams. Key points about dreams:

- We all dream, but many do not recall dreams in any detail.
- Most dreams are symbolic and invite questions rather than giving answers; rarely will a dream be predictive.
- Dreams operate at several levels. People who appear in our dreams usually represent parts of ourselves, rather than saying something about actual people whom we might know in our conscious life.
- Generally nightmares are simply trying to draw attention to something we are ignoring. If we face the 'terror' we often find that it represents part of our emotional life trying to find expression, and the nightmares cease. The exception is a nightmare with literal content – like a constant frightening replay of an actual event. These are more likely to be connected to trauma and have to be handled differently, usually with the help of a counsellor or psychotherapist

The Examen

In terms of developing self-knowledge, arguably the most useful practice, for us and for our directees, is doing the Prayer of Examen, described by Foster as a process embodying:

- an Examination of Consciousness: a time of reflection on our thoughts, feelings and actions, usually conducted at day's end; and
- an Examination of Conscience: a time in which we invite God to shine light on those areas which need cleansing or healing.[116]

In the Examination of Consciousness, we look back through the events of the day, to see where God has been at work and the nature of our response. We can do this in any way that fits our situation, but commonly choose to use our journal so we have a record of our discoveries. Some of us might choose to do our Examen while taking an evening walk, perhaps making a couple of notes about any theme which is beginning to emerge when we get home, but the important thing is to find a way that will work in our context.

---

116 Foster, Richard, *Prayer: Finding the Heart's True Home*, London: Hodder & Stoughton, 1992, pp. 27–36.

In its simplest form we can ask ourselves pairs of questions to help us recognize those things that give us life and energy or which drain us. The Linns[117] suggest things like:

- When did I give and receive the most love today?
- When did I give and receive the least love today?
- How was I most aware of God in my life today?
- How was I least aware of God in my life today?

Over time, the Examen can help us notice areas of strength and vulnerability and identify patterns in our responses which might need our attention, such as a tendency to avoid conflict or to keep silent instead of speaking out about something important.

We can do the simple Examen alone or we can use these questions as a basis for dialogue with our partner or family members, as a regular spiritual practice. Whatever way we choose, this tool for deepening self-knowledge and spiritual growth can help us become more able to discern God's leading.

In the Examination of Conscience, as the name suggests, we give God space to bring to our minds those things which hamper our ability to re-present Christ to those we meet and serve. We invite God to point out where we are falling short:

Search me, O God, and know my heart; test me and know my thoughts. See if there is any wicked way in me, and lead me in the way everlasting. (Psalm 139.23–24)

Foster helpfully points out that 'God is *with* us in the search . . . our petty rationalizations and evasions of responsibility simply will not tolerate the light of his presence. He will show us what we need to see when we need to see it.'[118]

Why is the Examen so useful? Foster would say that it produces within us 'the priceless grace of self-knowledge'. Learning more about ourselves enriches our spiritual lives, brings insight and interior freedom, and builds compassion for others. The more we know of ourselves the more of ourselves we can bring to God for healing and redemption and the less we will judge others.

✠

---

117 As described by the Linns in their book *Sleeping with Bread*. See Further Reading for details.

118 Foster, *Prayer: Finding the Heart's True Home*, pp. 29–30.

Reflection questions

⚭ What is your experience of searching for self-knowledge?

What tools have you used or are you using to learn more about yourself?

⚭ As you consider your prayer life, to what extent do you censor what you bring to God?

What sorts of things do you avoid taking to prayer? Why might this be?

⚭ What might help you incorporate the Examen of Consciousness into your day or week?

What might hinder this intention?

⚭ How has the Examen of Conscience been part of your prayer pattern or spiritual life?

Talk to God about any fears or doubts you have about regularly asking God to help you recognize areas in your character, behaviour or priorities which are falling short of God's standards.

4.2 Listening to our body, our soul and our spirit

Body

While we are busy paying attention to our directees, our inner thoughts and the prompting of God, we may overlook the vehicle through which God works and through which we experience the world: our bodies.

We may be used to thinking of our bodies in negative terms, unhelpfully comparing our shape, hair colour, weight and fitness with models of media-generated 'perfection'. But scripture reminds us that our bodies are a temple of the Holy Spirit (1 Corinthians 6.19). Made in God's image, we are stewards of the Spirit within us, responsible for and responsive to our bodies. If we listen well to our bodies we notice things like fatigue, dehydration, hunger or indicators of a malfunction such as pain, or a lump where a lump shouldn't be. To ignore such signals can threaten life itself.

Our bodies are designed for 'fight or flight'. Stress hormones are released whenever we are alarmed, preparing us for a response, helping us to avoid danger or to meet an important challenge. If we do not 'turn off' the stress response by relaxing once the perceived threat or need for improved performance has passed, or if we find ourselves in long-term stressful situations, the stress response remains 'activated' and continues to produce stress hormones until, eventually, we are left exhausted, prone to infection and accidental injury.

If we are to continue in long-term ministry we need to familiarize ourselves with our personal pattern of bodily reactions to stress and overwork. There will always be more people needing more help than we are able to give, and burnout is an unfortunately common result of our efforts to fill a sump-hole of needs, while ignoring our body's warning signs.

But our bodies are more than our reactions to stress. We are created as spiritual *and* sexual beings, invited by God to welcome the beauty and truth of our masculinity or femininity, the 'goodness' of our physical selves. For some, this is a tall order: upbringing, attitudes, experience, teaching or trauma affect our psychosexual development and leave many with sexual wounds of some description. Part of our journey with the God who loves us is to face the reality of our past hurts and begin to make it available to God for healing. We need to do this work ourselves so we can be sensitive companions for directees who, as they begin to allow God to come closer, may bring their sexual pain to spiritual direction.

An important part of embracing our sexuality is noticing if we are physically attracted to others, especially to colleagues or our directees. Perhaps our hearts lift when expecting a particular directee to arrive; or we are having erotic thoughts about them; or we find our bodies stirring when we sit with them in the same office. We all know of the damage done by ministers crossing professional and ethical boundaries designed to protect those to whom they have a pastoral responsibility. The attraction may be fleeting and 'harmless' but, after taking the matter to supervision, if it is clear that we are at risk of transgressing, it is time to arrange for the one-to-one meetings to cease. Making a referral to another spiritual director in such a situation demands tact, avoiding any implication that the directee is in any way at fault. If this is an isolated event it *may* possibly be addressed adequately in robust supervision and in our own prayer and confession; if not, personal counselling might be indicated.

Some of us are affected by chronic disability, daily struggling with small routines which others do without a second thought. The process of inviting God into what we might consider a severely impaired reality may be supported by both counselling and spiritual direction as we address issues of self-image, anger, frustration, exhaustion and pain. The question of healing is particularly relevant – and poignant – in the light of Gospel miracles and the activities of contemporary healers. Spiritual direction can be a safe context in which to speak of disappointment, hope and longing, and the nature of healing itself.

As we age we are faced with our mortality: we notice our bodies starting to slow down, stiffen up or silently sag. Whether this provokes a trip to the gym to help us retain what physical strength and suppleness we still have, and/or a grace-full acceptance of the truth of our physical diminution, we know that God wants to be with us in this stage of our lives as well. We are encouraged to bring to God our fears about failing faculties, our worry about falling, or losing our mind's sharpness, our petition for ongoing strength and the capacity to complete whatever God asks of us.

On a lighter note, as we journey closer to God it is not uncommon to discover that we want to *move* more in our prayer, to let our worship include our whole bodies rather than solely voice or mind. Dancing, raising one's arms, lying prostrate, using one's hands to express emotion, are all possible embodiments of prayer which can help energize us as we express ourselves more freely and fully.

Soul: mind

In this section I want to pay particular attention to 'self-talk', the inner conversations which run through our minds during the day, and at night if we are awake, sleepless or anxious. Of particular relevance here is the self-talk which hinders our ability to be present to our directees, i.e. self-talk which raises doubts about our competence or the working of God's grace.

The struggles between good and evil, between doubt and faith, between fear and freedom, take place within the mind. It is not surprising therefore that Romans 12.2 speaks of 'being transformed by the renewing of your minds', and 1 Peter 1.13 invites us to 'prepare our minds for action', so we may co-operate with the power and grace of God who is intent on liberating our minds from all that would hinder our growth in Christ. We can 'prepare' and 'co-operate' in a number of ways:

1 We can ask the Holy Spirit to guide our thinking, to strengthen our minds, to protect us from temptation and to reveal any issues which need our attention.
2 We can pay attention to the general *tone* of our self-talk. For example, are we calling ourselves names and putting ourselves down, or are we encouraging towards ourselves, building ourselves up in a healthy way, perhaps by acknowledging achievements or little victories over laziness or fear? Are we naturally pessimistic or optimistic in our thinking? Once we realize what the predominant tone is, we can ask God for the grace we need to talk to ourselves with more hope or with less violence. We can 'take every thought captive to obey Christ' (2 Corinthians 10.5), no longer entertaining put-downs or excessive self-congratulation but re-minding ourselves, using the words of John 15 which speak of sustained connection with Jesus, the vine, the source of life and fulfilment.
3 We can notice recurrent patterns of thought or themes. Faced with a vestry meeting, we might start to have panicky thoughts, telling ourselves that we don't have the skills to chair a meeting, we lack the personality to deal with extroverted opposition and so on. Or we may compare ourselves with a high-achieving sibling, neighbouring priest or respected writer and notice a familiar slide into self-doubt. As we notice these self-limiting ideas and the situations which seem to trigger them, we can bring them to prayer, confident that God will meet us in our reality and grace will indeed be sufficient for our needs.

4 We can journal about our fears and anxieties – identifying the details so that we can bring them one by one to Jesus for healing and freedom, instead of 'entertaining them', letting them gather weight until they threaten to overwhelm us. However, if these fears and anxieties do seem to be spiralling into uncontrollable negativity, or we are having thoughts of self-harm, then it is vital that we do not delay but seek help from someone we trust.

5 We can acknowledge our doubts, questions, theological wonderings and, instead of denying or repressing such ideas, we can bring them to God in prayer, discuss them in spiritual direction and, in time, find a way of living authentically with paradox.

6 We can own up to unhealthy or sinful thoughts or behaviours, because we know we are beloved by God. Through the sacrament of absolution or other meaningful assurance of forgiveness, we can be released from guilt and shame. However, if such thoughts persist and seem to be obsessive, and/or we are engaged in addictive behaviour, we can seek God's grace to face this and act – perhaps entering a 12–step recovery programme. Nothing is beyond the reach of God's love.

Soul: feelings

In some cultures people find it easy to express their feelings, but for others the opposite is true, and the 'stiff upper lip' prevails. Compounding this conditioning, in some Christian circles feelings are mistrusted or actively belittled, resulting in a lopsided spirituality biased towards rationality and analysis. If we discount our feelings, if we are unnerved by their intensity or embarrassed by their 'unsuitability', we can deny them adequate attention as we hurriedly 'offer them up to God'. In doing so, we risk the stress produced by repressing emotion – the energy inherent in our feelings has to find expression or it will eat away at our well-being. We also miss a valuable source of information about ourselves and clues to our God-given desires.

I remember being at a workshop on the spiritual life, run by a visiting Catholic speaker. In a break I was introduced to a woman who had two books of spiritual poetry published. I congratulated her on her work, but when I sat down I felt a wave of envy rise in me. It would have been easy to dismiss this response as 'unChristian', but instead, in the space for reflection that followed a few minutes later, I chose to let myself feel the envy, to explore it, to acknowledge it before God and then listen for what the Spirit might say. It soon became clear that this 'envy' was drawing my attention to a deeply held longing to give myself more fully to writing. I resolved to honour that longing – this book is part of that outworking.

In the sixteenth century St Ignatius developed an entire system of Christian spirituality by learning to pay attention to his feelings during months of enforced inactivity while healing from a war wound. His concepts of consolation and desolation, the practice of the Examen, and the spiritual exercises involving imaginative engagement with the Gospels, still inform much spiritual direction practice and spirituality, as we have already seen.

Feelings, then, may be described as valuable raw material for spiritual growth, giving us access to a different level of information about ourselves than our rational mind can provide. I can tell you what I think and, although this might reveal something about me, if I tell you how I'm feeling, I am sharing a different aspect of my inner life and personhood. Talking to God about our thoughts *and* feelings is essential, if we are offering God the truth about ourselves and our need of grace.

As spiritual directors, it is important that we are able to work with our own feelings or we will not be able to help directees work with theirs. Ferder provides a straightforward process for attending to feelings in spiritual direction or elsewhere. This process has four parts: Noticing, Naming, Owning and Responding.[119]

1 *Noticing*: a first step in working with our feelings is to pay attention to our physiological responses, as many feelings express themselves through a change in our bodies, for example blushing, sweaty palms, 'butterflies' in the stomach alert us to varying degrees of embarrassment or nervousness.
2 *Naming* is the next significant step in working with the emotional content of our lives, bringing the feeling 'out in the open'. However, although this might seem straightforward, many people lack an adequate emotional vocabulary and struggle to put their feelings into words.
3 *Owning* simply means that we acknowledge the feeling. We do not pretend it doesn't, or shouldn't exist. Emotions are neutral in themselves, they simply 'are'. In order for us to learn from them, we have to accept their reality in our lives, unpleasant though having to face the fact that we feel bitter or angry or let down may be.
4 *Responding*: our responses will vary according to the circumstances. If we feel frightened because there is a very large spider in our bathroom, we will instinctively run away. However, when we are not in danger, we have time to think through the possible responses and make a choice which will be life-giving.

Soul: will

What can I say about 'the will', except to agree with Paul's observations in his letter to the Romans, bemoaning the huge gap between his will and his actions: 'I do not understand my own actions. For I do not do what I want, but I do the very

---

119 Summarized from Ferder, Fran, *Words Made Flesh*, Notre Dame, IN: Ave Maria Press, 1986, pp. 49–66.

thing I hate' (Romans 7.15)? Paul knows how hard it is to align human will with the will of God, the internal battle that is waged:

> For I delight in the law of God in my inmost self, but I see in my members another law at war with the law of my mind, making me captive to the law of sin that dwells in my members. Wretched man that I am! Who will rescue me from this body of death? Thanks be to God through Jesus Christ our Lord! (Romans 7.22–25)

Jesus, who from the time of the temptation in the desert knew the interior battle as no one else could, remained resolute, his will in tune with the Father's. In Gethsemane, fighting to overcome a human's instinct for self-preservation, a human's fear of humiliation and pain, and faced with imminent arrest, he endured extremes of mental anguish, but still managed to say: 'My Father, if this cannot pass unless I drink it, your will be done' (Matthew 26.42).

Because Jesus spent time living within the constraints of a human body, because he experienced the interior struggle of the will and saw that dynamic in his disciples, God in Christ knows our struggle *from the inside*; God knows that our intentions are so often good, though unachieved; time and time again God assures us of forgiveness and a fresh start whenever we bring our weakness of will to God. When we honestly admit our failures, God meets us in this moment of confession and offers the Spirit to strengthen our will.

However, if we are not careful, constantly bemoaning our weakness of will can sabotage our spiritual life. Putting our shortcomings on centre stage and repeatedly giving them our full attention equates to spiritual pride and is another form of self-centredness. We are certainly encouraged to be honest about our weakness of will, to bring that to God, asking for the grace we need for the next hour or day or week. But then it is time to turn our attention to Jesus, focusing on his love and power and beauty and challenge, rather than on our failure of will.

Paul could have been sidetracked by the mysterious 'thorn in the flesh' which he repeatedly asked God to remove. Whatever this 'thorn' was, God did not remove it, and Paul himself believed that this was for a reason – *twice* in the same verse; (2 Corinthians 12.7), Paul said it was to keep him from 'being too elated', carried away by his 'exceptional' visions and revelations. Because Paul knew the reality of battling spiritual pride, he also knew his need of God and the truth of God's response: 'My grace is sufficient for you, for power is made perfect in weakness' (2 Corinthians 12.9).

Directees may reveal an involvement with pornography or confess an old crime that has been weighing on their mind; as we listen and help them attend to God's way forward for them, we may be faced with our own addictions or guilt. All of us struggle with living an upright life, with making consistently wise choices or sharing our resources with the less fortunate, with doing God's will. We may have times when we know that we are living out our vocation but, even then, there will be pockets of rebellion and patches of resistance, for self-interest still casts shadows across our motivation. We all experience temptation, but we can bring all to our Lord knowing that, though faultless, he experienced temptations too and is on our side.

Spirit

From a Christian perspective, the spirit may be described as that part of ourselves which:

- recognizes God and wants what God wants;
- rejoices when we make a move towards God;
- sings in the background of our consciousness, keeping us in contact with our Creator;
- honours the presence of gifts such as words of wisdom and knowledge, faith and healing, miracles, prophecy, discernment of spirits, tongues and interpretation (1 Corinthians 12.4–11);
- encourages the blossoming of love, joy, peace, patience, kindness, generosity, faithfulness, gentleness and self-control (Galatians 5.22–23);
- links us with others in prayer and intercession;
- always hopes for good, for freedom, for justice, for truth (Philippians 4.8);
- expresses and experiences intimacy with God.

The spirit is like a magnetic hand on a compass, pointing us constantly 'home', to the Way, to God. Prompted by the Spirit of God, our spirit reminds us of our relationship with God time and time again, as Paul describes in Romans 8.14–16: 'For all who are led by the Spirit of God are children of God. For you did not receive a spirit of slavery to fall back into fear, but you have received a spirit of adoption. When we cry "Abba! Father!" it is that very Spirit bearing witness with our spirit that we are children of God.' We see this 'spirit to Spirit' dynamic when we pray in tongues; bypassing the rational mind and carefully formulated mental prayer, our spirit directly communicates with God in a personal language of prayer. Our spirit is strengthened by this form of communication with God as we begin to express our fledgling love in a 'prayer of the heart' to the One who first loves us.

A similar 'spirit to Spirit' dynamic is in place if we have begun to pray apophatically – without the use of any symbols, structures, words or prompts from scripture or creation. In silence and solitude, we make our spirit available to God so that the Holy Spirit may communicate more of the self of God directly to our spirit in contemplation, and the transforming work of God in us is advanced.

Although we may be weak – physically, emotionally, even morally – our spirit's fundamental orientation (its 'default setting' if you prefer) remains focused on

God and constantly works with the Spirit of God to turn us back towards holiness. While our body may register feelings and our mind begin to make connections between cause and effect, it is in our spirit that we recognize 'consolation' or 'desolation', those subtle interior movements away from or towards God and God's purposes. Our spirit 'quickens' when we respond to God, as if a little burst of love lights our being as we turn once again towards home.

For those in the wider community for whom a specifically 'religious' description of the spirit might be less helpful, 'spirit' could be spoken of in terms such as:

- the fundamental energy of human beings;
- that part of ourselves that seeks the good;
- relational capacity: our ability to connect at a deep level with those we love; or
- the inner strength which enables people to endure extreme hardship and struggle.

✠

Reflection questions

- What aspects of your bodily reality do you want to bring to God in prayer?
- How comfortable are you with your own sexuality? Who might help you with any difficulties?
- How have you – or others you know – been affected by physical disability? How has that shaped your or their self-image, image of God or spiritual journey?
- Read Ferder's pattern for working with feelings and use it as you go through the next week. How comfortable are you with expressing a range of feelings?

4.3 Being aware of 'red flag' areas: parallel process and projection

Life circumstances can threaten our composure and capacity to listen to ourselves and others. If we are under any sort of pressure, ordinary daily hurdles can demand of our resources more than we have to give and we may get caught in awkward situations, make unwise decisions, or speak out of turn. Sometimes we echo Shakespeare's words and find that 'sorrows come not single spies, but in battalions',[120] in which case self-awareness and self-care are vital. To avoid losing

---

120 William Shakespeare, *Hamlet*, Act iv. Sc. 5.

our objectivity, it is wise for us to monitor our behaviour when we are in difficult circumstances, for example major life transitions, chronic personality clashes and unremitting pain – all of which require sustained energy.

Parallel process refers to the interpersonal dynamic in which one person's material reminds another person of his or her own circumstances. In spiritual direction this happens when directees' issues are similar to issues that their spiritual directors are working on themselves. Such parallel process may be of a relatively minor nature, such as both approaching a significant birthday. Or it can constitute a 'red flag' area into which we may proceed only with care, aware that we may lose our focus because what we are hearing resonates powerfully with our current reality and evokes strong feelings in us. For example, if you as director are worried about your child's health and the directee brings her concern for her sick child, immediately there is a risk that the similarity of situation will distract you from your primary purpose. Instead of heightening your empathy, parallel process may see you sharing details about illness and treatment, about fears and hopes. While this may bring short-term comfort to you both, it is not what you are there for – to help the directee find a way of bringing her feelings and fears to God which, in the long-term, will better serve the directee's needs.

Projection, a second inter-personal dynamic which can earn 'red flag' status, occurs when we unconsciously 'drape' some unacceptable or difficult aspect of our own personality or behaviour over someone else's shoulders. This ego defence is often revealed when we have a very strong response to someone. If, for example, we haven't come to terms with our tendency to control others, we may get very angry when someone else asks us to do something, and accuse them of being a 'control freak'. If we are ignoring our own gambling problem, we may be highly critical of someone else's loss at the races. Whenever we find ourselves reacting in a way that is disproportionate to the circumstances, we need to check and ask ourselves, 'What am I reacting to here? How does this relate to something in my own life or personality?' In prayer we can ask God for the grace to see what we need to see, so that we can address what we might be avoiding. As we grow in Christ and become more self-aware, we begin to withdraw our projections and become less critical of others.

Different 'red flags' will unfurl for us, depending on our own vulnerabilities and experience, our personality and faith journey. If, for example, we have been adopted and have not yet addressed some of the chronic grief and uncertainty that adoption frequently evokes, then adoption can be a 'red flag' area for us. Similarly, if we are still struggling to work through the implications of early abuse and directees begin to divulge abuse in their background, we may not be able to companion them as they deserve.

It is important to attend to our own issues as they come to our notice so they are less likely to colour inappropriately our responses to directees and their issues.

Our experience can then provide a compassionate backdrop to what the directee is saying.

✠

⚱ Listed below are some common situations which might put the working alliance between director and directee at risk. For each situation identify what you think the 'red flag' is, and note your response, as if you were the director:

- you are financially stretched and meet with a directee whom you know arranges mortgage refinancing and debt consolidation as part of his work;
- your nephew committed suicide six months ago and your directee, who is unaware of this, begins to talk about a suicide in his family;
- a woman with a daughter the same age as your daughter living overseas, shares her fears that her daughter will never return home as she has fallen in love with a man who lives in Japan;
- your partner is not interested in matters of faith or the spiritual life; your directee tells you how really helpful it is to talk to you about the things of God which her partner just can't understand;
- your father was an alcoholic; after your recent sermon on the wedding at Cana, your directee begins to talk about his difficulty with alcohol and the effect of his drinking on his family.

Noticing a 'red flag' does not automatically mean that we cannot work with particular directees; it simply indicates a need to discern carefully – in prayer and in supervision – whether or not we are going to be the right person to companion the directee. The strength and nature of our response to what the directee might be saying will also determine whether the 'red flag' points to a need for us to do some personal work – in journalling reflections, with our own spiritual director or supervisor and/or in counselling – before we continue. If we do discern that we can proceed, we are then responsible for making sure that our directees are safe and not exploited or disadvantaged in any way.

✠

Reflection questions

⚱ What did you notice about your responses to the 'common situations' listed above?

⸆ What are the current 'red flag' areas in your own life?
In what contexts might you be less effective because of these?
What might you do to address your 'red flag' areas?

⸆ How have you been aware of 'parallel process' in ordinary conversations? In ministry?

⸆ How have you been aware of 'projection' – in your own responses and in the responses of others?

4.4 Ministry supervision and spiritual direction

Taking time to listen to our own inner life, our ministry and our spiritual journey is mandatory, so that we can identify those issues which might impede our capacity to be an attentive presence to others.

We have already mentioned several ways in which we and our directees can listen to our inner lives; most of them are informal, low-key practices we can do ourselves, without referral to anyone else. However, these may not always provide adequate information or processing – many of us need the presence of another to help us go further, to challenge us to go deeper than we might do on our own. Spiritual direction and ministry supervision are two, more formal ways of listening to ourselves in the presence of a compassionate and skilled witness, for the purpose of helping us reflect on our journey with God, and on our ministry practice, and the way the two might interrelate.

Peer supervision

When asked about their supervision arrangements, it is not uncommon to hear ministers say that they meet regularly with one or two colleagues to talk about their work. This form of 'peer supervision' is likely to be quite informal, and possibly irregular, as commitments like funerals and urgent pastoral matters usually take precedence. Peer supervision is certainly less expensive than seeing a clinically trained supervisor or a psychologist, but unless the supervision session is set up with definite guidelines and the participants trust each other and are self-disciplined and competent communicators, such sessions can easily turn into 'talking shop': the focus slips, competitive elements surface and any deep work falls prey to self-protection. Worse still, breaches of confidentiality can be made if clear protocols aren't followed.

However, workable models of peer supervision do exist. Conroy describes a simple but effective process suitable for monthly gatherings of three or four spiritual directors, lasting about two hours:

- A case is presented by one spiritual director who provides background and a verbatim for study.
- The whole group reflects together, evoking deeper feelings and responses from the presenting director; working from a contemplative stance allows space for further insights to emerge in a safe, gentle, God-centred process as the director looks deeply into his or her practice.
- The group prays together in silence, listening for any insights relevant to what has been shared before offering any specific prayer; each person then offers 'one observation, insight, image, feeling, suggestion or question that can assist the presenting director's ongoing growth'.
- Finally, each person shares a learning from this peer supervision session; this may be about themselves, God, spiritual direction, spiritual growth, religious experience or about the supervision process.[121]

One-to-one supervision

I have already commented on the value of a minister or spiritual director being able to meet regularly with a well-trained supervisor. Such a supervisor should of course be able to maintain professional boundaries and facilitate our engagement with our ministry or spiritual direction practice, including areas of perceived failure, conflict or ineffectiveness. Sometimes supervisors are not readily available and we may struggle to find someone who is familiar with spiritual direction, even with what it is like to be a minister in this post-Christian age. We can still find supervision helpful as long as the supervisor we do choose can listen well and recognize stressors, can help us find ways through challenging situations, is able to help us when interpersonal dynamics are affecting the working alliance, and can recognize when personal issues require further attention and with whom this might be done.

Choosing a spiritual director

Choosing an initial spiritual director has been mentioned in an earlier section but, as we grow in our faith or our circumstances change, we may need to alter our spiritual direction arrangements, perhaps to a director of a different denomination, theological position, age, gender or someone in a different location.

Changing one's director is a matter of personal choice. Over a period of about 16 years I have had four long-term spiritual directors, and a few others when I have been on a variety of retreats. I know of other people who change their director

---

121 Conroy, Maureen, *Looking into the Well: Supervision of Spiritual Directors*, Chicago: Loyola University Press, 1995, pp. 91–105.

every year and say they find that helpful; perhaps I'm a bit suspicious, but I would wonder whether the decision to change might coincide with their director holding up a mirror to areas in which God might be challenging the directee to grow!

When a change is being considered, once you have sorted out who you might like to approach for spiritual direction, it can be helpful to have an initial exploratory session without obligation before making a decision about whether or not you can work together. It is also a good idea to build a regular review into the rhythm of your spiritual direction. Whether as directee or director, a review at three months, six months or annually can provide both parties with a chance to assess how the relationship is working, the directee's current understanding of spiritual direction, and expectations of what might be done differently or better. It allows both parties to disengage if it seems that their work together has come to an end.

✠

4.5 Counselling and therapy

It is relatively easy to commit ourselves to spiritual direction and supervision because everyone in ministry can be expected to have this type of support. In fact, because this requirement may be specifically written into ministry licensing arrangements or covenants, we are less likely to see these relationships as threatening the way we see ourselves.

However, it is a different matter when it comes to counselling or psychotherapy. Part of the difficulty lies in our role as 'priest' or 'minister'. We are the ones who are called on to help others; we are the ones who are there for a whole range of people when they are stuck or struggling, grieving or dying. What happens when *we* find each day a hurdle too hard to jump, a whirlpool of commitments into which we are being sucked head first?

Most of us find it very hard to admit to ourselves that we need help, that we are not coping or that something in our lives is bigger than we can handle. We may feel as if we do not have enough faith, or that if we were 'better Christians' we would not have become depressed or angry. Our family life may be less than perfect: we wonder how we can stand up in front of others and preach each week, when our own partner is threatening to leave, our teenage daughter is pregnant, or our son has dropped out of university.

Recognizing the need for help is one hurdle, being willing and humble enough to ask for it is another. Pride, shame, embarrassment, denial, a sense of failure, stubbornness, disappointment, self-deprecation have to be overcome if we are to receive the help we need. It is also very hard to know who to talk to. We worry about confidentiality and how others might see us if our 'weakness' becomes known. We worry that if we tell the archdeacon or the bishop that we are not coping, that will be the end to our 'career' in the Church. We may feel that we do not want to let our wardens, vestry or parish council know in case 'it gets out' and the whole parish starts looking at us sideways, waiting for signs of imminent meltdown.

A further complication is that it can be hard to find someone suitable to help us in our own geographical area. We may already have a relationship with local counsellors or therapists as members of our congregation for example, or as professionals to whom we refer others; it can be awkward to anticipate exchanging our collegial relationship for that of client/therapist. Consequently, it may be appropriate to seek counselling or therapy in another town so that privacy is protected and the mutuality of our local network is maintained.

Serious relational issues, unrelenting depression and anxiety, emergence of material from the past, sexuality issues, addictions and compulsions, crippling guilt or chronic grief can combine to challenge our self-image, deconstruct the way we see God and drain our inner resources. If we do not attend to these issues they will pop up again, particularly as we age and have less energy available to keep afloat in 'a sea of troubles'. However, by acknowledging that we are not functioning well, we allow others to enter our lives to bring hope and healing; in effect, we are responding to Jesus' invitation to bring our burdens to him. Counselling or psychotherapy can be a profound gift to help us through to a better appreciation of our true selves and a greater sense of empathy with others who struggle.

✠

Reflection questions

- ⚲ What is your own experience of supervision?
  What made that experience so positive or negative?
- ⚲ At the start of this book you reflected on your understanding of spiritual direction. Spend a few minutes doing so again in the light of further reflection and note any changes.
- ⚲ How easy or difficult is it to ask for help for yourself?
  How might the ease or difficulty vary depending on what sort of help you needed?
- ⚲ In your experience so far, have you ever needed to have counselling or psychotherapy?
  What was that experience like?
  Where was God in that experience?
  What impact did that experience have on your faith journey?

4.6 Self acceptance and self-care

Self acceptance

Self acceptance is an essential but often painful part of our maturing in Christ. Inevitably it will emerge as a theme in spiritual direction as people listen to God and pay attention to their own responses. The process is poignantly revealed in the series of interchanges between Peter and Jesus before and after the crucifixion. Quoting Zechariah 13.7[122] Jesus tells his disciples that all of them will desert him:

> Peter said to him, 'Even though all become deserters, I will not.' Jesus said to him, 'Truly I tell you, this day, this very night, before the cock crows twice, you will deny me three times.' But he said vehemently, 'Even though I must die with you, I will not deny you.' (Mark 14.29–31a)

Not long after, Peter is brought face to face with the truth of his moral cowardice as he denies Jesus three times (John 18.15–27). Peter cannot avoid his failure but Jesus later heals and restores him so he can take on the leadership of the disciples and build the Church of God.

Like Peter, we also have an ideal way of seeing ourselves. I think of a time when, as an exhausted and inexperienced new mum struggling to live up to my textbook image of motherhood, I found myself shouting, pounding my fists on the floor beside my child as I changed his nappy. I have never forgotten that moment when I was confronted with my capacity for violence, when I realized that I was not different or 'above' others, and began to view with more compassion those who lacked a supportive network.

This ideal view of ourselves is challenged each time we are confronted by something which we would rather not accept about ourselves. But according to Rowan Williams, the good news is that 'One of the chief sources of anxiety from which the gospel delivers us is the need to protect my picture of myself as right and good.'[123] When we and our directees come to know the God of infinite compassion, we realize that we no longer have to pretend in order to be loved – we are loved just as we are. Once this awareness becomes established, we are better able to look at the issue of forgiveness, particularly forgiveness of ourselves, as Tom Wright explores:

> It takes spiritual discipline to forgive others. It takes different, though related, spiritual discipline to forgive myself, to echo within my own heart the glad

---

122 'I will strike the shepherd, and the sheep will be scattered.'
123 Williams, *Silence and Honey Cakes*, p. 34.

and generous offer to forgiveness which God holds out to me . . . that sense of self-worth comes, not from examining myself and discovering I am not so bad after all, but from gazing at God's love and discovering that nothing can stand between it and me. Forgiving myself means recognising that I have indeed done sinful, hurtful, damaging things to other people, to myself and to God in whose image I'm made, and because God forgives me I must learn, *under his direction*, to forgive myself.[124]

Self-care

A stark reminder of the need for self-care can be found in pre-flight routines demonstrating use of an oxygen mask 'in the unlikely event of an emergency'. One thing always stands out for me: we have to attend to our own needs *before* we can be of use to anyone else.

We and our directees are challenged to take good care of ourselves so that we can be there for others without being overwhelmed. Many of us feel guilty if we restrict our availability or are slow to respond to a perceived need because, as Christians we are taught always to put our own needs second. However, 'dying to self' really has more to do with the letting go of the 'false self', the ideal face we show to the world so the 'true self', the 'loved-by-God-warts-and-all-self' can breathe and dance.

Good self-care prevents us from succumbing to exhaustion or 'retiring hurt' from a ministry we entered with such high hopes. We and our directees can benefit from some or all of the following elements of self-care:

- *Time management* – we and our directees lead such full lives that prayer is often squeezed out. Those who make listening prayer a priority, however, often discover that the day flows more smoothly, they are more aware of the Holy Spirit's promptings, less stressed, and more creative in their responses to the issues they face.
- *Regular health and wellness checks* – for example cholesterol and anaemia checks, breast self-examination and mammograms, cervical and prostate cancer checks.
- *Recreation* – indoor hobbies and exercise out of doors, times to unwind and connect with creation and/or our creativity but also space in which to listen to God and ourselves as we engage in contemplative activities such as gardening, fishing, making bread, embroidery or wood-turning.
- *Relationships* – ensuring we have a network of support, informal as well as

---

124 Wright, N. T., *Evil and the Justice of God*, London: SPCK, 2006, pp. 106–7. Emphasis mine.

formal. Meeting friends for coffee, or going with our partner to see a film or have dinner is as important as having regular spiritual direction and supervision.

• *Reflection* – regular time alone with a chance to mull things over using journalling or the Examen; creating space simply to 'be' with God.

• *Adequate rest* – adequate sleep, getting regular time off, taking short breaks during the day. This will be more likely to happen if we ask those we live and work with for their co-operation in planning meetings, evening commitments, weekend leave and so on. It will also depend on:

• *Setting limits.* Learning to say 'No' seems to be one of the hardest things for ministers to do. If you find this difficult and it is affecting your health and ministry, enrol for an assertiveness course – often run through night classes at local schools or community colleges.

• *Practise the prayer of petition* – learn to bring your own needs to God in humble confidence, asking for the grace you need, trusting God's provision

Soaking prayer

Flora Slosson Wuellner, aware that ministers often risk burnout, suggests that when we experience spiritual exhaustion and inner fatigue, we lay aside all forms of prayer and reading, even intercessory prayer, confident that God will take care of those for whom we normally pray, while we rest. She suggests using the following 'soaking prayer':

Make your body comfortable and at rest . . . Think of God's warmth and light surrounding you, as if you lie in the sun, or a pool of refreshing water if the sun image is too hot! You may wish to let your body slowly and gently rock from side to side as if being cradled. Or you may just wish to lie very still and let God's light and breath flow slowly and deeply into every part of your body . . . your whole self is washed in God's presence. After a few minutes of soaking prayer, lay your hands gently on your heart, abdomen, your forehead, over your eyes and pray *very slowly*:

The living love of Jesus Christ now fills me . . . calms me . . .
heals me . . . renews me.

Touch or think of any part of your body that is in special need and pray this prayer of Christ's indwelling presence. Use words that you feel are right for you.[125]

---

125 Wuellner, Flora Slosson, *Feed my Shepherds*, Nashville: Upper Room, 1998, pp. 124–5.

Learning to take good care of ourselves is not self-indulgent, but a necessary part of ensuring that we are fit for the ministry to which God has called us, and can better accompany those we meet in spiritual direction.

✠

Reflection questions

🕯 Have you ever been in a situation in which you have thought yourself able to act in a particular way but have been unable to live up to your expectations of yourself when the time came? You may like to talk to God about what that was like, if you have not done so before.

🕯 What is there about yourself that you currently find hard to accept?
   With whom are you comparing yourself?
   How might you bring these less accepted parts of yourself to God in prayer?

🕯 What issues around forgiveness – of others or yourself – still need to be addressed?
   How might you do this?

🕯 Re-read the 'Elements of self-care' and make some notes about your current situation. Add to your list anything else that you need, then spend ten minutes in 'soaking prayer'.

Suggestions for further reading

Dreamwork

Bowater, Margaret, *Dreams and Visions*, Auckland: Tandem Press, 1997.
Savary, Louis M., Berne, Patricia H. and Williams, Strephon Kaplan, *Dreams and Spiritual Growth: A Judeo-Christian Approach to Dreamwork*, New York: Paulist Press, 1984.

Personality and preferences

Bergin, Éilís and Fitzgerald, Eddie, *An Enneagram Guide: A Spirituality of Brokenness*, Mystic, CT: Twentythird Publications, 1993.
Fowke, Ruth, *Prayer and Personality*, Guildford: Eagle, 1997.
Michael, Chester P. and Norrisey, Marie C., *Prayer and Temperament: Different Prayer Forms for Different Personality Types*, Charlottesville, VA: Open Door, 1991.
Wilson, Shirley, *Offering Spiritual Direction to Extroverts*, New Zealand: Spiritual Growth Ministries, 2001. Full text: <www.sgm.org.nz/research_papers.htm>.
Zuercher, Suzanne, *Enneagram Spirituality: From Compulsion to Contemplation*, Notre Dame, IN: Ave Maria Press, 1992.

Self-knowledge, self acceptance and self-care

Benner, David, *The Gift of Being Yourself: The Sacred Call to Self-discovery*, Downers Grove, IL: InterVarsity Press, 2004.

Ferder, Fran, *Words Made Flesh*, Notre Dame, IN: Ave Maria Press, 1986.

Linn, Dennis, Sheila Fabricant Linn and Matthew Linn, *Healing Spiritual Abuse and Religious Addiction*, New York: Paulist Press, 1994.

——*Sleeping with Bread,* New York: Paulist Press, 1995.

May, Gerald, *Addiction and Grace*, New York: HarperSanFrancisco, 1991.

Sturt, Agnes and John Sturt, *Created for Love: Understanding and Building Self-esteem,* Surrey: Highland (IPS), 1995.

——*Created for Intimacy: Discovering Intimacy with Yourself, Others and God*, Guildford: Eagle (IPS), 1996.

Wuellner, Flora Slosson, *Feed my Shepherds*, Nashville: Upper Room, 1998.

Supervision and ethics

Conroy, Maureen, *Looking into the Well: Supervision of Spiritual Directors*, Chicago: Loyola University Press, 1995, pp. 91–105.

Gula, Richard, M., *Ethics in Pastoral Ministry*, New York/Mahwah NJ: Paulist Press, 1996.

5

Listening and Responding to Others

Introduction

In this section, we are going to see how the principles and practices of contemplative incarnational spiritual direction infuse a range of common ministry situations, presented in dialogue format. Like all scenarios, there is a limit to the amount of detail which can be included, but I have attempted to give them a reality which stems from experience while disguising details to protect privacy. I hope the examples will enable you to get a feel for spiritual direction in action, formally and informally as we consider some of the basics and some of the more difficult issues which may arise.

To get the most out of the dialogues, approach them as if you are the 'minister', formally offering spiritual direction or informally listening with spiritual direction 'antennae' at the ready! If you are able to speak the dialogues aloud, or role-play the dialogues, this will give them more immediacy. Instead of reflection questions at the end of each section, questions will be interspersed in the dialogues so you can get some idea of how you might respond to what is going on and can practise paying attention to your own experience as you listen deeply.

Bringing it all together: spiritual direction in one-to-one conversations

5.1 Listening to disappointment or anger with God – Beth

We start with the story of Beth, a priest who began regular spiritual direction six months ago. As Dot, her spiritual director, opens the door to Beth, she notices Beth's husband, Leo, driving away. They settle down in Dot's study and Beth launches into a conversation about her son and his girlfriend. Dot listens and, when Beth stops for a breath, says:

Dot   I noticed that Leo dropped you off today.
Beth   Yes – I'm not supposed to drive for another week.
Dot   What's been happening?

Beth   Well, I had surgery three weeks ago – a mastectomy – so Leo's ferrying me round.

Dot   Oh, Beth! I'm so sorry to hear that!

Beth   Oh, I'm fine – I don't have to have any further treatment, so that's good, and I'll be back on deck next week.

Dot   That seems very quick!

Beth   Well, no point hanging around is there? Haven't got time to put my feet up – there's lots of people far worse off than me and there aren't enough chaplains to cover the place as it is.

Dot   What sort of leave did your doctor suggest?

Beth   Well he'd like me to have six weeks off! Six weeks! Never had that sort of holiday in my life!

Dot   I wouldn't call it a holiday – six weeks recovery after that sort of surgery sounds a great idea!

Beth   Well, I feel fine, like I said, and I don't see any reason to let someone else take over my work.

Dot   What's it been like for you going through this, Beth?

Beth   I've just gone and got on with it – that's what you do isn't it? No point complaining or shouting at God about it.

Dot   Is that what you'd like to do? Shout at God?

Beth   I'd like to give him a piece of my mind, that's for sure!

Dot   You sound pretty annoyed.

Beth   Well, wouldn't you be? When I think of all the years I've put in for God – 20 years lay ministry before I was ordained – and all the things I've sacrificed, all the struggles – how can he do this to me?

Dot   Is that what you think ? That God did this to you?

Beth   Well didn't he? *(Her voice is getting louder)* I think it stinks – the whole thing stinks! I don't know how I'm going to go back into the surgical ward, and Leo's scared to come near me, and there's a new chaplain who wants more work . . . but I don't want to let anyone down.

Dot   It sounds like a hard place to be in, Beth. What would you like to say to God?

Beth   I can't say what I'd like to say.

Dot   What would you like to say?

Beth   Dot, I'm a priest – how can I tell God I'm absolutely fed up with him, I'm supposed to help other people deal with their own stuff, not get caught up in those sorts of feelings myself!

🜂 Take a few minutes to note your reaction to the above scenario.

Consider what life issues are significant for Beth.

As her spiritual director, what clues can you pick up that help you get a clearer picture of who Beth is, and who God is in Beth's eyes (her image of God).

✠

Your initial response to Beth may vary: for example, you may have been distracted by an imminent mammogram appointment of your own or you may have thought about someone you love who has just had this sort of radical surgery – both examples of parallel process. You may have been confronted by your own fear of cancer or experienced a human mixture of compassion for Beth's distress and disapproval for what you consider her inadequate self-care. This scenario reminds us of the importance of noticing our own 'stuff', and how mentally putting it to one side, to be raised later in supervision, frees us to attend to the directee.

In companioning Beth, Dot may have noticed the following:

- Uncertainty and fear about the continuity of Beth's chaplaincy position.
- Fear of a change in the relationship with her husband after the mastectomy.
- Unspoken fears about her attractiveness as a woman and her sense of femininity.
- A deep attachment to her work.
- Trying to 'get back to normal' as soon as possible without doing the emotional work that a healthy recovery involves.
- Stoic independence bordering on 'martyrdom'.
- A discrepancy between Beth's 'espoused theology'[126] – what she has expressed to Dot, talks about to others, and thinks she believes, i.e. that God is a God of love and mercy – and Beth's 'operant theology' – the thoughts and ideas about God out of which she is actually responding, i.e. that God is punitive and untrustworthy.

All of these have a place in spiritual direction and, as Dot and Beth continue to meet, each will come into focus as the Spirit moves. All are influenced by the way Beth sees herself and sees God, and so it is to this that priority is given. Sadly, from what she has shared so far, it seems that Beth sees God as indifferent, unjust, ungrateful and downright malicious. There is no sense of a God alongside Beth in her suffering, someone with whom she can share all that troubles her.

It is not uncommon to meet people who struggle with anger and disappointment, and this can precipitate a faith crisis as the relationship between the person and the God whom they believe in is tested by their circumstances. Spiritual direction, as we have seen, encourages people to be honest with God, no matter what

---

126 For a fuller description of these terms see: Ruffing, Janet, *Spiritual Direction: Beyond the Beginnings*, New York: Paulist Press, 2000, pp. 59–64.

they feel. It is particularly hard, however, for those who are in ministry to notice, name, own and express what they consider to be 'negative' feelings towards God.

It is also hard for us to listen to another's anger; we may even feel afraid of its expression, worried in case emotions get out of hand. Dot could have defended God and reassured Beth (and herself) that God *does* care. Instead, by her careful listening, repetition of potent words or phrases and perceptive questioning, Dot has helped Beth bring her disappointment and anger with God to the surface. From this point, Dot would encourage Beth to express her feelings and thoughts, her truth directly to God, no matter how 'ugly' or 'inappropriate' that truth may seem to Beth. There are several ways of doing this:

- Assuring Beth that God is able to handle whatever she says to God, i.e. it is all right to be angry with God, to communicate her truth to the God who loves her.
- A space may be offered for Beth to begin to do this verbally there and then – with or without Dot present.
- If Beth is struggling to put her anger and disappointment into words, Dot can provide paper and crayons, with the invitation to 'put some colour on the page that says something about how you are right now'. Covering a page with red or black lightning flashes or question marks for example can begin the process of accessing and expressing feelings that Beth might not be able to articulate directly. Dot will be attentive to the Spirit as she watches Beth, so she can offer appropriate support as Beth moves towards real – albeit angry – connection with God.
- Dot may invite Beth to choose and read aloud one of the Psalms of Complaint, for example Psalm 13 or 22, both of which start from a place of desolation and move to a sense of God's consolation. If this does not appeal, Beth might like to write her own.

🕯 How would you hope to bring this session to a conclusion?
What issues/feelings/attitudes might form part of future spiritual direction sessions?

✠

It is important for Dot and Beth to finish the session together well. This may mean with prayer, and perhaps with anointing for Beth (if she is comfortable receiving this ministry and Dot is able to offer it), and an arrangement for another meeting the following week. When someone is in the middle of a major life challenge, it is wise not to leave it too long before the next spiritual direction session.

As she prays for Beth between sessions, and from her experience as a spiritual director, Dot may discover other possible ways forward for Beth to consider over a longer period, for example:

- An invitation to record or journal her experience from the cancer diagnosis to the present day.
- A look at her sense of vocation and its expression.
- Further praying with relevant scripture, for example Mark 5 where the woman touched the hem of Jesus' garment – even if Beth might initially feel like tearing the garment to shreds!
- Asking the Holy Spirit to help her write a letter to her husband about her deepest fears.
- Encouraging Beth to reflect on her image of God at various points in her life and how this relates to her current situation; who has God been for her, and who is God for her now?
- Working out, perhaps with Dot's help, a way to pray her 'Goodbye'[127] to the person she was before the operation, to acknowledge where she is and, when she is ready, to pray her 'Welcome' to the person she is becoming

All that Dot does will have the goal of helping Beth re-establish an honest and open relationship with God, trusting that, as this develops, God will more than meet Beth in the difficult areas of her life.

✠

5.2 Listening in places of pain, vulnerability and abuse – Tom

Inevitably as directees become more open to God's indwelling love and boundless compassion, they will come face to face with things in their lives which need healing. Even directees who think they have 'dealt with' past pain may be surprised when a memory surfaces during prayer, or something touches them deeply. Often, bemused, they will say to their spiritual director, 'But I thought I'd dealt with that!' In situations like this, God is inviting a deeper engagement with what has emerged – perhaps so the directee can look at the event or memory from another perspective, or experience Jesus as present in a way that was not possible when the issue first surfaced.

I recall the first time the issue of my paternal identity was raised. I had a dream in which a maternity nurse, holding me as a newborn, entered my mother's room. She looked uncertainly at the three men present: no one claimed me. That dream

---

127 See Rupp, Joyce, *Praying Our Goodbyes*, Notre Dame, IN: Ave Maria Press, 1998, for suggestions.

helped me begin to face my grief about my unknown father. Since that dream, however, more work has been done as different versions of the 'finding my father' story surfaced when old taboos began to lift and the keepers of the family myths died. The latest 'version' occurred unexpectedly in my prayer time last year with a replay of the old dream, this time with Jesus present. As the maternity nurse entered the room, Jesus reached out and said quite clearly, 'Give her to me. She's mine.' My searching and longing for my birth father is being resolved – all I need to know is that I belong to Christ.

In spiritual direction it is not uncommon for issues such as deep grief, shame, guilt, abuse, relational isolation, family feuds, the effects of addictions or suicides and much more, to come to the surface as directees' image of God changes and their sense of self strengthens. As they begin to believe they are loved by God, as they come to know that God is on their side, they are enabled to enter places of pain.

Earlier we met Tom and Mary. We'll pick up their dialogue where Tom has just told Mary that he had taken the step of inviting a neighbour for a meal:

Tom   Just as we were finishing dinner, before we watched the football, Stan said, 'This is an answer to prayer, Tom.'

Mary   What was that like for you – to hear Stan say that?

Tom   It's . . . it means that he knows about Jesus and prayer too . . . and . . . it means that I'm an OK person . . . in spite of what I've done.

Mary   You're an OK person . . .

Tom   Yes – even though . . . *(he hesitates and Mary waits . . .)* I . . . I haven't told anyone about this, but . . . it's really been on my mind an awful lot lately . . . *(he hesitates again)* . . . years ago, when I was a young boy . . . about eight or nine . . . an uncle came to stay with us. He wasn't a real uncle, just a friend of my Dad's. I had to share my room with him because we lived in a small house and there was nowhere else . . . and, in the night . . . *(he takes a deep breath . . .)* in the night he used to come across to my bed and . . . make me do things . . . it was awful . . . and I didn't want to do it . . . but he said it was our special secret and not to tell anyone or I'd get into trouble. And so I never spoke up . . .

⏾ Take a few minutes to note your reaction to Tom's revelation.

What questions are going through your mind? What feelings are you noticing?

How would you respond to Tom?

✠

Mary may be surprised, even shocked, by what Tom has said. If she has never encountered sexual abuse before, she may wonder about her ability to be alongside Tom as he deals with painful memories, or who she could refer him to. Her first response, however, must be to attempt to convey that she is on Tom's side and does not judge him. See what you think of her response and compare it with your own notes above.

Mary   Oh Tom . . . I don't know what to say . . . how awful for you . . .
Tom   I didn't ever tell Betty. I was too ashamed. She sometimes asked me why I had no men friends, but I never told her.
Mary   This must have been a huge weight to carry around all these years by yourself.

Tom's story raises the issue of the difference between shame and guilt. We have already heard Tom say things like 'in spite of what I've done' and that he was 'made to do things'. Guilt refers to those feelings and thoughts we have in response to an action, to something we have *actually* done wrong (real guilt) or something we *think* we have done wrong (false guilt). Part of Tom's journey towards recovery will involve accepting he was not at fault for what happened.

Shame, on the other hand, strikes at the heart of who we are, it affects our *being*. It's not a question of there being something wrong with what I've done so much as there being something wrong with *me*. As such, it is particularly crippling, stunting emotional and psychological development and limiting a person's capacity for healthy relationships. Shame often forms a barrier between people and God. That is why in spiritual direction we help people embrace the truth that God loves them *for who they are, just as they are*. They do not have to *do* anything to be loved by God: that is the scandal – and the wonder – of grace. Tom's earlier retreat experience of God's unconditional love broke that barrier and freed him to begin to work through the current implications of his earlier abuse.

🕯 As we pick up Tom's story, keep your own responses and questions in mind.

Rarely meeting Mary's eyes, Tom tells Mary more about what happened, revealing a pattern of regular sexual abuse for six months while the 'uncle' was staying, and a sexual assault experienced when he was an Army conscript in his late teens. He comes to the end of his story and looks directly at Mary for the first time:

Tom   You do believe me don't you?
Mary   Yes I do, Tom. It's horrible to think that you were put through this abuse by people who should have been trustworthy. But . . . I don't have any experience in helping people work their way through this sort of thing.

153

I'm not sure how best to help you – it might be better for you to talk to someone else . . . someone who knows more than I do.

Tom   I'd rather talk to you.

Mary   Well, you can still do that, of course. We can talk about what's happening for you and where Jesus is in all of this. But I know a couple of really good counsellors who have a lot of experience.

Tom   I don't really want to tell anyone else.

Mary   I'm not surprised. It must have taken a lot of courage to tell me. But Tom, I can say that I would trust either one of these two counsellors if I had something like this to work through.
(She gives him the details of the counsellors – one male and one female – and they talk a little further about the benefits of seeing someone who has more experience than Mary)

Tom   Well, I'll think about it – and I guess I can sit down and talk to Jesus about it and listen and see what we come up with. But if I don't want to see them, will you still listen to my story?

Mary   I'll do my best, Tom – we can listen together for how God will help you through this.

✠

The issue of competence and referral is crucial but raises complex questions:

- How can we companion someone through recovery from abuse if we have no training or background in such a difficult area?
- How can we encourage a referral to someone who does have the expertise if our directee prefers to work with us?
- Do we maintain a spiritual direction relationship with a directee who is having psychotherapy or counselling for abuse issues, or wait until after they have made progress towards healing?
- If we do have counselling skills, can we offer a dual contract, with the focus of each session determined by the needs of the directee? And, of course:
- What happens if we have not yet done the hard work from our own abusive background?

Thankfully, supervision is the place where all of the above can be discussed. And we can take steps to make sure we know the contact details of reputable counsellors or therapists to whom referral can be made, should we encounter issues which lie beyond our competence.

I recall some years ago, knowing hardly anything about working with abuse, accompanying an abuse survivor who had already done a lot of work in psychotherapy and spiritual direction in another city. For years 'Kim' had dissociated herself from her body as she unconsciously defended herself from painful memories. Now it was Advent and she wanted to talk about how she might reconnect with her body. I didn't have any idea what to say or suggest, apart from being silent and listening.

As we sat together in that silence, both of us waiting for the Spirit, the connection was made: the Word became *flesh* – God in Jesus had a *body*. We talked about the infant Christ coming to us at Christmas. We talked about how babies gradually discover their bodies – one toe, then ten, the curves of ears and cheeks, the flexibility of fingers. 'Kim' was able to name God's invitation to her: gently to get to know her body, as a baby would, as Jesus did, encountering the mystery of the incarnation. We were both thankful for the Holy Spirit's leading. We both felt touched by grace.

🕯 This topic may be painful for some readers. If that is the case, please make sure you talk about this with someone you trust. There are many resources available to assist us as we grieve or recover from various forms of abuse. We do ourselves and those whom we companion in ministry a service if we do our own work in this area, hard though it might be.

5.3 Listening for transitions and crises in a person's faith – Kelly

🕯 Before you read this dialogue, you may like to re-read the material in Chapter 3, section 3.5 about different models of spiritual growth. Then, as you read or role-play the dialogue, keep in mind the question: 'Where might Kelly be on her spiritual journey?'

Rob, a recently appointed minister, is clearing up quickly after the 9.30am Eucharist, so he can drive to the neighbouring village for their 11.30 service. Kelly is tidying the books and chatting to him about her family and her plans for the summer holidays. Suddenly she blurts out:

Kelly   There must be *more* to being a Christian than this, Rob!

Rob   Gosh! Where did that come from? Sounds like you're pretty fed up.

Kelly   I'm not only fed up – I'm bored witless if you want to know the truth. I only keep on coming here because Russell's in the choir. Honestly, Rob – it's nothing personal – but I just keep on hearing the same old stuff all the time, the same prayers, the same hymns.

🜊 Before we go any further with this dialogue, just consider how you would feel if you were Rob, Kelly's minister.

✠

Feelings of defensiveness, annoyance, disappointment, failure, anxiety could all form part of your response, and it would be easy to slip into self-protection mode. However, if Rob understands something of the dynamics of spiritual growth, he will see cause for optimism because Kelly's discomfort could be the catalyst for a new impetus in her spiritual development – if she receives helpful spiritual direction.

Knowing he has to leave shortly, Rob attempts to get a bit more background:

Rob   You were here before I started last year, Kelly. How long have you been coming to St Anne's?

Kelly All my life – I was baptized here, taught Sunday school, met Russell in the youth group and we got married here when we'd finished university. The children were baptized here and Ali and Stephen were married here last year.

Rob   What do you think you might be missing out on?

Kelly I don't know really – it's just that – there must be more to church than coming here once a week to sing the same old songs and hear the same old lessons – there *must* be . . .

Rob   You sound convinced.

Kelly More like desperate!

Rob   It's important that you find whatever this 'more' is, then.

Kelly Yes – the old answers don't stack up any more; the old ways of praying don't mean what they did; I don't want to throw the whole thing away, but I don't want to trudge along like this for the next 30 years either.

Rob   I've got to head off to St Agnes' in five minutes – but I can tell you about a couple of options that might help. I see several parishioners individually once a month for spiritual direction, to talk about their faith journey – what's working and what's not, that sort of thing. I'd be happy to see you on that basis too. Or, if that doesn't appeal, there's a small group starting soon, next week actually. Five people at the moment, a bit like you, people who are looking for something more from their faith. Carol is going to introduce some ways of praying with scripture. Everyone can try it and there'll be coffee afterwards and time to talk if people want.

Kelly I've done lots of Bible study before, but I've never actually prayed with scripture. Let me think about it and I'll get back to you. What night was it going to be?

Rob   Monday at 7pm for about an hour. At Carol's place. Just go along if you'd like to.

Kelly   OK. I rather like the idea of talking to you one to one though, if you've got the time. You mentioned about being on a faith journey; I hadn't thought of it that way before. Journey means movement doesn't it, and I'm certainly stuck at the moment.

Rob   I'd be happy to see you. Just get in touch with me when you've had time to decide what you want to do. I must be off now, Kelly, over to St Agnes'. God bless you.

🕯 What are the key issues here for Kelly?

What did you notice about how Rob responded to Kelly?

✠

Once Rob got over Kelly's surprise outburst, his main concern was to try to get some idea of where she might be on her faith journey within the five minutes he had available. Her brief comments are enough to indicate a readiness to explore her beliefs and practices and, before he leaves, Rob is able to offer her a couple of options to consider. He does not condemn her for her point of view and, as one adult to another, leaves the choice to her, giving her time to reflect, trusting that God is at work.

It is important to consider for a moment the added factor in this dialogue – the time pressure which Rob is under, the next commitment which prevents him from exploring Kelly's disappointments in more depth. Even if we are meeting more formally and have set aside an hour together for spiritual direction, a directee can still bring up important material near the end of a session. In either case, it's no use getting annoyed or asking why the matter wasn't raised earlier. Instead we can:

- be fully present to the directee rather than thinking about the next commitment;
- indicate how much time is available before the session together has to come to an end;
- acknowledge what has been shared, for example a significant dream, a spiritual experience;
- encourage directees to do further exploration, for example TTAQ (Title, Theme, Affect, Question – see Chapter 4) for dreams, journalling about their experience, talking to God about it, identifying their feelings, thinking about relevant scripture passages if appropriate;
- offer another meeting time; depending on the nature of the content and the well-being of the directee, this may be within the week or the following week;

- trust the Holy Spirit that what has been begun, in and with the directee, will continue.

If Kelly chooses to go to the group exploring praying with scripture, the sort of process involved is covered in Chapter 6. If she chooses to go to see Rob for one-to-one spiritual direction, Rob would begin by asking Kelly what she is hoping for in her conversations with him; between them they would clarify his role as 'companion on the journey' rather than 'resident expert'. They would set up an initial agreement to meet for a few sessions and agree to review their work together, then go on to see if spiritual direction sessions were helping Kelly or not.

Rob would ask Kelly to share with him her faith story to date – what has been important and what has been difficult, especially her current frustration with her church experience. Rob would encourage her to be honest, and would try to give space for her spiritual longings to emerge. He might offer some information about different steps on the faith journey for Kelly to take away and read so she can see that she is not alone in her desire for 'more'. Further sessions will build on this beginning, and will cover some or all of the following:

- *Exploring prayer.* What does Kelly do when she prays? What does she think prayer is? What is her pattern of prayer? Where does Kelly think God is when she prays?
- *Religious experience.* Has Kelly had some awareness of God or something that was outside her normal understanding, for example a synchronicity of events, answered prayer?
- *Image of God.* How would Kelly describe God? With which of the Persons of the Trinity does she connect most readily? How does she think God works in the world?
- *Her attitude towards scripture* and any patterns of regular engagement with the Bible.
- *Life events.* What major events in Kelly's life have affected her faith, caused her to question, or to give thanks?
- *If she has experienced loss or grief.* How was God involved or absent during that time? What questions about God and her faith still remain unanswered?

Primarily though, Rob will be encouraging Kelly to begin to be honest with God and to pay attention to her experience – perhaps encouraging her to use a spiritual journal to reflect on key moments in her daily life, or to record what surfaces when she prays with scripture or attends a worship service. Always he will be wondering, with Kelly, 'What might God be doing here? What might God's invitation be in this?'

5.4 Listening for barriers, blocks and resistance – Marie

We can't resist a vacuum – in order to *resist* there must be *something* drawing us *towards* itself which we can refuse to accept – and in our directees that something is God's call to deeper relationship. Resistance, then, is an expected part of the spiritual journey; we can look at it positively as evidence that God is at work.

Most of us are initially hesitant when faced with change of any sort. It's what we do with this hesitation that is important in our spiritual growth. When this hesitation or resistance is expressed directly to God, we see God's affirmation and reassurance. Communication is two-way and the relationship of trust and response to God's call deepens, for example when Ananias speaks out his understandable reluctance to go to 'Brother Saul' in Acts 9: 'Lord, I have heard from many about this man, how much evil he has done to your saints in Jerusalem . . .', God responds to Ananias with encouragement, direct instructions and reassurance of God's continuing presence. Indirect or unconscious resistance is a different matter. When a pattern of thinking or behaviour hinders people's movement towards God and they cannot bring their honest concerns to God, they will also miss out on God's support or guidance.

In spiritual direction we look for signs of resistance and hints of hesitation as we listen to our directees.

Marie is an articulate older woman whose husband Walter died two years ago. She has met her minister Chris four times over the last six months to talk about her spiritual life. We enter the dialogue in mid-conversation:

Chris   Has anything come to you as you've been journalling during the last month?

Marie   Well, to be honest, I haven't actually given the journal a chance. I've got lots of thoughts . . . and I think 'I must write that down, I must write that down', but then things sort of get in the way and I don't get round to it.

Chris   What gets in the way?

Marie   Oh, you know – just things – the cat to take to the vet, the shopping, going to bowls, chores around the house – that sort of thing. There's always something that needs doing.

Chris   Life can be very full. What's happening in your prayer life?

Marie   You see, this word 'prayer' is interesting as well. I wonder if we all mean the same thing by it? And prayer during the service is tricky because I don't know the people they're praying for. How can I pray for someone I have no image of? I don't see the point of this – it's just a jumble of words, not my conception of the word 'prayer' at all.

Chris   What is prayer for you?

Marie   Well it's ... uumh quietly ... er ... (*sigh*) ... just talking ... er ... (*sigh*) ... just ... going through images, I suppose ... (*another sigh*) ... going over things quietly ... just kind of spiritually communicating I suppose ... (*another sigh*).

🕯 Put yourself in Chris's shoes. What would you be feeling and thinking? What indicators of possible 'resistance' have you noticed in the above dialogue?

✠

It is important for spiritual directors to be able to recognize resistance in one of its many forms, for example:

- the directee starting to feel negative towards prayer or avoiding it altogether;
- the directee missing spiritual direction appointments or arriving late; or
- the directee keeping the focus on intellectual discussion, not personal experience or feelings.

Chris has noticed several other signs of possible resistance in Marie:

- Not having done any reflection/journalling since their last appointment.
- Moving away from the immediacy of the question on her personal prayer practice to the 'safer ground' of criticism of corporate prayer recently experienced at a formal service.
- Keeping the discussion focused on thoughts rather than on feelings.
- What seems a persistent pattern of doing everything *but* making time for God.

As well as recognizing signs of possible resistance, Chris will be considering possible causes, for example:

- Marie is still grieving for Walter and she may not have much energy to pray actively.
- There may be issues around her image of God which get in the way of her prayer, for example does she blame God for Walter's death?
- Is Marie trying to be self-sufficient, to live her life without God's help and direction?
- Is she afraid of losing control of her life if she gets closer to God?

When we have carefully reflected and prayed for our directee and we sense that there is resistance, one way forward is to address the resistance in the spiritual direction session itself. We can raise the topic with the directee, perhaps by mentioning the way people initially hesitate or resist change in life, including their spiritual life. Offering several examples from scripture can be another useful way for the resistant directee to engage with the issue prayerfully and without any sense of condemnation. Another possibility is to offer space within the spiritual direction session for the 'too busy to pray' directee to have time with God there and then, and this is what Chris is going to do now.

Chris   There's a lot of sighing, Marie. What's going on for you right now?

Marie   I don't know – well, I suppose I'm feeling tired. Life's so different since Wally died – I'd really like to have a regular pattern of prayer but life feels like being on a treadmill at the moment and I'm running out of steam.

Chris   How would it be if we were to stop for a few minutes – and you had that time just to be with God. You could sit quietly or you might even like to picture yourself on that treadmill, wanting to slow down – you could simply tell God what it's like for you now. I could stay here or go into another room for the next ten to fifteen minutes, whichever you prefer. What do you think?

Marie   Well, I'm not too sure if I can imagine anything, but I don't mind just sitting quietly – but I'd like you to stay with me.

Chris   That's fine, I won't interrupt you – you just let me know when you're ready to continue and we can take it from there. *(Chris starts to pray silently and Marie closes her eyes)*

§ What do you notice about the way Chris responds to Marie?
How would you feel and what would you think about offering a directee this sort of space?

✠

It would not surprise me if, after a time of quiet, Marie reported something like this:

Marie   That was really peaceful. It's funny, but it made me think of a time when I used to sit with my mum on the front porch of our house – I had three brothers and a sister, so it was special to have time with Mum on my own. We'd sit on the step in the sun and shell peas – and it would be warm and peaceful and I'd sort of lean against her knee.

Chris   Leaning against her knee, you'd feel absolutely secure – would you like to go back to that memory for a moment . . .

Marie   Yes . . . *(Marie closes her eyes again)*

Chris You can feel the sun . . . the warmth . . . and the comfort of your mum as you lean against her knee.

Marie Mmmh . . . *(a long pause)* . . . it feels . . . it's bigger than Mum somehow.

Chris Bigger somehow . . . *(another long pause – Chris continues to pray and watch Marie, who looks very calm)*

Marie *(She suddenly smiles)* It feels as if I'm leaning against God's knee – and God is saying to me: 'Just sit on the porch with me, dear Mae, and we'll get through this together.'
   (Chris remains quiet)

Marie Mae was Mum's pet name for me. *(She closes her eyes again)* There's such love in God's voice. *(There are tears slowly running down her cheeks; Chris is also moved; they sit silently for a few minutes until Marie sighs again, this time in deep peace)*

Chris God is taking care of you, just like a loving mother . . . *(Marie nods but doesn't speak, so they spend the remaining few minutes in silence)*

Of course, this is an imaginary dialogue and we can't know if this is how God would have met someone in Marie's situation. However, as spiritual directors we *can* trust God to meet each directee as may be best for that person. Sometimes that will mean that God will meet the directee during the spiritual direction session and we will know ourselves to be on holy ground. If that doesn't seem to happen, we can still trust that if the directee genuinely desires to meet God, sooner or later something *will* happen in response to her making even the smallest space to listen to God.

As we gain confidence, we learn to follow the Spirit's leading and risk inviting the directee into space and silence; we wait, we take time to pray, and we respond to whatever has happened during the directee's time of silent reflection. Even if Marie were to report 'Nothing happened', at least Chris would have had time to listen for the guidance of the Spirit so that she can respond more grace-fully to Marie:

- Chris may introduce her to 'soaking prayer', which we looked at in Chapter 4, section 4.6 – that form of prayer in which exhausted people imagine themselves resting in a safe, undisturbed place as they soak up God's love like the warmth of the sun.[128]
- Chris may encourage Marie to explore the treadmill image more fully, perhaps writing about it or drawing a diagram of all the things in her life that make up the 'running out of steam' feeling.

---

128 See Wuellner, Flora Slosson, *Feed My Shepherds*, Nashville: Upper Room, 1998, pp. 124–5.

- If Marie wanted to pray with some scripture, Chris could offer several passages for her to choose from. 'Come to me all who are heavy laden and I will give you rest' (Matthew 11.28) would certainly be one of them!

It is a work of the Spirit that when we prayerfully offer this sort of space for directees, something helpful and relevant frequently emerges. I think of one directee who, left alone in my study for ten minutes with God, said she had been drawn to look closely at the pattern on my small rug. She noticed a square with a small cross at the centre and arrows running off it at each corner. Through that pattern she recognized that she too was running off in all directions and she knew that she needed to stop and stay quietly in the centre with God. We were both amazed!

Resistance can also hide under the guise of a *counter-movement* in which we are 'sidetracked' into activities which take us away from God or God's best purposes. Much counter-movement is towards things that are safe or familiar, things that keep us busy and get in the way of our actually spending time with God. Much that seems worthy – both individually and as a community of faith – can in fact be a counter-movement if it draws us into spending our time and energy on things that are not what God wants us to be doing. How do we know what God wants? By adopting a contemplative stance – spending time in discernment, listening to God as individuals and corporately, listening to the needs of the local communities, and listening to ourselves.

5.5 Listening to issues around sexuality – Henry

Keeping in mind the focus of Chapter 4 – listening to our own responses and noticing and attending to our own 'red flag areas' – consider the following dialogue between 18-year-old Henry and his neighbour and friend Kim, a pastoral worker in their church.

Kim knows that Henry's faith has always been important to him, and he wonders what has prompted Henry's visit:

Henry You know I'm going to London to study, don't you?
Kim Yes, your mother did mention it. You got a scholarship, I hear – congratulations!
Henry Thanks – it was a surprise but I'm really thrilled. It's exactly what I want to do *(he talks about the details of the course and job opportunities)*. I'm really looking forward to it – it'll be wonderful to be in a big city.
Kim A bit more freedom to be yourself?
Henry Yes – to be my real self *(silence)* . . . Kim, can I tell you something?

Kim   Of course.

Henry   And you won't tell Mum and Dad?

Kim   Anything you say remains with me, Henry. I give you my word.

Henry   Do you remember that guy who came to stay with us last year?

Kim   The exchange student? Paulo, was that his name?

Henry   Yes – Paulo – he was with us for four months and during that time I
        realized . . . well, I was . . . attracted to him. It was like a whole different
        way of feeling about someone – something I'd never felt with the girls
        I've been out with. It's like there was never any real spark in me – until I
        met him, and I . . . Nothing happened, Kim. But I felt alive when he was
        around, and when he left I got quite depressed and Mum thought it was
        because I'd always wanted a brother. But it wasn't that. Paulo is straight I
        know, because we still text each other and he's always going on about his
        girlfriend. But – girls just don't interest me, Kim. I think I'm gay.

☍ Take some time to notice your response and any questions or issues that
surface for you.

✠

Kim's response to Henry's revelation will depend on a number of factors, including the nature and extent of his experience of being with gay people, his theology
and that of the church he and Henry attend, his understanding of human psychosexual development, and his relationship with Henry's family. Personal issues for
Kim may be triggered too: there may be unfinished business stemming from his
own sexual history, for example sexual experimentation at school; or he might
have a son Henry's age.

☍ Consider Kim's possible responses and notice *your* reaction to each one:

- Repulsion – a turning away from all that the word 'gay' conjures up.
- A strong urge to help Henry explore a heterosexual orientation and lifestyle.
- Remembering a passing but intense attraction to someone his own gender
  while an adolescent.
- Feeling caught between his own compassion for Henry and the publicly
  stated negative stance of his Church towards homosexuality.
- Suspending judgement, encouraging him to say a bit more about how he
  felt towards Paulo.
- Remembering the struggles a cousin had before 'coming out' about her
  sexual orientation.

- An unconditional compassion for him.
- Concern that he might be heading for eternal damnation.
- A mixture of several of the above.

⚱ As the scenario stands, both spiritual director and directee are male. If the directee in this scenario were Henrietta instead of Henry, would this affect your responses? Why?

In society – and in spiritual direction – discussing any matters of sexuality can be awkward or embarrassing. Issues around homosexuality in particular are complex, emotive and potentially divisive of family and congregation. However, wherever we – or Kim – might stand on the homosexuality continuum between absolute revulsion and unqualified acceptance, Henry and directees like him need a safe place in which to discuss their sexuality and its implications. Initially, Kim may find himself doing some or all of the following:

- Checking Henry's safety – he has already mentioned depression; suicide of adolescents who suspect they are gay is a real risk.
- Maintaining confidentiality so long as Henry is not at risk of self-harm.
- Helping Henry talk further about his developing awareness of his sexual orientation.
- Looking at the implications for Henry and his family and the question of if, how, or when he might 'come out'.
- Exploring Henry's support network.

As is customary in spiritual direction, Kim will be praying for Henry between meetings, knowing that the Holy Spirit can guide them both at this time. During their conversations, although much of their discussion will centre on how Henry is addressing the above issues, Kim's focus will always return to helping Henry pay attention to what God may be saying, inviting, calling him to do and be as he travels this road of self-discovery. Thus there will be:

- conversation about questions of faith that arise for Henry;
- exploration of Henry's image of God;
- discussion about how Henry is currently relating to God and what's happening in his prayer.

Kim will take any issues emerging from his spiritual direction of Henry to supervision so he can make sure his own 'stuff' does not prevent him from attending to Henry's pastoral and spiritual needs appropriately. If Kim has little or no experience of working with someone in Henry's position, his supervisor can help Kim consider the appropriateness of referral or will help Kim monitor his own level of anxiety or inadequacy as together they consider possible ways forward.

Whenever issues around sexuality surface during spiritual direction, we try to provide a calm, listening presence; we concentrate on helping the directee to address the issue, to keep communication with God alive, and to pay attention to what God might be saying about the situation.

5.6 Listening for signs of isolation, low self-esteem and vulnerability – Evan

Evan is an unmarried man aged 35 who is in Harry's evening Bible study group. He shyly asks to see Harry after the other group members have gone home. Harry has to go and pick up his son from music practice so he makes an appointment with Evan for the next day at lunchtime. They meet in a local café.

Harry   This is a nice place – I've driven past it a few times but never been in.

Evan   I come here most days – it's got a friendly feel to it and the food's good. It's nice to sit here and watch the people and wonder about their lives.

Harry   Are you on your own a lot then, Evan?

Evan   Well, my work's not exactly social, as you know. Being a dentist, I don't really get to have much of a conversation with people.

Harry   How do you find the Bible study group?

Evan   I'm enjoying the reading and the discussion. I mean, some of the people there have a lot of experience and it's good to hear their ideas and stories. It'd be nice to have some younger people in the group though, nearer my age, people I could hang out with a bit, perhaps.

Harry   What do you do for recreation at the moment?

Evan   Oh well . . . I walk quite a lot – the park, the riverside walkway – it's good to get outside after being in the surgery all week. And I like to go to concerts sometimes – and then there's the internet – I usually spend time in the evenings surfing the net.

Harry   What sort of sites have you found interesting?

Evan   Well – a whole range of things really – sometimes I go into chat rooms and see who's there and what's going on. There's one that I often visit because it has some people who breed Siamese cats – we had Siamese when I was growing up and I've often thought I'd like to breed them.

You have probably noticed that Harry asks three open-ended questions here, ones beginning with 'What . . .' and 'How . . .' which are more likely to elicit a fuller response than a simple 'Yes' or 'No'. Jesus knew the value of asking open-ended questions to invite deeper reflection and focused attention:

- 'What are you looking for?' asked of two of John's disciples in John 1.38.
- 'What do you want me to do for you?' asked of the blind beggar in Luke 18.41.
- 'Why do you see the speck in your neighbour's eye; but do not notice the log in your own eye?' asked of a crowd of followers in Luke 6.41.

Harry has only a limited understanding of Evan's life from a few comments made at the Bible study group, so he takes his time to build up a more complete picture, before asking:

Harry   What was it that you wanted to see me about?

Evan   Well – it's probably a bit silly really, but it's just that I feel as if no one at church cares whether I turn up or not. You would, I know, but all the others – I'm sure they wouldn't notice if I wasn't there.

Harry   I am sorry that you're not feeling part of the church yet, Evan. It can't be pleasant, feeling sort of out on the edge.

Evan   It's horrible – it was like that at school a lot of the time and even at uni, in the hostel – sorry, it sounds a bit lame, but when I came to St Peter's, I hoped that I'd find someone, some people to share things with, you know . . .

Harry   So you've felt like this before, at school and when you went to university – this sense of wanting to connect with people but it's just not happening?

Evan   Yes – all my life really. I know I'm a bit shy, but I'm getting fed up with being on my own . . . it's really hard and I don't know how much longer I can continue *(he looks down at his feet)*.

🕯 Notice your response to this last statement by Evan. What's going through your mind?
How do you feel? How might you want to respond?

✠

Harry takes a deep breath, prays, before saying very gently:

Harry   When you say you 'don't know how much longer you can continue', what do you mean, Evan?

Evan   Well – sometimes I wonder what's the point of it all.

Harry   Are you thinking about harming yourself in some way?

Evan   No – of course not *(there is a short pause)* . . . well, to be honest, I did think about suicide last year but I realized I wouldn't have had the guts to go through with it! *(He smiles ruefully)*

167

Harry So you had a plan?

Evan   Not specifically – it didn't get to that point. I got really low but I've got
       a good GP who's been helping me and I can really say that's behind me
       now, especially since I'm beginning to get to know more about God and
       have started back at church – it's just that I'm lonely and it takes a lot of
       energy to try to meet other people. Sorry to moan!

Harry No need to apologize, Evan. I'm glad to hear that you've got an under-
       standing GP. Have you seen him recently?

Evan   Yes – I go every three to four weeks just to have a talk and monitor my
       medication. He's a no-nonsense chap and I trust him. He says I'm doing
       well and I know that I'm definitely less anxious than I was a few months
       ago.

Harry It sounds like you've been in a really difficult place. Would it be helpful for
       us to meet again to talk about what's happening for you and to see where
       God might be in the midst of all you're going through?

Evan   Yes, I'd like that.

🕯 What have you noticed about Harry's approach?
  What questions emerge for you as you read this section?

If you have experience of working with people who are at risk of self-harm, you
will no doubt know the importance of being direct with them to establish the
level of risk, what their support network is, how often they think of self-harm or
suicide, whether they have a detailed plan.

  If you have not got that experience – and many ministers do not – then you
will appreciate that Harry has made a brave choice to be direct with Evan, using
a series of closed questions to get the information he needs to help him assess the
risk of Evan harming himself. Harry has a responsibility to ensure that someone
who even hints at self-harm is able to get the help he needs promptly if the risk
is imminent. If Evan had indicated that he had a detailed plan and had frequent
suicidal thoughts, Harry would need to arrange a GP appointment at once or
access a mental health team in the area.

  However, Harry quickly establishes that the risk has receded and Evan has got
support from a health professional with whom he is in regular contact. Harry will
be aware from this point on that Evan's mental health may be a factor in their
work together and so will bring any lack of experience in this field to his next
supervision session.

The next portion of the dialogue takes place six months later, during which time
Harry and Evan have met regularly – usually every three or four weeks – to talk
about Evan's life and to find out more about relating to God, as an adult child

would to a loving parent – something Evan lacked in his early life. In addition, Evan has continued to attend the study group and is beginning to talk more freely with the other members. Harry thinks things are going well, and is surprised when Evan doesn't turn up on time for his next meeting.

Evan   Sorry about being late – I got a bit preoccupied! In fact I nearly forgot our appointment but my computer reminded me just in time! I've got something to tell you. You know ages ago how we were talking about my wanting to breed Siamese cats? Well, you probably won't believe this but I met a woman who wants to do the same thing – she lives in Canada – and we've been having this conversation about how to set up a breeding cattery.

Harry   So you met her on the internet and you've been keeping in touch?

Evan   Yes – every day I text or email her while I'm at work, and then when I get home and when the time zones are right we get on the net and chat away to each other. She's a lovely person and she's even talking about setting up a cattery and wants me to go into partnership with her. It would mean fronting up with about £50,000 to get under way – she's got a good job too and has her eye on a small property in Vancouver that could be a great starting point.

Harry   £50,000 seems a lot of money, Evan.

Evan   I know, but I've got plenty saved – after all, as I said to her, I'm earning good money and I own my own house already and I've got nothing else I really want to spend it on.

    ☺ Now what's going through your mind?
    What questions does this development raise about the role of a spiritual director?

✠

Here is a lonely young man apparently finding happiness through a relationship with someone he has met on the internet. Whatever our personal experience of internet-initiated relationships, common sense rings warning bells. Evan has revealed details about his personal financial situation and is being asked to contribute to a venture which might be judged dubious. What does Harry do? What is his ethical responsibility if he sees someone with whom he has a close pastoral relationship moving towards something that could cause personal disappointment and possible financial loss? Does he pour cold water over Evan's enthusiasm and jeopardize their work together? Does he stay silent and hope and pray that the woman has good intentions? Does he raise questions and risk undermining Evan's

169

self-esteem and embryonic happiness? How can he invite Evan to involve God in this decision?

This is a good example of a time when coming from a contemplative stance is vital. If Harry is paying attention to God and to himself as he listens to Evan's story, a wise way through may be found:

Harry I'm not sure how to respond to this news, Evan. Can we take a few minutes in silence – just to have some space and time to reflect?
Evan Well, you've mentioned the value of taking time to reflect often enough over the last few months, so yes, I don't mind. *(They spend a few minutes in silence)*
Harry I'm just wondering, Evan. How are you praying about this decision?
Evan Praying about it? Why should I be praying about it? It seems perfectly logical to me.
Harry Well, we've talked quite a lot about God being interested in the whole of our lives and wanting to help us make good choices.
Evan Do you think I'm making a mistake?
Harry I don't know. I'm just wondering whether it might be a good idea to invite God into the whole thing – talk to God about how you're feeling, what you're hoping for . . . that sort of thing. There are some solid Christian methods of making choices and I'd be happy to look at those with you if you'd like to. After all, God cares about you and wants only the best for you . . . and so do I.

Harry is keeping to a spiritual direction focus here by emphasizing to Evan the value of talking honestly to God about what is happening for him and encouraging him to apply Christian discernment practices. At the same time, Harry expresses his personal concern as he invites Evan to take more time to make his decision.

5.7 Listening for transference and counter-transference – Ted, Sally

Ted Thanks so much for taking the time to see me – I know you're really busy.
Ruth No problem, Ted. What do you want to talk about?
Ted Well, I really like your preaching – it brings the scripture to life for me; you must have done a lot of study to know about what went on in biblical times. I've got a few questions about prayer; and I thought you'd know the answers, so here I am!

🕯 What's your reaction to Ted's comments?

Within two statements we already see the potential for an unhealthy spiritual direction relationship. Ted approaches Ruth as if she is someone above him in status, knowledge or power, transferring onto her a way of relating that emerges from his childhood response to significant adults. Let's look at two different ways Ruth might respond to Ted:

Ruth   *(smiling)* Well, thank you Ted. It's good to know you like my preaching. I always put a lot of time into it and it's great to know it's appreciated. I'm not sure that I've got all the answers about prayer though, but let's hear the questions and I'll see what I can come up with.

or:

Ruth   *(smiling)* Well, thank you Ted. It's nice to know my preaching is appreciated. A lot of people have questions about prayer, so you're not alone! I'm happy to listen to your questions about prayer, Ted, and to help you find out some answers for yourself. If you'd like to, we can look at what prayer is and who God is for you, and we can talk about what happens when you pray.

In the first response, Ruth is 'buying into' Ted's transference. Acting out of what is called counter-transference, she is overly gratified by his comment about her preaching and willingly takes on the 'expert' role he wants to assign to her. If this continues, their whole relationship may reflect this dynamic and will work against Ted's spiritual growth. It may make Ruth feel good, but it won't help Ted grow in his relationship with God. He is looking to Ruth to do the work for him.

In the second response, Ruth resists responding to Ted's transference and immediately takes steps to ensure that Ted understands her role. She affirms his interest in prayer but adopts an adult–adult style of communication, talking to Ted straight away about the value of him doing his own exploring and her willingness to listen and help him find his own way with God.

✠

Let's look at the example of Sam who has been seeing Sally, a woman in her early twenties, for spiritual direction for a few months. She has willingly talked about her journey, until today when she arrives late:

Sam   Hi, Sally – good to see you. *(A few minutes general conversation follows before Sam says):* What would you like to bring to spiritual direction today?
Sally   I haven't got a clue. *(Her tone is abrupt)*

Sam	Oh . . . well, let's take a few moments and see what comes to mind. *(There is a rather strained pause)*
Sally	I don't really know what I want to talk about. In fact, I really wonder what I'm doing here talking to you about all this God stuff – I mean, you can't even prove God exists, can you?
Sam	Well . . . *(he is interrupted)* . . .
Sally	It feels a bit like being at school – coming to the teacher and getting my homework checked.

☙ What might be going through your mind if you were Sam?

Without realizing it, Sally has transferred her reactions to someone in her past onto Sam and this is upsetting the working alliance. It would be understandable if Sam felt confused, defensive or indignant. Unsettled by her rudeness, he may become tentative in his response to her, replaying an unconscious dynamic that belongs to *his* earlier interactions with critical adults. In other words, counter-transference would be operating.

He might back down, assuming the situation is his fault:

Sam	Oh, dear me, I'm really sorry, Sally. I only wanted to help you find out more about God. I feel awful that I've let you down.

Or square off for a fight:

Sam	Of course you're not coming to get your homework checked! How on earth could you think that I'd treat you like a naughty child! Surely you think more of me than that!

✠

As spiritual directors, we need to be alert, suspecting counter-transference if we find ourselves:

1 being depressed or annoyed during or after conversations with certain directees;
2 experiencing fearfulness or loss of confidence as a result of a directee's disagreement or anger;
3 having difficulty putting aside people's possible status in the Church or in society when focusing on their spiritual life;
4 intervening in the directee's life outside the direction setting;
5 dreaming about the directee;

6 having a sudden change in interest, either an increase or decrease, in the directee;

7 experiencing a strong desire to discuss the directee with others;

8 feeling concern about one's reputation if the direction relationship succeeds or fails;

9 asking the directee for favours or help with non-direction-related matters;

10 wanting to impress the directee;

11 having difficulty grasping blocks in the spirituality of a directee that are similar to one's own problematic areas;

12 avoiding discussion of a particular directee in supervision.[129]

As the person responsible for the smooth functioning of the spiritual direction relationship, it is up to the director, Sam, to respond to Sally's unexpected criticism without being drawn into an argument or self-defence. So, using his normal tone of voice (not 'wounded' or whining!) he may say something like:

Sam	I'm really surprised to hear that, Sally. Last time we spoke you said you'd been finding our sessions helpful. I'm wondering what has changed since then?
Sally	It's just that you asked me about that journalling stuff last time, and when I haven't done any I feel guilty.
Sam	Does that feeling remind you of anyone or anything in particular? *(Sally stops and thinks)*
Sally	Well, actually – it reminds me of when I used to go to maths and Mr Smythe would look at me and I'd know he knew I hadn't done any work. And I'd get a real ticking off which made me feel sick – and that's how I was feeling as I came here today, because I hadn't written anything in my journal.
Sam	Do you think that you ought to journal all the time?
Sally	Well, that's what you said.
Sam	I'm sorry if I gave you that impression, Sally – it's certainly not what I intended. Keeping a spiritual journal is just something that some people find helpful to keep track of their journey with God. It's not meant to be a straitjacket.
Sally	I thought you wanted me to journal every day?
Sam	You can journal as little or as often as you want to. What have you been trying to do?
Sally	Well, I bought a big scrapbook and started to write in it every day – but it sort of fizzled after about a couple of weeks. I'd been trying to understand

---

129 Summarized from Wicks, Robert J., 'Counter-transference in Spiritual Direction', in *Human Development*, 6(3), Fall 1985.

that book you said I should read – what was it called, *Meeting Jesus Again* or something, but I wasn't getting anywhere.

Sam   Sally, I think there are a couple of things that need clarifying. First your journal is for your eyes only – yours and God's. No one else need ever see it.

Sally   Aren't you going to ask me to show you?

Sam   No, I'm not – if you have something that you want to talk to me about from your journal, that's fine – but it's your journal and your choice. The other thing that you mentioned – my wanting you to read that book. As I recall, we talked about several books, so that you could choose one that *you* wanted to read. It's *your* faith journey, Sally. My job is not to tell you what to do or think but to walk alongside you for a while, listening to where your story and God's story connect.

🕯 What do you notice now about Sam's approach?

What spiritual direction issues does this dialogue illustrate for you?

Sam and Sally have weathered a potential disturbance in their relationship because Sam was able to take a non-defensive stance. Whatever he may have been feeling (and remember he can take his responses to supervision for further reflection if necessary), he managed to keep focused on what he was there for. Sam was also prepared to apologise for any misunderstanding to which he may have contributed. He did not blame Sally for her interpretation of events but sought to clarify areas of confusion when he realized that Sally was uncertain about his role.

Even though at their first meeting Sam may have clearly stated that spiritual direction is about the directee's journey with God, it can take some directees a while to get used to exercising the freedom of choice which this approach encourages. Sam is reinforcing for Sally that she is the one responsible for her own spiritual journey and he is a companion on the way. Although he may sometimes offer a range of resources to help her on that journey, the choice always remains hers as she prays and reflects on her growing relationship with God.

5.8 Listening to someone from a different faith tradition – Jenny

Hazel calls in to see Alan, a terminally ill parishioner, and his daughter, recently returned from overseas.

Hazel   *(Coming out of Alan's bedroom)* We've had a good talk but he says he's ready for a rest now. *(They sit down with a cold drink)* This can't be easy, Jenny. How are you doing?

Jenny   Oh, you know, OK most of the time and then it just sort of sweeps over me and I go down to the bottom of the garden with a cushion and just shout into it – yell and howl and cry – it's not fair – Dad's a good man.

Hazel   He is a good man. It must be hard to come home and see him going down-hill like this.

Jenny   When I went away he was fine – still digging his garden and going for walks with Toby and he was making plans for us to have a holiday together in Nepal – he always wanted to see the really high mountains. Now he'll never get his wish . . . *(There is a thoughtful silence)*

Hazel   What's it like for you, being back here after your time away?

Jenny   Well – I wouldn't want to be anywhere else of course because I love my dad and it's the most important thing for me to be here with him, but there are some things I really miss.

☨ Take some time to notice what you are thinking as you look back through this dialogue.

Hazel may have left Alan's bedroom relieved that she now knows what funeral arrangements he wants; or she may be preoccupied, wondering about whether he acknowledges Christ as his Saviour. She may be thinking about the next couple of weeks, her busy schedule and hoping that Alan doesn't die in the middle of it, or she may be personally sad to see her parishioner, someone she's known for several years, nearing the end of his life.

However, whatever Hazel's thoughts, she quickly pays attention to Jenny, conveys empathy for her sad homecoming and establishes enough of a relationship for Jenny to give a truthful answer to Hazel's concern, rather than a stoical rebuff. After their first bit of conversation, although she has noticed it, Hazel is choosing not to respond immediately to Jenny's comment 'It's not fair', but to keep it in her mind for later.

Hazel   What sort of things do you miss?

Jenny   The rhythm of each day is so different here – I find it hard to meditate when there's so much noise and when there's no one else around who knows what it was like in that Buddhist monastery. I mean, I was there for a year and now it feels kind of remote, as if I experienced it in another life somewhere and it has nothing to do with the life I live here and now.

☨ Now what are you thinking? Feeling?

If Hazel has little experience of, or knowledge about Buddhism, she may adopt a defensive position of uninformed superiority and shut down the conversation by implying that what Jenny has experienced is going to lead her away from God; or she may feel a little unsettled, even afraid, of someone who is travelling a different spiritual path. Hazel may briefly share something of her own struggles to practise listening or centring prayer in the midst of busy, noisy, city life; or, noticing the longing Jenny is expressing, give her space to share a bit more about it. And that is what Hazel chooses to do by asking one simple, open question:

Hazel What was your meditation practice there, Jenny?

With this simple question, Hazel is demonstrating presence, respect and a willing-ness to find out more about Jenny's spirituality and how it may resource her as she attends her father in his dying. Where that conversation will lead them, God alone knows; Hazel's task is to be a vehicle of God's grace, not a source of more dis-ease and pain.

5.9 Listening to someone who is grieving – Alex

We use the term 'grieving' to describe the normal process people go through as they adjust to *any* significant[130] loss in their lives. The length of this process varies according to the person's attachment to what has been lost, and the circumstances. In a major loss, such as that of a life partner, grieving can extend for years.

One of the gifts we can give our directees is to walk alongside them as they mourn, knowing that times of major loss are also times of potential growth if people are well supported. We can better support them if we have done our own grief work and know some of the dynamics of grieving. Courses in pastoral care normally cover the process of grief, death and dying, so I will only mention briefly some major contributors.

Elisabeth Kübler-Ross's foundational work[131] described a five-part model of grief *in the dying*: shock and denial, anger, bargaining, depression, and accept-ance. This was initially interpreted by many of those working with the dying as a strictly linear model, with the expectation that all dying people would pass through each 'stage'. Nowadays, while this model can still be a useful tool, we know that not everyone goes through all these phases, nor does everyone reach 'acceptance'. People tend to die as they have lived – facing reality or denying it, talking a lot about what is happening, or doing their anticipatory grief work in the privacy of their own minds, with one or two trusted friends – or not at all.

---

130 The significance of the loss is determined by the person who experiences it, not by anyone else.

131 Kübler-Ross, Elisabeth, *On Death and Dying*, Macmillan, 1976.

Westberg's book *Good Grief*[132] has been in print since it first appeared in the 1960s. It lists ten 'stages' on the journey of the bereaved: shock, emotional release, physical reactions, depression, anger, guilt, idealization (for example putting the deceased or homeland on a pedestal), realization (for example the deceased had his faults, the 'old country' wasn't perfect), new patterns of living and, finally, living with the loss. When this model was first introduced, and to some extent even today, those companioning the bereaved can still expect or encourage them to move neatly through the sequence, irrespective of the individual nature of their loss. However, if you have grieved a major loss, you know that the process is not neat and tidy but can be messy, exhausting and unpredictable. Reality is more like the model recently developed by Stroebe and Schut[133] who noted that grieving people tend to 'oscillate' between times of being focused on what they have lost (loss orientation) and adjusting to change, and times of moving back from the demands of grieving to give themselves space (restoration orientation). In effect, people can only deal with their loss for so long and need to distance themselves periodically from the truth of the loss.

Alex's wife Sadie died three months ago. The vicar, Tom, who has visited twice since the funeral, has not been able to arrange for the interment of Sadie's ashes, as Alex refuses to talk about it. Meg, the parish pastoral worker, is 'sent' to visit with instructions to see if Alex is ready to 'do something about the ashes'. Having visited Sadie several times, Meg is known to Alex, but this is her first visit since the time immediately after Sadie's death.

🔔 If you were Meg, how might you feel about being sent to visit with this specific task in mind? How would you prepare?

The first few minutes are spent in general conversation about the funeral.

Meg   How are you really getting on, Alex?

Alex   It's very quiet now that the family's all gone back to their lives – my grand-kids are a noisy bunch! Sadie always got on with them better somehow, so in a way it's quite good to have the place to myself, but I have to admit, it's lonely without her. I didn't realize how much we did together until after she'd gone – just little things, you know, like preparing dinner together. Something Sadie insisted on, always said, 'I'm not going to leave you so helpless you can only boil an egg!' *(He smiles)*

Meg   Judging from these muffins, Sadie taught you a lot before she died.

---

132 Westberg, Granger E., *Good Grief: A Constructive Approach to the Problem of Loss*, Augsburg Fortress, published in Australia by Desbooks, Thornbury, 1992.

133 Stroebe, M. and Schut, H., 'The Dual Process Model of Coping with Bereavement: Rationale and Description', in *Death Studies*, 23(3), 1999, pp. 197–224.

Alex   She certainly did – not just cooking but courage, real courage, Meg. I don't know if I could have endured what she went through with such determination and sheer guts.

Meg   She was very brave, Alex. I admired her, I really did.
(There is silence for a moment as they remember Sadie; Meg prays, takes a deep breath)
Tom was wondering where you're up to in your thinking about Sadie's ashes.

Alex   I wondered if he'd sent you round!

Meg   Well, he thought it might be easier for you to talk about it with me – but there's no rush, you know, Alex; nothing has to be done until you're ready.

Alex   I don't know – I mean I've got them sitting over there *(he gestures towards the corner and Meg notices the wooden box on the mantelpiece)*. You probably think I'm silly, but it's sort of like still having her around somehow . . .

Meg   I don't think you're silly Alex.

Alex   But I don't suppose I can have them there for ever.

Meg   What's the hardest thing – when you think about her ashes not being here?

Alex   It's like the final step – the last connection with her would be gone.

Meg   You don't want to give up that tangible sign of her presence? *(He shakes his head and there is another silence)* What would make it easier for you to release these ashes?

Alex   . . . If I could just believe that she was all right, somewhere better.

Meg   It's hard for you to believe that right now?

Alex   I don't know where God is any more – everything's just gone flat. I make myself get up in the morning, but the days can be quite long. Sadie was a good woman – she shouldn't have had to go through this. I mean, I don't blame God for her death – her mum and sister had the same cancer, but I just don't seem to feel God's presence any more.

Meg   What was it like before?

Alex   Well, when I was outside – walking in the woods or fishing down at the river – I'd often have a sort of feeling that I was somehow part of everything. And then when Sadie and I went to some choral services, the music would just *(he touches his heart)* get me right here – and somehow it was wonderful, and I'd know I was linked to something special, something that would last . . .

Meg   . . . to something eternal . . . even to God?

Alex   Yes – to God. And that's not happening any more – I sort of feel a bit numb most of the time and I guess if I'm honest, Meg, I've lost Sadie, and now I'm scared I've lost God too.

⚷ What issues seem uppermost for Alex at the moment?

✠

Meg has enabled Alex to face and name what he is afraid of – the disappearance of the God whom he has experienced through creation and music. It would be easy for Meg to slip into 'fix-it' mode or to utter platitudes assuring Alex that there's no chance he'll lose God. However, her first response is to offer Alex the chance to say a little more about what he is afraid of:

Meg   You're scared that you've lost God too? Can you say a bit more about that?

Alex   Well, God's always been part of my life – one of my favourite childhood memories is of sitting in the stable with my pony one Christmas and smelling the hay and thinking about the baby Jesus smelling that same sort of smell all those years ago. And when I met Sadie it was as if I knew somewhere deep inside that God had given her to me.

Meg   And now you're worried that God's left you on your own, just when you need God more than ever?

Alex   That's about it. *(There is silence for a minute. Meg wonders whether she should respond to the 'left alone' theme which Alex has expressed or whether to invite him to look more closely at his daily experience to see if there are any glimpses of God's presence. She opts for the first, choosing to approach it through Jesus)*

Meg   If you think about Jesus – are there any times when he felt really alone?

Alex   Well, his disciples weren't much use to him in the Garden, were they, or later when they all ran away – he must have felt alone. And then, of course – he said, didn't he, something like, 'My God, why have you forsaken me?' when he was on the cross?

Meg   Yes, he did – 'My God, my God, why have you forsaken me?'

Alex   He must have felt more alone than anyone could ever feel. *(They are both silent)*

Meg   So Jesus would understand how you are feeling at the moment.

Alex   Yes *(thoughtfully)*, I guess he would. At least I've got people I can call if I feel low.

Meg   So you've got people to ring if you need them?

Alex   Yes, I have, but, well, when I think about it I haven't actually needed to. Most days something's happened that's got me out of the house, or cheered me up a little bit.

Meg   What sort of things?

> *(Alex talks about neighbourly care, a surprise invitation to join a walking group, regular calls from a friend)*

Meg   As you remember all those things, Alex – what's happening for you?

Alex   Well, as I think about it, there seem to have been a lot of small things that have helped me since Sadie died – nothing spectacular, just a steady stream of small things that are making it a bit easier.

Meg   'A steady stream of small things that are making it a bit easier.' Shall we just sit with that for a moment . . .

Alex   *(He pauses for a minute)* There's that saying, 'thank God for small mercies' . . . Perhaps God's meeting me in different ways at the moment – in all the little things that make life without Sadie a bit more bearable.

Meg   What would that mean for you – if God were present in every act of kindness and love you're experiencing through your family and friends and neighbours?

Alex   Well, to be honest, Meg, I've never thought of it that way before – that when people are kind it's like God's caring for me through them – gosh – that's what Sadie would call 'a big thought'!

A fortnight later, Alex rang the vicar and arranged for the interment of Sadie's ashes.

Of course, for the purposes of this book the dialogue has been condensed – it may take longer for Alex to be able to name any glimpses of grace in his world as he grieves; it may take longer for him to see the care of friends as an indicator of God's care for him. However, this dialogue tells us that while we need to honour people's grieving, in spiritual direction we ignore the core of our practice if we do not gently invite them to notice tiny moments of consolation and comfort, the 'small mercies' which, if acknowledged, can bring a touch of respite into the rawness of grief.

In doing this, we are not trying to minimize or 'spiritualize' the loss; we don't encourage people to take a short cut in the process of grieving but to receive any glimpses of grace as 'food for the journey' as the road of recovery unfolds. We do not manufacture meaning to fit into our preconceptions that God is at work; we simply *attend* to what we are hearing in the life of the other, trusting the Spirit to reveal signs of God's grace.

5.10 Listening for the 'dark night' or the perceived absence of God – Derek

As usual, imagine that you are a minister, listening with your spiritual direction 'antennae' up. Pay attention, too, to your own inner responses as you read aloud or role-play this dialogue.

Sandy is surprised when Derek, a middle-aged priest from another denomination whom he has met a few times at the ministers' monthly lunch meeting, phones and asks if he can come and see him.

Sandy   You've got something on your mind, Derek?

Derek   Yes, I have – thanks for making time to see me. I really didn't want to talk about this with my wife or with any of my colleagues. *(Silence)*

Sandy   Well – just take your time. *(Long pause)*

Derek   It's . . . well, to put it bluntly, the problem is that God has disappeared.

Sandy   Disappeared?

Derek   Yes – completely. All the ways I've prayed and felt close to God in the past have just stopped working. I've used the Daily Office for years and it's always fed me and helped start off the day well . . . and even writing sermons, the intellectual wrestling with concepts and working out how best to get them across to others which I really enjoyed, that process just seems flat and empty now, although I go through the motions. It's like the tide has gone out and left me high and dry.

Sandy   'High and dry' – what's that like for you, to be 'high and dry'?

Derek   It's lonely . . . and it scares me. I mean, I'm supposed to be the one who helps everyone else get closer to God, and now here I am feeling as if God's done a runner.

Sandy   You're wondering how you can possibly lead others if God's vanished?

Derek   Yes – sometimes I feel like a hypocrite standing up there preaching about God's presence and love when all I feel is God's absence and . . . *(he hesitates, lowering his head)*

Sandy   *(Very gently)* . . . and what, Derek?

Derek   *(Tears fill his eyes, and almost in a whisper)* . . . it feels like he's abandoned me . . . I don't know why, I've given my whole life to him, and although it's been hard at times, I've known a real joy in my ministry – but now . . . *(another long pause)*

Sandy   It feels like the whole thing's turned to custard?

Derek   Exactly.

🕯 Note your responses and then consider what you think could be happening for Derek.

In companioning Derek, Sandy would initially have some or all of the following in mind:

- Providing a safe environment in which Derek can talk without risking condemnation.
- Helping Derek connect with any scriptural examples of people experiencing a sense of God's absence (for example Jesus on the cross, Psalm 13).
- Encouraging him to share his feelings honestly with God or Jesus in spite of their 'absence'.
- Wondering exactly how Derek is praying, what is and is not happening.
- Trying to gauge whether this felt sense of God's absence is moving Derek away from God or whether Derek's commitment to God remains unwavering or is actually intensifying.
- Wondering if Derek is clinically depressed.

If Derek trusts Sandy enough to continue to meet regularly for spiritual direction, then further exploration would include the possible *causes* of this perceived absence of God. These may be:

- *personal*, for example Derek's paying less attention to God; unexpressed anger or disappointment with God; rebellion; or engaging in inappropriate behaviour;
- *life circumstances*, for example major transition; depression; family illness or chronic pain; loss or grief; exhaustion;
- *God's activity*, i.e. a movement initiated by God to draw Derek closer in love, although it won't appear positive to Derek at first.

If the causes are *personal*, Sandy would help Derek face these and take appropriate steps, for example if Derek had been neglecting his spiritual practices, he would agree to making time for prayer a priority and sharing inner feelings with God to bring his prayer life back on track. If in spiritual direction Derek identifies any areas of sin and is ready to acknowledge his shortcomings, the question of *confession* arises. How this is done will vary according to both Derek and Sandy's traditions:

- It may be primarily a verbal prayer of confession that takes place during the spiritual direction session, followed by a sharing of scriptures which speak of God's mercy and Sandy's reminder of God's forgiveness.
- If Derek is from a sacramental tradition and Sandy is not, then Sandy could encourage Derek to consider seeking the ministry of Reconciliation or Confession of a Penitent, in which Derek could receive a formal assurance of absolution according to the ritual of his tradition.

- If both Sandy and Derek are from a sacramental tradition, they can discuss whether or not Sandy should act as priest to Derek or whether Derek would prefer to go to someone else. If Derek wants Sandy to hear his confession, they may decide to do this by meeting at Sandy's church for a special time of prayer and absolution. This sets the act apart and indicates a temporary shift in Sandy's role to that of confessor.

☙ What part has the ritual of confession and absolution played in your own spiritual life?

If this is not part of your tradition, how do you experience God's forgiveness?

How might you help others receive assurance of God's mercy?

If the causes stem from *life circumstances*, spiritual direction would help Derek acknowledge the difficulties and losses, seek appropriate support, ask God for what he needs, assess adequate self-care and be alert for signs of grace in the middle of these circumstances.

Because spiritual dark nights and depression can both include feelings of hopelessness and emptiness, and can affect a person's thoughts, motivation and confidence, spiritual directors need to be able to distinguish between them. Sandy would compare what he knows of depression with his understanding of the 'dark night' – perhaps using Gerald May's guidelines:

1 Dark-night experiences are not usually associated with loss of effectiveness in life or work, as are primary depressions. Often, in fact, the individual is mystified at how well he or she is continuing to function. This is especially true in terms of the individual helping others on their spiritual journeys.
2 Surprisingly, sense of humour is usually retained after dark-night experiences. This humour is not cynical or bitter as it might be in mild depression; it retains an almost sparkling quality.
3 Compassion for others is, if anything, enhanced after dark-night experiences. There is little or none of the self-absorption seen in clinical depression.
4 In the dark night, one would not really have things otherwise. While there may be great superficial dissatisfaction and confusion, the most honest answer, the deepest response is that in spite of everything there is an underlying sense of rightness about it all. This is in stark contrast to primary depression, in which one's deepest sense is of wrongness and, consciously at least, the desire for radical, even miraculous, change is pervasive.
5 A person experiencing the dark night does not seem to be pleading for help, as does a clinically depressed person. Explanations and evaluations may be sought, but seldom is there communication of anything like 'Get me out of this.'

6 Very subtly, yet perhaps most importantly, one does not generally feel frustrated, resentful, or annoyed in the presence of a person undergoing a dark-night experience. While such feelings are common in working with depressed people because of their own internalized anger, one is much more likely to feel graced and consoled with someone experiencing the dark night.[134]

If this sense of God's absence does not seem to stem from personal or life issues or depression, Sandy would help Derek explore the probability that God is at work in a new way in Derek's life. Perhaps there is the beginning of a shift from kataphatic prayer to apophatic prayer[135] and/or the onset of the classic 'dark night' as described by St John of the Cross, during which all that has hitherto helped Derek stay connected to God is stripped away:

> . . . the losses experienced in prayer that John describes with the metaphor of darkness are caused by an intensification of contemplation or *God's self-communication* to the person, which purifies the person, first at the level of the sense, and then at the level of the spirit, so that, eventually, the entire person may be one with God, transformed in divine knowledge and love.[136]

Sandy's next step is to take time to help Derek articulate in some detail what is happening in his prayer life so that together they can discern Derek's *readiness* for a possible change to contemplative prayer. John of the Cross would encourage spiritual directors to look for the presence of three signs which together indicate that a person is being led by the Holy Spirit towards greater union with God:

1 The person no longer finds meditation – on scripture, symbols from nature, particular events, etc. satisfying or attractive or helpful in building relationship with God.
2 There is a reluctance to engage the senses and the imagination to help the person connect with God – almost a sense of having explored all the words and images of faith as far as one can.
3 There is a growing desire simply to be lovingly aware of God, even to 'waste time' with God, and to let the rational faculties quieten. Active meditation ceases.[137]

Sandy would be aware that the first two signs together could be the result of life circumstances and/or mental health issues. But the presence of the third sign along

---

134 May, Gerald, *Care of Mind, Care of Spirit: a Psychiatrist Explores Spiritual Direction*, New York: HarperCollins, 1992, pp. 109–10.

135 See Chapter 3, section 3.1, Praying – movements in prayer.

136 Culligan, 'The Dark Night and Depression', in *Presence, An Internationl Journal of Spiritual Direction*, 10(1), February 2004, pp. 9–19, italics mine.

137 Adapted from Culligan, 'The Dark Night and Depression'.

with the other two indicates this is God at work in Derek, fanning the flame of desire for more of God than can be received and known through the human will, intellect or imagination:

Sandy   Can you tell me a little bit more about how your prayer life has been over the years?

Derek   Well, many years ago I used to talk to God a lot during the day, then gradually that somehow began to give way to spending more time meditating – you know, I'd imagine myself in the Gospels as someone Jesus was talking to and letting myself respond to him; there were some really moving encounters which I still remember clearly. And I'd have a list of people to pray for and tick off when prayers got answered and I used to really enjoy the liturgical colours of the year, and favourite hymns; and things in creation – birds, butterflies, the fragrance of a rose – that sort of thing would remind me of God, help me feel closer to him.

Sandy   So prayer was spoken aloud, you were using your senses a lot, noticing things in creation, praying for others, meditating on scripture was fruitful.

Derek   Well, yes – I think I've prayed that way for a long time.

Sandy   And more recently?

Derek   Over the last few months it's been getting quieter – actually when I come to think of it, instead of rattling off a long list of people, I sort of sit and in my imagination I just bring them to God, but even that's starting to change. It's like there's something going on inside me – it's almost like God's up to something and I'm just 'turning up' – does that make any sense to you?

Sandy   There are times when God quietens our sensory self, and our mind's activity. We 'turn up' as you put it, and put ourselves at God's disposal – so God can work directly in our spirit.

Derek   That's what it feels like – I just turn up and God does what God wants to do – there's no striving to make anything happen.

Sandy   And that's totally different from how you used to pray?

Derek   Yes – it's such a contrast that I thought I must be doing something wrong.

Sandy   For some people it's a natural part of their spiritual journey. Would it be helpful if you could read a bit about this sort of prayer?

Derek   Yes, that would be a good idea. *(They spend a few minutes looking at books and articles before Derek makes his choice)* Do you think God's bringing about this change in my prayer?

Sandy   Well, something is happening. How about you have a look at these and then give me a ring and we can talk about it some more if you'd like to.

Neither Sandy nor Derek knows when or how or even whether 'the tide' will return – something fundamental may well have shifted for Derek, but there is hope that he will know a new intimacy with God, a greater level of trust and a new awareness of God in his deepest centre.

What spiritual direction issues are raised for you as you read this dialogue?
What is your experience of 'dark night' places in your prayer life?
What personal questions arise for you from this material?

The primary role of a spiritual director working with someone experiencing an unsettling change in their prayer is to recognize what *may* be happening, provide a safe space in which to explore the reasons behind the change, and help discern whether God is leading the directee into a prayer of greater intimacy. Even if directors have not experienced this form of prayer themselves, they can still offer informed understanding, companionship and encouragement. Familiarizing ourselves with the traditional concepts of growth in union which were introduced in Chapter 3, section 3.1, are important in companioning someone like Derek.

Suggestions for further reading

Dark night/The perceived absence of God/Disappointment with God

The Bible, e.g. Psalms 13, 22; Isaiah 45.
Burrows, Ruth, *Ascent to Love: the Spiritual Teaching of St John of the Cross*, London: Darton, Longman and Todd, 1987.
Culligan, Kevin, 'The Dark Night and Depression', in *Presence: An International Journal of Spiritual Direction*, 10(1), February 2004.
May, Gerald, *The Dark Night of the Soul*, New York: HarperSanFrancisco, 2005.
Walsh, J., (ed.), *The Cloud of Unknowing*, New Jersey: Paulist Press, 1981 (Classics of Western Spirituality series).
Yancey, Philip, *Where is God When it Hurts?*, Grand Rapids, MI: Zondervan, 2002.

Grief, loss or abuse

Cochrane, Jeannie, *Spiritual Abuse*, New Zealand: Spiritual Growth Ministries, 2000. Full text: <www.sgm.org.nz/research_papers.htm>.
Reeve, Nancy, *Found Through Loss*, British Columbia: Northstone, 2003.
Rupp, Joyce, *Praying our Goodbyes*, Notre Dame, IN: Ave Maria Press, 1988
Westberg, Granger E., *Good Grief: A Constructive Approach to the Problem of Loss*, Augsburg Fortress, published in Australia by Desbooks, Thornbury, 1992.

Sexuality and spirituality

The Bible: The Song of Songs.

Cotter, Jim, *Pleasure, Pain and Passion: Some Perspectives on Sexuality and Spirituality*, Exeter: Cairns Publications, 1988.

Couvela, Stephanie, *Celebrating Celibacy: Sexuality, Intimacy and Wholeness for the Single Adult*, Cambridge: Grove Books, 2007.

Larsen, Ron, *Spiritual Direction and Gay Christians*, New Zealand: Spiritual Growth Ministries, 1999. Full text: <www.sgm.org.nz/research_papers.htm>.

Ruffing, Janet K., *Spiritual Direction: Beyond the Beginnings*, New York: Paulist Press, 2000 (Chapter 4, 'Love Mysticism in Spiritual Direction').

Whitehead, Evelyn E. and Whitehead, James D., *Wisdom of the Body: Making Sense of our Sexuality*, New York: Crossroads, 2001.

6

Spiritual Direction in Parish, Chaplaincy and Community Contexts

6.1 The contemplative stance

In this section, you will hear not only my 'voice' which has accompanied you for many pages, but also the 'voices' and gathered wisdom of others[138] – parish ministers, chaplains and a community worker, who are also spiritual directors in the contemplative incarnational tradition. Like them, we can choose to approach every encounter, every activity, every meeting from a contemplative stance, *trusting* that God is already at work in people's lives, *listening* to the Holy Spirit, to others and to oneself, *watching* for signs of God's grace, *exploring* people's everyday experience, *wondering* with them about their sense of God's presence or absence, or the shape of God's invitation to growth. As Brian Hamilton, Anglican vicar and spiritual director, comments:

> The change of focus in pastoral ministry to that of spiritual director means that whenever I am with people in a variety of ministry situations, I am constantly asking myself: 'How can I foster this person's, or this group's relationship with God? Are there signs of God's voice or activity in this person's life? Can I help this person become aware of such activity?' When I do this I realise that, '. . . being a spiritual director doesn't mean introducing a new rule or adding another item to [my] ever-extended job descriptions, but simply rearranging [my] perspective: seeing certain acts as eternal and not ephemeral, as essential and not accidental.'[139] . . . I simply call attention to what is already happening.[140]

---

138 To protect their identity and that of their faith or work communities, the following *noms-de-plume* are used: Anna, Tim, Kevin, Dani, Ian, John, Winnie, Zoe, Andrew, Christine, Richard. Their material was communicated to me in 2007 and is not published elsewhere.

139 Peterson, Eugene H., *Working the Angles*, Grand Rapids, MI: Eerdmans, 1987. p. 153.

140 Hamilton, Brian, *Spiritual Direction as the Model for Pastoral Ministry*, Spiritual Growth Ministries Trust: New Zealand, 2001, p. 4. For full text see <www.sgm.org.nz/research_papers.htm>.

Whatever our context, learning to minister from this perspective makes a difference not only to others but to ourselves and can help us avoid the sort of frustration which Richard, a mature Methodist minister, describes:

> Parish ministry was different from my expectations. Meetings, church politics, toeing the church line and espousing the ethos of the denomination, became mixed up with the personal privilege of being trusted with people's trauma . . . At 58, I felt time was running out and if I didn't make a claim for the spiritual ministry I felt called to, I might as well give it all up.

Richard's dilemma surfaced at a time when he had the support of a small group outside his parish who encouraged him to enter a spiritual directors' formation programme. The two-year process, which included regularly seeing a spiritual director, and attending a seven-day silent, directed retreat, helped Richard give God space to re-form his entire outlook. Now, although still involved in some administration, Richard and his ministry have changed:

> I have felt held up by Christ . . . I have gone from finance meetings involving millions to being one on one with a directee and have found that feeling of 'sinking into God's presence' at both . . . Not only has Jesus changed the burden of ministry but ministry has changed in other ways. Pastoral visiting has become special. Dying people share their fears and their hopes of God. In meeting people anywhere the skills and insights of contemplative spiritual direction have made a difference . . . even when picking up hitch-hikers while travelling about the district, people have opened up in a way I hadn't experienced before . . . I am invited into God's conversation with a complete stranger. I see all of it (*ministry*) as being in God's presence with so many different people in so many different kinds of places . . . for me this is joy . . . that 'lightness' of living is within me.

This brief glimpse into Richard's journey highlights the new energy and hopefulness permeating ministry and life as the focus of parish ministry moves back to the traditional 'cure of souls', to paying attention to the ways God is already reaching out to people in their prayer or life experiences.

This focus can also form the core of much chaplaincy work, as Anna describes:

> Spiritual direction takes seriously the ways in which people experience the divine/Spirit in their lives . . . treating these experiences with respect and inviting people to savour and explore these experiences, can open up a new spiritual space for people or deepen an existing relationship . . . (even) in a context in which secularism and rationality are often lauded. Chaplaincy which grows out of a contemplative posture, which is informed by spiritual direction as a model,

cultivates moments of silence. For me this is expressed in a variety of ways: caring for a physical space (*the chapel*) which offers a haven of silence in the middle of campus life, offering contemplative prayer opportunities which make room for silence and also in what I carry with me as I go about the campus: space in me for silence, space to allow the other to speak into, space to listen to oneself speak . . . Letting conversations enjoy moments of silence invites the possibility that we will hear God speak.

Tim also speaks of the importance of 'space':

Chaplaincy is for me a ministry of hospitality – of opening and holding open a space, a sacred space, for each person or group I have contact with as I 'loiter with intent' around the campus. The contemplative stance of spiritual direction facilitates a generous and compassionate attentiveness to the other, to God, and to myself. People talk to me because of who I am as well as who/what I represent. I am perceived as both a safe person and a safe place.

This focus frees us to approach each conversation with expectation and the possibility of blessing, not only for the person to whom we are listening, but for us as well; regularly hearing how God is at work in the lives of others is deeply encouraging.

✠

Reflection questions

⚱ Reflect on where you are in your own ministry – you might want to draw a diagram or timeline to show the shape it has taken so far, noting the high points and struggles.

⚱ How does Richard's frustration and longing to reclaim the spiritual focus of ministry resonate with your own story?

⚱ Re-read Anna's comments about chaplaincy being informed by spiritual direction practice and principles. How does this description relate to your context?

⚱ What is your experience of 'holding open a sacred space' for others?
How do you respond to the idea of being 'a safe person and a safe place'?

6.2 Spiritual direction in pastoral ministry

Two questions will be addressed in this section. First, 'What are the pluses and minuses of offering regular spiritual direction to our parishioners or people we meet in our chaplaincies?'

Zoe, vicar of a large urban parish, believes that parish clergy should offer spiritual direction 'as part of the tools of their trade'. For parishioners who want individual spiritual direction, Zoe's practice is to offer them three or four individual sessions, after which people are referred 'either to a group that can support this exploration, or to a spiritual director, or to both'.

Winnie is also a vicar, but she chooses to have longer-term directees. She only accepts as many directees as the time she has allotted allows. Her parishioners sometimes worry but, Winnie says, 'It is not an issue of boundaries, or of role confusion, but knowing how busy a parish our size is, they're concerned that they're being unfairly favoured by getting an hour of my time every month!'

Ian, a Baptist pastor, comments with enthusiasm:

As often happens after discovering a new tool, I was sold on the benefits of spiritual direction for any who expressed an interest. I quickly developed a clientele among parishioners and others. At first I was convinced that a commitment to professionalism and regular supervision would sort out any difficulties arising from relating to parishioners in a dual role. And in many ways the ministry of spiritual direction has been glorious in the lives of my directees. It has been thrilling to see people grow in God as they have explored their spiritual lives through direction. In my early zeal, I felt vindicated: I had found something that worked . . .

But there are some cautions to negotiate:

- Too many directees may take time away from other essential tasks.
- Resistance to spiritual growth may surface and cause unrest.
- Managing dual roles with directees who are also colleagues or parishioners requires discipline.

Zoe also noted: 'Those who go to their own clergy for spiritual direction may find that the clergy have an unspoken agenda for their participation in the parish; attention-seeking people may ask for pastoral counselling or spiritual direction, so clergy need discernment and good boundaries to handle this.'

Unlike our contact with those who *seek us* out, in parish visiting and in chaplaincy walkabouts, *we* may be the ones initiating contact. So the second question has to do with how the 'routine' pastoral visit moves from social conversation (valuable though that is for relationship-building between minister and parishioner), and into the building of the parishioner's relationship with God? Being alert for conversations that have the potential to open up areas of spiritual need and exploration, welcoming questions as harbingers of growth, is part of the process, as Dani, a retired Presbyterian minister, describes:

> When one elderly parishioner asked me, during a visit to her home, if I could teach her how to write a spiritual journal, I realized that here was an opportunity to help people to journey further with God. So I collected some quotes on journalling and used these to help her and others, as the idea caught on, to reflect and write up their discoveries. Then, when I visited, we would sit with a cup of tea and discuss what they'd written about . . . And, unless there was a very good reason not to, I would read a suitable Psalm or Gospel portion and pray with each individual around the things we had been discussing. This also helped to focus my pastoral work on *people's lived experiences of God and grace* as well as the issues of the day. It became such an important part of home visits that if it looked liked I might leave without doing this some would remind me of it!

Ian also discovered that spiritual direction skills and attitudes could be applied more widely than with committed directees in structured sessions. When visiting, he keeps in mind the question: 'What is the Holy Spirit doing here in, with and around this person?' He listens for content that reveals people's spiritual needs, i.e. issues around guilt and forgiveness, meaning, hope and purpose, fear of death, or difficult life experiences which raise questions about the nature or existence of God. By asking questions such as, 'Where do you think God might be in this?' or 'How are you praying about this?' Ian moves the focus to the person's relationship with God, however tenuous or ambivalent that might be.

Andrew is pastor of a small, rural parish with people from nine different denominational backgrounds. When he visits, he talks with people about their daily lives, alert for points of connection and ways of going deeper. He avoids jargon, instead using everyday language to help people engage with the spiritual life. For example, he speaks about prayer as 'noticing God's active role in our everyday lives', or draws on Margaret Silf's understanding that 'we are at prayer whenever we are really living true'.[141] He encourages people then to 'notice the times, the moments in their lives when they are living true to their calling'.

Christine, working in a university chaplaincy, notes examples of meeting people 'where they are at: for women who feel alienated by the Church, then the creation, gardening or art work may be a way to connect with their spirituality. *Find out*

---

141 Silf, Margaret, *Landmarks: An Ignatian Journey*, London: Darton, Longman and Todd, 1998, p. 135.

what they like doing and . . . recognize the life-giving Spirit at work. Let them name it in their own way . . . People in 12-step recovery programmes will talk quite easily about *Higher Power, a Power Greater than myself.* I've learned a lot from people in recovery and although the language is different, I meet and recognize God in the encounter.'

In chaplaincy or community contexts, spiritual direction conversations can occur with people who have left the church scene years ago, people like 'Eve' who is described by tertiary chaplain, Kevin:

> Eve grew up in the Christian Church, served in a high-profile ministry and now has no connection to Church. She maintains a vibrant faith in Jesus Christ and needs opportunities to talk through her frustrations and confusions with her own spirituality. Initially she carried lots of guilt about no longer going to church but still professing to be Christian. She was confused about the role of the Bible in her life and her lack of interest in the 'quiet time'. With gentle exposure to contemplative prayer and the writings of Joyce Huggett and Thomas Merton, Eve has discovered new parts of the Christian tradition. She continues to need accompanying on her journey of discovery but is no longer afraid to venture into new territory.

Although few of us in parish ministry might expect to be approached by people of other faiths for help with their spiritual life, in chaplaincy or community work this can be part of the territory. Kevin and Tim have both worked with Buddhist students, but had quite different experiences:

> Nick is a practicing Buddhist here as an International Student. He has struggled to connect with the expression of his ethnic Buddhism in this area and asked if I could help him practise his meditation. Initially this meant lending him my office, but then he asked for my involvement in the meditative practice and help in reflection of this practice in the rest of his life, especially study. Through personal contacts with a sensei in another Buddhist tradition I have become aware of how to accompany Nick on his spiritual journey. He has introduced me to a number of Buddhist writers and I have introduced him to some material from John Main and the World Community for Christian Meditation. We can comfortably enjoy fellowship in meditation and discuss the experience. This has greatly enriched our spiritual journeys. (Kevin)

> A student I'm currently working with has journeyed through five years of Buddhist philosophy and meditative practice to encounter only frustration and dissatisfaction. He has come to me to explore 'Christianity' and has discovered that being a follower of Jesus is to engage experientially with a living Being (he was both shocked and excited by this). I have encouraged him to incorporate

193

a modified centring prayer into his meditative practices and to simply sit and listen attentively for Jesus to 'speak' to him. We have trialled this and just last week he described our time together as 'a place and time of profound peace. I've always been striving for this [peace]. Here I can just be and feel it!' The journey continues! (Tim)

✠

Reflection questions

⚮ How do the above comments on spiritual direction and pastoral ministry compare with your own understanding and experience of offering formal spiritual direction in a parish or chaplaincy setting?

⚮ What elements of contemplative spiritual direction practice would sit well with your pastoral visiting style and focus?

⚮ If you were to offer spiritual direction in your context, what boundaries might you put in place?
What language or terminology would work well for those you meet in your ministry context?

⚮ How would you feel and what would you think if, like Kevin and Tim, you were approached to companion someone from another faith? What resources do you have to draw on to respond to these types of requests – for example people, information, personal experience, etc.?

6.3 Group spiritual direction, quiet days and longer retreats

Many people would never go to see a spiritual director one to one, so providing spiritual direction in a small-group context is a helpful alternative. Group spiritual direction from a contemplative perspective involves a simple rhythm of silence, personal sharing, silence, response from the group, and silence, continuing until all have had a turn. Rose Mary Dougherty speaks of this gathering as 'a community of discernment':

In group spiritual direction, although there is usually less time for attention to individuals, people often become aware of God's ways in their hearts as they hear how God seems to be present for others and as they become conscious of God's presence with them as a group. God breaks open the tiny vessels they each have built to contain God. They come to expect God in surprising places in their lives and the lives of others.

In group spiritual direction people learn to listen to God's Spirit at work in

194

them for others in the group. Thus there is a collective wisdom available for each person.[142]

This structured form of spiritual direction requires a high level of trust and guaranteed confidentiality, and may develop out of an existing house group or be a group gathered specifically for this purpose .

Opportunities for less formal group spiritual direction already exist in many congregations, for example Dani helped his home group 'begin to talk about their spiritual journeys by beginning each meeting with a question for reflection. 'What am I thankful for this week?' was non-threatening and usually brought a full response. The Bible study that followed emphasized the spiritual teaching of the passage and avoided debates about 'head' stuff or textual technicalities so that folk could shift the focus to 'praying the scriptures' and enjoying the fruit of that. Over time the questions deepened until we were discussing some very profound insights, discoveries, pains and delights. We also developed greater trust and the encouragement to share the faith with one another.'

Winnie finds that spiritual direction material is particularly valuable for Lenten study, for example 'Deepening our prayer life' looked at biblical meditation, using a spiritual journal, and understanding prayer as 'relationship with God'. Over the six weeks of Lent, people met in small groups to look at the material, and the Sunday sermons supported the theme.

A form of group spiritual direction can take place in church meetings such as vestry or parish council by making space for hospitality and sharing of religious experience, as John[143] describes:

Four years ago I began a year-long experiment. The 14-member vestry met monthly from 7.30 to 9.30pm, starting with different members in turn sharing a short devotion with prayer, followed by a standard agenda. The meetings felt spiritually arid, members sometimes expressing vague feelings of dissatisfaction.

I proposed, and we agreed, that the vestry would meet bi-monthly for business, and in the intervening month would meet for fellowship and a pot-luck meal in different members' homes. After the meal a vestry member, and sometimes a staff-member would share some significant experience of God in their recent life or work.

To begin with the results were startling. People enjoyed the social aspect of meeting together, and we were getting to know each other much better simply by

142 Dougherty, Rose Mary, *Group Spiritual Direction: Community for Discernment*, New York: Paulist Press, 1995, pp. 35–6.

143 John's parish has 450–500 worshipping on a Sunday, with seven full-time and three part-time staff.

chatting over the meal. When people began to share recent and sometimes quite dramatic God-events in their lives, the evenings developed a real depth . . . there was a real sense of God's presence. The meeting would shift into a prayerful mode, and a much deeper sense of prayer began to emerge. Members looked forward to future meetings with anticipation. I had a real sense of helping people learn to pay attention to God.

However, as the parish was in the middle of building a new church, vestry was particularly busy and decisions needed to be made promptly. John continues:

As the opening day approached, we changed one social night to a business night because some urgent decisions needed our attention. With hindsight I suspect that what spiritual directors know as 'resistance' emerged. We didn't return to conducting such meetings, and in the full flush of enthusiasm of moving into a new church, the momentum was lost. I am no longer in that parish but I would definitely like to try that experiment again.

John's experience shows us how easy it is for pressing issues to divert us. The resistance that John identifies reminds us to be alert for this dynamic in any group setting – or in individuals whom we might see for spiritual direction, as Ian discovered:

Some parishioners wrestling with areas of resistance began avoiding asking for spiritual direction sessions: 'You're too busy,' they said. Others found themselves unable to deal with their resistance, and left because church – or myself – somehow became equated with their dark-night struggles. A small group found the ideas around spiritual direction (especially my appreciation of Catholic writers) or the practice of it so threatening that they reacted to me with open hostility. In retrospect, undertaking spiritual direction with parishioners has been a mixed experience. For some, it's opened up a whole new world of spiritual journeying. For others, their own reluctance has allied itself with my shortcomings, resulting in difficulties. However, I am not about to give up this ministry. I am continuing to offer spiritual direction to parishioners, but with lessened expectations of directees and myself.

Whether with individuals or with a group, we work towards bringing resistance to the light of day, acknowledging it as a normal part of humanity's response to the invitation to move closer to God. We recognize, however, that people move towards God at their own pace; for whatever reason, some will prefer to meet with God in ways that are familiar.

We have considered some of the more likely expressions of group spiritual direction, but there are others:

196

i Having someone *other than their pastor or priest*, act as spiritual director to a faith community:

> Through monthly two-hour sessions with staff, Brother John directs the group spirit of a Catholic parish. As a contemplative listener he gathers the staff members with questions: 'How are you coming to this meeting today?' 'How has the Mystery of God been present to you in your ministry this week?' His function is to listen for what is not being said as well as to what is being said – to notice and lift up for the group's reflection the times when there is energy and the times when things get quiet. Both are important occasions for attending to undercurrents that would otherwise go unnoticed. As director, he is particularly attuned to the primary movements of God, and so he listens in the rest of the meeting for the relationship between what the staff first shared and the 'business' of the organization revealed through its agenda items, budget and process. After a break, the group moves to a different room. Following five minutes of silence, they reflect together on how the mystery of God has been present in the meeting that day, in both the time of personal reflection and in the structures of their life together as a ministry team.[144]

ii Approaching *children's ministry* from a contemplative perspective, such as that developed in *The Catechesis of the Good Shepherd*. This model is based on the understanding that 'God and the child already have a unique relationship with one another, particularly before the age of six, and the growth of this relationship should be assisted by the adult, but *directed by the Spirit of God* within the child'.[145] Adults prepare a sacred space or 'atrium' which welcomes children's exploration and reflection using tangible symbols of Gospel stories, starting with the Good Shepherd. Silence, prayer, worship, discovery and deepening unfold in an unrushed and reverent environment as children respond to the Spirit within them. As good 'spiritual directors' the adults don't answer the children's questions with explanations or opinion but with open-ended or naïve questions, trusting the Spirit to help children find their way to a truth that builds their relationship with God.

iii Offering youth ministry from a contemplative perspective: noticing what God is already doing in young people's lives and group interactions; encouraging youth to pay attention to their spiritual experience or key moments; modelling a commitment to prayer; listening to God for how best to enhance God's work among the young. Mark Yaconelli's book, *Contemplative Youth Ministry:*

---

144 Lommasson, Sandra, 'Tending the Communal Soul', in *Still Listening: New Horizons in Spiritual Direction*, Norvene West (ed.), Harrisburg, PA: Morehouse, 2000.

145 Information brochure. For further details see: <http://www.cgsusa.org/> or Further Reading section.

Practising the Presence of Jesus, provides an excellent resource for a form of contemplative group spiritual direction.

Quiet days and retreats

Providing opportunities for people to spend time with God in silence and reflection can be like offering sips of water to someone who is dehydrated after a marathon. It is natural for those of us who value contemplative spirituality and spiritual direction to want to make them available to others but, in line with earlier comments about 'attending to our own spiritual journey', we cannot offer these sort of contemplative retreat opportunities to others with integrity, unless we ensure that we have a silent, directed retreat week each year and take other shorter times of reflection as they become available.

If a parish has no experience of being offered retreats of any sort, a 'quiet evening' or day retreat can be helpful. A brief introduction to praying with scripture and to short times of silence and reflection can act as a 'taster' for those who are wondering about contemplative spirituality, spiritual direction or going on a longer retreat. Using a theme relevant to the season, space can be provided for people to have time alone with God, as well as time to share with another person, or acknowledge the gifts or questions of the day if they wish. Personal, individual spiritual direction can be available as part of the day for those who request it.

Alternatively, a 'retreat in daily life' may be run in parish or chaplaincy contexts. In a typical format, retreatants commit themselves each day to 30 minutes of praying with scripture and 30 minutes exploring their prayer experience with a prayer companion or spiritual director. This format originated in the work of Fr John Veltri SJ who wanted to make the Ignatian Exercises more accessible. It is particularly suited to people who cannot afford, or travel away to a residential retreat, but who are intentional about growing in their faith.

Offering residential retreats will depend on factors such as costs, venue and availability of experienced spiritual directors, but are well worth the effort. If you are not able to offer these yourself, there may be people in your congregation who can do this with your support. There is no doubt that if people make themselves available to listen to God in this way, spiritual growth will occur, often in unexpected but totally appropriate ways as God's grace touches them. (See Further Reading for resources which give a more detailed coverage of retreats and quiet days.)

✠

Reflection questions

⚮ What is your experience of formal or informal group spiritual direction?

⚮ How do you respond to the idea of offering an opportunity for informal group spiritual direction in an existing group of which you are a part?
What pitfalls or benefits might this present?

⚮ To what extent have you been aware of 'resistance' in any group context of which you are a part? How was that resistance handled?

⚮ What are the pluses and minuses of having a spiritual director from outside the congregation regularly facilitate the reflection of leadership such as vestry or parish council?

⚮ How might you start to offer opportunities for people to experience a contemplative retreat?
What resources will you need? What support is there in your context?

⚮ Reflect on your experience of Sunday school and/or young people's ministry as you were growing up. To what extent did these foster your *relationship with God* as well as your knowledge about God?

6.4 Worship, teaching and preaching, programmes and discernment

As well as helping people grow in their prayer life, key aspects of contemplative spiritual direction can underpin our worship services, inform our preaching and teaching, aid our discernment, and guide our activities and mission.

Worship and liturgical life

In worship we offer our selves to God as fully as we can, aware of our creaturehood and of God's awesome 'Otherness'. We offer adoration and thanksgiving and, as we delight in God, we come to know something of God's delight in us. Integrating some or all of the following suggestions can give space for this mutual communication to deepen.

Using the Psalms

In reading aloud or singing the Psalms, we express words of celebration, lament, struggle and thanksgiving and build up the capacity to share our truth with God, as Jesus did on the cross.[146] Walter Brueggemann reminds us that psalms connect with us in settled times of orientation, in the disruptions of disorientation and the

---

146 Psalm 22.1, 'My God, my God, why have you forsaken me?'

hope of new orientation. Aware that there is a tendency in many churches to use psalms which focus predominantly on God's love and provision, he argues for serious use of the complaint Psalms because through them we are invited 'into a more honest facing of the darkness' and 'because even in the darkness there is One to address . . . the power of the darkness is strangely transformed, not by the power of easy light, but by the power of relentless solidarity'.[147] He also makes the point that the Psalms speak not only to the individual but consistently point to issues of justice in the context of community life.

Giving space for silence

Prayer books generally indicate appropriate places for silence during the liturgy. However, those leading worship often move directly on to the next set of responses, losing the opportunity to pause and reflect. Dani suggests:

- In the prayers of confession offer a verse or two of scripture and give space for reflection before drawing it together with words of cleansing and forgiveness.
- After the homily or sermon, offer two minutes of silence and a statement to reflect upon, for example 'Today I heard God say to me . . .'
- Prayers of intercession can also be led in a contemplative way, giving time to imagine the people or situation prayed for with the invitation to visualize it/ them made whole, healed, helped or blessed.
- Serving Holy Communion in silence can be a welcome change and can offer a profound sense of presence and community.

Slowing down

Closely linked with a lack of silence is the speed with which the words of many services are said. Slowing down a little is a contrast to the frenetic activity of much contemporary life. It need not make the service longer, but allows space for words to convey their meaning more fully and models attentiveness to that which endures.

Offering services which draw on the contemplative tradition of the Church

Material is readily available for those who wish to offer services which include substantial opportunity for reflection, engagement with evocative symbols, simple prayers, silence, relevant readings from a range of sources including – but

---

147 Brueggemann, Walter, *Spirituality of the Psalms*, Minneapolis: Augsberg Fortress, 2002, p. xiii.

not solely – scripture, meditative music, meaningful ritual and hospitality.[148] It is not difficult to produce your own services from scratch if you, or someone in your faith community, have the time and talent and passion for offering people an alternative to the busy-ness and noise of much contemporary worship. Such services are often a gentle way of meeting the needs of people on the edges of the Church or those who may be drawn to something that is a bit different from their current understanding of religious observance. Christine shares her experience of a special service on campus:

> We chaplains joined with the School of Music to put together a service of song and readings to take us through from the sung Hosanna of Jesus' entry into Jerusalem; Holy Thursday had the symbol of a towel and basin with the sound of water poured, Good Friday, three songs performed and then an Easter Song. My role was to link the songs with readings chosen from an inclusive lectionary. This appealed to a wide range of people, some of whom hadn't been inside a church for many years. The soft drape of white cloth on a plain cross spoke of resurrection to come. The university chapel was *safe* for them to gather. Food followed! *This was a contemplative experience with few explicit prayers, rather a prayerful atmosphere where the use of music and readings from scripture and other sources, invited us into God's presence.*

Preaching and teaching

When we are preparing sermons or other input we not only exegete the scripture as we have been taught, we also *pray with* the scripture, giving room for the Holy Spirit to reveal something not seen before in the passage. Winnie also includes 'spiritual direction'-style rhetorical questions: 'What is God saying to me as an individual and us as a community through this passage . . .?' and the sermon may sometimes merge into a guided meditation at some point.

Over time, all the key themes we have explored in one-to-one spiritual direction will *naturally* emerge from the readings, prayers or theme for the day, enabling us to:

- remind people that religious and spiritual experience happens, not just between the pages of the Bible, but today, to anyone, anytime;
- help people to be honest with themselves and with God;
- encourage people to think of God as being present and active in *every* person's life – not just in the lives of churchgoers;

---

148 The Taizé, Iona and Lindisfarne communities all produce material suitable for contemplative worship; see Further Reading.

- help people learn to pay attention to God in the midst of everyday life;
- introduce ways of praying with scripture;
- talk about and practise discernment as individuals and as a congregation;
- be honest about the questions that difficult circumstances raise, for example after a parish family loses a longed-for baby, or a tragedy touches the innocent;
- share some ways of looking at change and movement on the spiritual journey;
- make sure that when Jesus' cry from the cross, 'My God, my God, why have you forsaken me?' echoes in parishioners' lives, the challenges of the perceived absence of God are addressed;
- encourage people to question and express their doubts, feelings, hopes and longings;
- explore how the way we see God can affect our spiritual journey;
- honour people's creativity and giftedness.

We can also offer or support others in offering focused teaching and resources related to growth in the spiritual life. Ian began a reading group within the church to explore aspects of Christian spirituality; Winnie ran a spiritual formation course at the end of one year and those who completed the full course acted as facilitators in the following year's Lenten groups; Richard writes a weekly article about God in everyday life, for parishioners to share with others. At her university, Anna often provides talks or workshops on 'discernment' and sees the opportunity 'to be alongside people as co-discerner, and to listen well to the decision-making process as one of the most significant places spiritual direction informs the practice of chaplaincy'.

Prayer

As prayer is explored at some length in Chapters 3 and 5, brief comments follow.

Andrew says, 'I have a growing belief that my chief role as a pastor is to teach people to pray.' It follows, then, that we set an example to others by committing ourselves to a daily rhythm of prayer and reflection and regular *lectio divina*, giving God space in silence to free us to grow in faith and service. We can also support those who are responsible for leading intercessions, sharing resources, discussing different options in their own prayer practice.

We can help people to pray individually whenever and wherever we get the opportunity. And in a parish context, it is not difficult to offer corporate prayer opportunities such as the Daily Office or Eucharist; some chaplains will have a chapel or room in which to offer prayer, or a regular service. On special occasions or after national or international tragedies, we can provide an opportunity for people to gather and share a simple act of lament, remembrance, hope or silent reflection. This not only connects people with the mystery of life, death and resur-

PARISH, CHAPLAINCY AND COMMUNITY CONTEXTS

rection, but witnesses to the capacity of the Church to hold and help people as they process their disorientation, trusting that new life will emerge.

Programmes and discernment

In some contexts, chaplains may have the opportunity to offer workshops, or conduct sessions on such topics as spirituality, discernment, grieving and ethics. However, apart from those who work in prisons, chaplains will generally have little opportunity to offer programmes which run over a number of weeks; staff and students are often already committed either to their study and work responsibilities or to their own faith communities.

The parish context is entirely different. Programmes or short-term studies are a normal part of parish life and are often used to help people learn more about their faith, the Bible and Christian discipleship. During the last decade, for example, the Alpha Course has entered church life globally, and has been found by many to be a useful tool for refreshing some who have been Christians for a long time, and for introducing others, including those in prison, to the faith. There is no denying that programmes have their place. However, programmes may also be problematic:

- if they cater predominantly for people who are in the early phase of exploring their spiritual journey and do not meet the needs of those faithful Christians who could be described as 'Searching' (O'Hare) or as 'Critic' (Fowler);
- if they promote one faith stream[149] and ignore or deny the value of others;
- if they reinforce the 'external authority' of the leadership rather than helping people learn to take responsibility for their own spiritual growth, guided by the Spirit;
- if they put extra demands on people and actually reduce their capacity to pray or to serve.

If we are spending a high proportion of our resources (leaders, time and money) on programmes and activities which are well intentioned but not actually God's call for our faith community *at this time and in this place*, we are unconsciously engaging in that most subtle form of resistance – 'counter-movement'. Even apparently 'worthy' activities can distract us from doing what God wants us to do, if we are not taking the time to stop and give space for the Spirit to reveal God's way forward, individually and corporately.

How do we discover what God is doing? We use the tools of discernment, we use the spiritual direction practices described in this book: stopping, listening to

---

149 Foster, Richard, *Streams of Living Water*, London: HarperCollins, 1998: Holiness, Social Justice, Evangelical, Incarnational, Contemplative, Charismatic.

God and to each other, waiting, wondering together as a faith community, asking evocative questions, paying attention to dreams or pictures as they emerge, watching and listening for signs of need in our neighbourhood, noticing energy for outreach and opportunities for mission. The contemplative stance underpins all of this.

God equips us for service, as long as we *make the time* to discern, are willing to set aside personal agendas, are open to risky possibilities, welcome the creativity of God and don't make choices just because something is cheap or easy to run, or has worked elsewhere. This approach requires a form of leadership that is, among other things, courageous, collegial, enabling, honouring of others' gifts, willing to delegate and personally secure in Christ.

Much is being written about 'fresh expressions'[150] of church and the need for outreach into our communities. But *before* we make choices about how we reach out or offer alternatives, I believe we must offer to God a listening space in our hearts – individually and corporately – so we and those whom we companion will be better able to receive the direction and enthusiasm of the Spirit, and be guided in the practical outworking of God's fresh expression of church, God's invitation to growth and service.

✠

Reflection questions

- ⸙ How do you respond to the assertion that 'my chief role as a pastor is to teach people to pray'?
- ⸙ What examples of the Church holding and helping people as they process their disorientation have you been part of? What worked well? What might have been done differently?
- ⸙ Take a moment to list the church-based programmes you have been involved in so far in your faith journey. Then assess the extent to which your participation in these programmes has helped your spiritual growth.
- ⸙ How does your faith community make decisions, particularly those relating to opportunities for mission or outreach? What worked well? What might have been done differently?
  To what extent has the contemplative process been part of that decision-making?

150 See for example: The Archbishops' Council, *Mission-shaped Church: Church Planting and Fresh Expressions of Church in a Changing Context*, Australia: Willow Publishing (under licence to Church House Publishing), 2005.

6.5 Spiritual direction and building bridges to the community

In his book *emergingchurch.intro*, Michael Moynagh writes:

> The Acts of the Apostles links the early church's growth to the way the first Christians enjoyed the favour of all the people (Acts 5.12–14). Initiators of emerging church might ask, 'What would we have to do to win the favour of the people around us?' The answer of course is 'to love them to bits'.
>
> What might that actually mean? Following best mission practice, it will almost certainly involve some form of service. Time and again Jesus did not start by proclaiming the gospel but with acts of service – healing and other forms of kindness.
>
> Meeting the real needs of people – 'consumer' needs such as having fun, and 'community' needs such as supporting single parents in looking after their children – will increasingly be the kernel of new expressions of church[151]

This book began with a story and, as we near the end, another story deserves attention – the story of a community offering significant service and actively using contemplative spiritual direction principles to help people connect with 'hints of the holy'. Much of this story will be told in the words of Bruce Maden, a spiritual director who is chief executive officer of Te Aroha Noa[152] Community Services. This unashamedly God-inspired community has, for the past 18 years, been building bridges of hope in the multicultural state housing area[153] it serves in Palmerston North, New Zealand. It is the premise of Maden's research that 'God is in the neighbourhood and that contemplative incarnational spiritual direction is uniquely equipped with a tradition and practice that can assist people to embrace the quest to encounter ultimate reality'.[154] Maden starts the story with some background:

> Te Aroha Noa originated out of the Central Baptist Church and operates on a semi-autonomous basis in a secular environment. Using Christian values to inform its work, it provides an extensive range of services[155] for young families. While a few services are provided solely by professionally trained staff, the

---

151 Moynagh, *emergingchurch.intro*, Oxford: Monarch, 2004, pp. 185–6.

152 This name was given to the community by Archbishop Winiata; its literal translation is 'unconditional love', its colloquial rendering is 'love with no strings'.

153 The locality is often described as an area of high social and economic deprivation.

154 Maden, Bruce, *God is in the Neighbourhood*, New Zealand: Spiritual Growth Ministries, 2006, pp. 7–8. Used with permission. For methodology and full text see <http://www.sgm.org.nz/research_papers.htm>.

155 Including Early Childhood Centre, Social Work and Counselling Services, and First Steps Adult Education.

majority involve the community in the co-provision of services, so Te Aroha Noa has a strong degree of community ownership.

The 'culture of care' or 'heart' of Te Aroha Noa is primarily conveyed through the 'telling of stories'. Stories of growth and development, stories of change are shared in the safe environment of the community centre; dominant stories that might diminish a person's potential are de-constructed and alternative stories of capacity, resourcefulness and resilience are re-constructed.

Woven within this 'culture of care' is a responsiveness to the spiritual. Te Aroha Noa's vision statement testifies to its intention: 'To be a God-Inspired Community Unleashing the Potential of all People(s)'. Not only does it want to *assist* its surrounding community but, increasingly, it is challenged to *become* community – *To Turangawaewae*, 'A Place to Belong'.

Throughout every aspect of Te Aroha Noa we are training our antennae to discover beneath the surface of all those we encounter the 'suppressed signals of spirituality' in the depths, the fire, the passion and in God. We have decided to stand against accepting people's version of themselves as the true version. We look beneath the surface and discover deeper longings, unexpressed dreams, God-saturated moments and a hunger for life other than it is. We see only extra-ordinary people!

Within this context, the 'spiritual' or the 'wairua' is not seen as describing something separate from, or a component of, but as infused into all that is – comprehensive and integrative. The Spirit of Christ is seen as already in the neighbourhood, already at the heart of all that is and wanting to be noticed, embraced and called forth. My research recorded many stories within both individual and group settings that support the premise that spiritual or religious experience is widely encountered by many with little or no religious involvement. When a permission-giving environment is created and constraints to expression removed, people share experiences of prayer being answered, the strange falling into place of events, the sacred in nature, an awareness of the presence of God and in one story a sense of the presence of evil.[156]

At Te Aroha Noa, Maden says, 'we aim to increase relational consciousness',[157] by assisting people to become more aware of their relationship with self, others, their world and God. The spiritual director[158] in this community:

- trusts 'the Loving Presence to know how best to encounter all who form part of the community';

---

156 Maden, *God is in the Neighbourhood*, p. 10.

157 Hay, D., Nye, R. and Hunt, K., *Understanding the Spiritual Life of Children*, University of Nottingham, 1998.

158 Maden is highly intentional about his own spiritual growth, and works out of a deep personal awareness of the love and grace of God.

- listens to people's stories alert for the Christ within, for signs of grace;
- encourages people to use their own language and ways of naming the sacred;
- helps community participants (directees) to reflect on their experiences, for example by introducing open-ended questions into conversations to help them notice, and dialogue more deeply with, the reality they are experiencing:

  - What do you think is really going on here?
  - What does this event mean for you?
  - In the midst of this mess, what do you think is the best direction to take?
  - If you were open to a divine Presence existing, what do you think that Presence would be saying to you now?

- helps people to connect the detached happenings (and 'key moments') of their lives to their deeper longing for the divine (which they may not know they have), for example by asking:

  - From these experiences, what understandings are you developing about God or the Divine Presence?[159]

Maden believes that, as the influence and presence of the institutional Church diminishes, communities need an informal network of 'anam cara' (soul friends) to help create an interpersonal climate in which 'neighbours' (directees) 'become progressively free of fear, spiritually perceptive, generous, able to assume responsibility and to take initiative in the spiritual life'.[160] Already this is happening. At Te Aroha Noa people are acting as 'soul friends' for each other, and the truth of God is being discovered organically:

> Often much of the 'directing' happened in group contexts and subsequently 'directing' conversations were seen to be emerging in everyday interactions. Community members would be heard sharing 'I think I had one of those "God Moments" we were talking about' and their friend or colleague would be heard asking them questions that further engaged the person in deeper spiritual exploration. It appears as if a context has been created where all are on a spiritual journey and all are responsible for encouraging and guiding their fellow travellers.[161]

A further consequence of this strengthening spiritual awareness and deeper 'relational consciousness' is its effect on the community in which people live:

---

159 Maden, *God is in the Neighbourhood*, p. 12, reference to Hay, Nye and Hunt, *Understanding the Spiritual Life of Children*.

160 Schneiders, Sandra, 'The Contemporary Ministry of Spiritual Direction', *Chicago Studies*, Spring, 1976.

161 Maden, *God is in the Neighbourhood*, p. 15.

Women have shared about how they have decided to stand against the prevalent culture of alcohol being needed at all events by holding a 'Mothers Day' party where there was no alcohol, and against family violence, calling the police whenever violence occurs in their street.[162]

And stories are shared such as this one from a relatively new Maori staff member who, in response to being asked to reflect on her experience, said:

> I notice I *korero* (talk) with *Atua* (God) more. I've been more aware of a sense of *Atua* going before me and bringing events about. I've become more aware of *ringaringa aroha o Atua* – the loving hands of God, personally guiding my life. I also find myself sometimes being prompted to offer *karakia* (prayer) – like the other day I had to go and visit a *whanau* (family) and I felt an inner voice telling me to offer a *karakia*. I wouldn't normally do that. So before I got out of the car I said a *karakia* and as I approached the front door of the home I could hear a furious verbal argument occurring inside. Normally I would have felt afraid in these circumstances, but this time I felt safe and protected and so I just knocked on the door and I think I helped restore harmony in the home. I'm now thinking about how *Atua* is in my life on a daily basis. I don't know how this has all happened. Somehow the *wairua* (spirituality) of this place is deeply affecting me.[163]

Te Aroha Noa came into being because a few prayerful people made time to listen and discern God's call for them, researched the needs of the community, were willing to take risks, trusted God's provision, *and* were prepared to struggle with the theological and practical implications of offering 'love with no strings': serving people with no hidden agenda of 'bringing them into the Church'. Maden's research at Te Aroha Noa shows that:

> . . . it is possible to create a sacred space, a holy place, in the neighbourhood where a community of people grow in paying attention to the 'Word' in another. Spiritual Direction in the Contemplative tradition, can guide people to become increasingly aware of their spiritual experience and key moments. They are freed to speak out about encounters with the Mysterious Other, God or simply the 'Weird'. Stories can be shared and people learn to ask questions of each other to support the emerging understandings of the divine. Questing is honoured and people can learn to respond to the deepest reality, the Christ, in each other.[164]

---

162 Maden, *God is in the Neighbourhood*, p. 14.
163 Maden, *God is in the Neighbourhood*, pp. 12–13.
164 Maden, *God is in the Neighbourhood*, p.19.

This is 'emerging Church', although that term might not make sense to those who are part of Te Aroha Noa. They simply know that they are accepted, listened to and helped to notice the presence of God in their ordinary days, and to change the patterns of abuse and violence, failure and fear that have been part of their lives for far too long. God is indeed in the neighbourhood.

✠

Reflection questions

- ⚱ Read Maden's full research paper (see <www.sgm.org.nz/research_papers. htm>) and notice what arises in you. Take your discoveries to God.
- ⚱ What does this story have to say to you about living out the consequences of your growing intimacy with God?
- ⚱ What implication does Maden's work have for the church community to which you belong?
- ⚱ Who might join you in listening intentionally to God for insight into outreach and service?
- ⚱ As you consider a 'fresh expression' of Church, how might the development of an informal network of *anam cara* be part of the planning or visioning?

Further reading

Bridges into the neighbourhood/workplace spirituality

Bellingham, Lois, *Integrating the Active and the Contemplative in the Workplace: The Weaving of a Seamless Garment*, New Zealand: Spiritual Growth Ministries, 2005. Full text: <www. sgm.org.nz/research_papers.htm>.

Harris, Myree, 'Spiritual Direction and Encounters with the Marginalised', in *Presence: An International Journal of Spiritual Direction*, 13(2), June 2007, pp. 49–55.

Maden, Bruce, *God is in the Neighbourhood*, New Zealand: Spiritual Growth Ministries, 2006. Full text: <www.sgm.org.nz/research_papers.htm>.

Moynagh, Michael, *emergingchurch.intro*, Oxford: Monarch, 2004.

O'Donohue, John, *Anam Cara: Spiritual Wisdom from the Celtic World*, London: Bantam, 1999.

Contemplative models for pastoral ministry

Hamilton, Brian, *Spiritual Direction as a Model for Pastoral Ministry*, New Zealand: Spiritual Growth Ministries. Full text: <www.sgm.org.nz/research_papers.htm>.

Peterson, Eugene H., *The Contemplative Pastor: Returning to the Art of Spiritual Direction*, Grand Rapids, MI: Eerdmans, 1989.

Group spiritual direction

Cavaletti, Sofia, *The Religious Potential of the Child: Experiencing Scripture and Liturgy with Young Children*, Chicago: Liturgical Training Publications, 1992.
Dougherty, Rose Mary, *Group Spiritual Direction: Community for Discernment*, New York: Paulist Press, 1995.
Helm, Nick, *Soul Spark: A Short Course Exploring Prayer and Spiritual Growth*, Cambridge: Grove Books, 2006.
Lillig, Tina, *The Catechesis of the Good Shepherd in a Parish Setting*, Chicago: Liturgical Training Publications, 1998.
Lommasson, Sandra, 'Tending the Communal Soul', in *Still Listening: New Horizons in Spiritual Direction*, Norvene West (ed.), Harrisburg, PA: Morehouse, 2000.
Smith, James with Graybeal, Lynda, *Spiritual Formation Workbook*, London: HarperCollins, 1999.
Yaconelli, Mark, *Contemplative Youth Ministry: Practising the Presence of Jesus*, Grand Rapids: Zondervan, 2006.

Retreat resources

Pickering, Sue, *Creative Ideas for Quiet Days*, Norwich: SCM-Canterbury Press, 2006. Includes material for 12 Quiet Days and copiable resources.
Retreats in daily life see <http://www.jesuits.ca/orientations/bob/retreat.htm> for details and copiable resources, accessed 10 February 2008.
Silf, Margaret, *Soul Space: Making a Retreat in the Christian Tradition*, London: SPCK, 2002.
Vennard, Jane E., *Be Still: Designing and Leading Contemplative Retreats*, The Alban Institute, 2000.

Conclusion

Tilden Edwards, part of the team at Shalem Institute in Washington DC, writes:

> Spiritual guidance out of a Christian tradition at its best is not meant to be a narrow 'in-house' affair (though it often has been treated as such), but *a personal bridge* to the Ground of all human life . . . available for all people yearning to touch that Ground more firmly.[165]

The 'spiritual direction' bridge that was introduced at the start of this book, the bridge that helps connect you – and helps you connect others – with the God of grace, has been taking shape, chapter by chapter, and question by question.

As you have engaged with the material and reflected on your own spiritual journey, I have been doing the same. Together we have considered the core elements of spiritual direction in the contemplative tradition, the shift in focus back to 'the cure of souls', and the centrality of listening – to God, to ourselves and to others.

We have seen how the spiritual director, trusting that God is already at work in all people, consistently helps the directee 'pay attention' and respond to God's initiative; and how both rely on the Spirit to direct the next step of the journey. Dialogues have helped demonstrate some of the dynamics and practices of contemplative spiritual direction with people who were angry with God, grieving, frustrated, uncertain, searching, vulnerable, or wondering about God's nature, or presence.

We have been reminded of the importance of being in spiritual direction and supervision ourselves, of 'practising what we preach' and doing our own 'work', so we don't get in the way of those we companion, and can fearlessly respond to God's call, wherever that might lead us. We have seen how, in the companioning of others, we too are blessed and our ministry given new hope and purpose.

We have had a 'taste' of the way contemplative spiritual direction principles and practices can infuse parish life, inform chaplaincy practice and enhance mission and community development. While we may begin our intentional ministry of spiritual direction in the context of one-to-one meetings, God's purposes may take us, or our directees, beyond the familiar as we respond to God's passion for the lonely, the poor and the disadvantaged.

---

165 Edwards, Tilden, *Spiritual Friend*, New York: Paulist Press, 2002, p. 8. Italics mine.

Aware of the findings of ongoing research into religious and spiritual experience, and empowered by the Spirit of God, we can engage in spiritual conversations with anyone, anywhere, helping them 'listen to their lives' and discover God, the Loving Presence within them, within everyone.

Whether we describe ourselves as spiritual director, soul friend, midwife to the soul, keeper of the campfire, or champion of grace;[166] whether we accompany a few or many, singly or in groups, for some months or many years; wherever our ministry is offered, our privilege and prayer is to assist our directees to recognize and respond to the Spirit who calls them – and calls us – ceaselessly, faithfully, towards the fullness of Love, made visible in Christ, waiting to be recognized at the centre of our being.

Although we may begin rather tentatively, concentrating very hard, as if we are trying to cross a scary three-wire bridge, gradually our ministry of spiritual direction will change and deepen as we give more and more of ourselves, and the process, over to the work of the Holy Spirit.

Gradually we will find ourselves unselfconsciously attending to the Spirit, listening with the directee for signs of God's break-through presence, helping the directee recognize God's firm invitation or gentle touch, or waiting with them in God's silence.

One day we will sit with a group and hear people sharing stories of graced encounter with the Holy One; we will watch others being encouraged to trust the reality of God and take another step closer towards building a community characterized by love.

One day we may be part of a team that hears God's invitation to move into the neighbourhood in service and love, and we will start to listen for stories of God's presence in the midst of everyday life.

One day it will be like coming around a corner and suddenly finding stretched out before us the stunningly beautiful Second Severn Crossing – a broad and airy span, appearing gently ahead of us, taking us and our directees on a journey to discover more of the ALL of God.

There may still be no bridge to Skomer Island,
but each of us can, with God's help, become 'pontifex',
bridge-builders with others on the journey home to God.
Contemplative incarnational spiritual direction gives us
the 'tools' and the 'set of plans'.
The Spirit kindles our creativity. Jesus shows us how it's done.
God welcomes us at the point of union
and, together, we celebrate our homecoming, with silence and with singing.

---

166 A term I first heard from a colleague, Warren Deason.

THE BRIDGE

There are times in life
when we are called to be bridges,
not a great monument spanning a distance
and carrying loads of heavy traffic,
but a simple bridge to help one person from here to there over
some difficulty
such as pain, grief, fear, loneliness,
a bridge which opens the way
for ongoing journey.

When I become a bridge for another,
I bring upon myself a blessing,
for I escape from the small prison of self
and exist for the wider world,
breaking out to be a larger being
who can enter another's pain
and rejoice in another's triumph.

I know of only one greater blessing
in this life, and that is,
to allow someone else
to be a bridge for me.

Joy Cowley, *Aotearoa Psalms*,
Pleroma Christian Supplies, Otane, New Zealand, 2008. Used with permission.

Bibliography

Archbishops' Council, *Mission-shaped Church: Church Planting and Fresh Expressions of Church in a Changing Context*, Australia: Willow Publishing (under licence to Church House Publishing), 2005.

Ashton, Lloyd, 'A Man for all Seasons', in *Anglican Taonga*, 22, Spring 2006.

Bakke, Jeannette, *Holy Invitations*, Grand Rapids, MI: Baker Books, 2000.

Ball, Peter, *Journey into Truth: Spiritual Direction in the Anglican Tradition*, London: Mowbray, 1996.

Barry, William A. and Connolly, William A., *The Practice of Spiritual Direction*, San Francisco: HarperCollins, 1982.

Benner, David G., *Sacred Companions*, Downers Grove, IL: InterVarsity Press, 2002.

——*Desiring God's Will: Aligning Our Hearts with the Heart of God*, Downers Grove, IL: InterVarsity Press, 2005.

Bonhoeffer, Dietrich, *Letters and Papers from Prison*, SCM Press and Macmillan, 1971.

Bourgeault, Cynthia, *Centring Prayer and Inner Awakening*, Cambridge, MA: Cowley, 2004.

Brother Lawrence, *The Practice of the Presence of God* (trans. E. M. Blaiklock), London: Hodder & Stoughton, 1981.

Brown, Simon, *Mission and the Art of Spiritual Direction*, New Zealand: Spiritual Growth Ministries, 2002. Full text: <www.sgm.org.nz>.

Brueggemann, Walter, *Spirituality of the Psalms*, Minneapolis: Augsberg Fortress, 2002.

Buechner, Frederick, *Listening to Your Life*, San Francisco: HarperOne, 1992.

Burghardt, Walter A., 'Contemplation: A Long Loving Look at the Real, in Church', Winter 1989. Quotation accessed at website: <http://www.shalem.org/resources/quotations>, 3 December 2006.

Calvin, John, *Institutes of the Christian Religion*, 1536 edn, trans. Ford Lewis Battles, Grand Rapids, MI: Eerdmans, 1995.

Catechism, *A New Zealand Prayer Book*, London: Collins, 1989.

Conroy, Maureen, *Looking into the Well: Supervision of Spiritual Directors*, Chicago: Loyola University Press, 1995.

Cornwell, Bernard, 'Cakes and Ale', 2005, quoted in *The Week*, 9 July 2005, No. 519, London: Dennis Publishing Ltd, pp. 44–5, from *Family Wanted: Adoption Stories*, Sara Holloway (ed.), Granta Books.

Culligan, Kevin, 'The Dark Night and Depression', in *Presence: An International Journal of Spiritual Direction*, 10(1), February 2004.

Doctrine Commission of the Church of England, *The Mystery of Salvation*, London: Church House Publishing, 1995.

Dougherty, Rose Mary, *Group Spiritual Direction: Community for Discernment*, New York: Paulist Press, 1995.

Ferder, Fran, *Words Made Flesh*, Notre Dame, IN: Ave Maria Press, 1986.

Foster, Richard, *Prayer: Finding the Heart's True Home*, London: Hodder & Stoughton, 1992.

——*Streams of Living Water*, London: HarperCollins, 1998.

Hall, Thelma, *Too Deep for Words: Rediscovering Lectio Divina*, New York: Paulist Press, 1988.

Hamilton, Brian, *Spiritual Direction as the Model for Pastoral Ministry*, Spiritual Growth Ministries Trust: New Zealand, p. 4. Full text: <www.sgm.org.nz/research_papers.htm>.

Hawker, P., *Soul Survivor*, Canada: Northstone, 1998. (Republished as *Soul Quest*, Canada: Wood Lake Publishing, 2007.).

——*Secret Affairs of the Soul*, Canada: Northstone Publishing, 2000.

Hay, David, *Religious Experience Today: Studying the Facts*, London: Mowbray, 1990.

——*The Spirituality of the Unchurched,* conference paper of British and Irish Mission Association, 2000. Full text: <www.martynmission.cam.ac.uk/BIAMSHay.htm>.

Hay, D. and Hunt, K., *Understanding the Spirituality of People Who Don't Go to Church*, University of Nottingham: Centre for the Study of Human Relations, 2000.

Hay, D., Nye, R. and Hunt, K., *Understanding the Spiritual Life of Children*, University of Nottingham, 1998.

Huggett, Joyce, *Listening to God*, London: Hodder & Stoughton, 1986.

Jamieson, Alan, *Called Again – In and Beyond the Deserts of Faith*, Wellington: Philip Garside, 2004.

——*A Churchless Faith: Faith Journeys Beyond the Churches*, London: SPCK, 2002.

Jones, Alan, *Soul-Making: The Desert Way of Spirituality*, San Francisco: HarperCollins, 1989.

Jung, C. G., *Modern Man in Search of a Soul*, London: Kegan Paul, 1933.

Keating, Thomas, *Foundations for Centring Prayer and the Christian Contemplative Life,* London: Continuum, 2004.

——*Open Heart: The Contemplative Dimension of the Gospel*, New York: Continuum, 2002.

Kübler-Ross, Elisabeth, *On Death and Dying*, Macmillan, 1976.

Larkin, Ernest E., *The Three Spiritual Ways* <http://carmelnet.org/larkin/larkin081.pdf>.

Leech, Kenneth, *Soul Friend: Spiritual Direction in the Modern World* (revised edition), Harrisburg, PA: Morehouse, 2001.

Lommasson, Sandra, 'Tending the Communal Soul', in *Still Listening: New Horizons in Spiritual Direction*, Norvene West (ed.), Harrisburg, PA: Morehouse 2000.

Lovinger, Robert J., *Working with Religious Issues in Therapy*, New York: Jason Aronson Inc., 1984.

Mabry, John R., *Faith Styles: Ways People Believe*, New York: Morehouse, 2007.

Maden, Bruce, *God is in the Neighbourhood*, New Zealand: Spiritual Growth Ministries, 2006.

May, Gerald, *Care of Mind, Care of Spirit: A Psychiatrist Explores Spiritual Direction*, New York: HarperCollins, 1992.

Merton, Thomas, *Thoughts in Solitude,* Boston: Shambala, 1993.

Michael, Chester P. and Norrisey, Marie C., *Prayer and Temperament: Different Prayer Forms for Different Personality Types*, Virginia: The Open Door, 1991.

Mother Teresa, *Come Be My Light*, Brian Kolodiejchuk (ed.), New York: Doubleday, 2007.

Moynagh, Michael, *emergingchurch.intro,* Oxford: Monarch, 2004.

Newsom, Carol A. and Ringe, Sharon H. (eds), *Women's Bible Commentary*, Louisville, KY: Westminster John Knox Press, 1998.

O'Hare, Breige, 'Opening to Love: A Paradigm for Growth in Relationship with God', in *Presence: An International Journal of Spiritual Direction,* 10(2), June 2004.

Peterson, Eugene H., *The Contemplative Pastor: Returning to the Art of Spiritual Direction,* Grand Rapids, MI: Eerdmans, 1989.

—— *Working the Angles*, Grand Rapids, MI: Eerdmans, 1987.

Pope John XXIII, *Journal of a Soul*, London: Four Square Books (The New English Library Ltd), 1966.

Pritchard, Sheila, *The Lost Art of Meditation: Deepening Your Prayer Life*, London: Scripture Union, 2002.

Reed, P. G., 'An Emerging Paradigm for the Investigation of Spirituality in Nursing', *Research in Nursing and Health,* 15, 1992.

Ruffing, Janet K., *Spiritual Direction: Beyond the Beginnings*, New York: Paulist Press, 2000.

Rupp, Joyce, *Praying our Goodbyes*, Notre Dame, IN: Ave Maria Press, 1988.

St Patrick's Breastplate, trans. Mrs Cecil Francis Alexander, in *Hymns Ancient and Modern Revised*, Norwich: SCM-Canterbury Press.

Savary, Louis M., Berne, Patricia H. and Williams, Strephon Kaplan, *Dreams and Spiritual Growth: A Judeo-Christian Approach to Dreamwork*, New York: Paulist Press, 1984.

Schneiders Sandra, 'The Contemporary Ministry of Spiritual Direction', *Chicago Studies,* Spring, 1976.

Silf, Margaret, *Landmarks: An Ignatian Journey*, London: Darton, Longman and Todd, 1998.

Steere, Douglas, in *Weavings*, IX(3), Nashville,TN: The Upper Room.

Stroebe, M. and Schut, H., 'The Dual Process Model of Coping with Bereavement: Rationale and Description', in *Death Studies*, 23(3), 1999.

Tacey, David, *The Spirituality Revolution: The Emergence of Contemporary Spirituality,* Sydney: HarperCollins, 2003.

Thornton, Martin, *Spiritual Direction: A Practical Introduction*, London: SPCK, 1984.

Veltri, John, *Retreats in Daily Life*, <http://spiritualorientations.com/bob/retreat.htm>.

Ward, Reginald Somerset, *A Guide for Spiritual Directors*, London: Mowbray, 1957.

Welch, John, *Spiritual Pilgrims: Carl Jung and Teresa of Avila*, New York: Paulist Press, 1982.

Westberg, Granger E., *Good Grief: A Constructive Approach to the Problem of Loss*, Augsburg Fortress, published in Australia by Desbooks, Thornbury, 1992.

Wicks, Robert J., 'Counter-transference in Spiritual Direction', in *Human Development*, 6(3), Fall 1985.

Willard, Dallas, *Hearing God*, London: HarperCollins, 1999.

Williams, Rowan, *Silence and Honey Cakes: The Wisdom of the Desert*, Oxford: Lion, 2003.

Wright, N. T., *Evil and the Justice of God*, London: SPCK, 2006.

Wuellner, Flora Slosson, *Feed My Shepherds*, Nashville: Upper Room, 1998.

Index

CPSIA information can be obtained
at www.ICGtesting.com
Printed in the USA
LVHW100256300719
625770LV00010B/99/P